MW00625712

THE ORIGINS OF U.S. NUCLEAR STRATEGY, 1945-1953

Also by Samuel R. Williamson, Jr.

AUSTRIA-HUNGARY AND THE ORIGINS
OF THE FIRST WORLD WAR

ESSAYS ON WORLD WAR I: ORIGINS AND PRISONERS OF WAR
(*co-editor*)

THE ORIGINS OF A TRAGEDY: JULY 1914
(*editor*)

THE POLITICS OF GRAND STRATEGY:
BRITAIN AND FRANCE PREPARE FOR WAR, 1904-1914

Also by Steven L. Rearden

THE EVOLUTION OF AMERICAN STRATEGIC DOCTRINE:
PAUL H. NITZE AND THE SOVIET CHALLENGE

FROM HIROSHIMA TO GLASNOST:
AT THE CENTER OF DECISION
(*co-collaborator with Paul H. Nitze*)

HISTORY OF THE OFFICE OF THE SECRETARY OF DEFENSE: THE FOR-
MATIVE YEARS, 1947-1950

PAUL H. NITZE ON FOREIGN POLICY
(*co-editor*)

PAUL H. NITZE ON THE FUTURE
(*co-editor*)

PAUL H. NITZE ON NATIONAL SECURITY AND ARMS CONTROL
(*co-editor*)

THE ORIGINS OF U.S. NUCLEAR STRATEGY, 1945-1953

SAMUEL R. WILLIAMSON, JR.
and
STEVEN L. REARDEN

St. Martin's Press
New York

First published in the United States of America 1993

Printed in the United States of America

ISBN 0-312-08964-3

Library of Congress Cataloging-in-Publication Data

Williamson, Samuel R.
The origins of U.S. nuclear strategy, 1945-1953 / Samuel R.
Williamson, Jr. and Steven L. Rearden.
    p. cm. — (The Franklin and Eleanor Roosevelt Institute
series on diplomatic and economic history)
Includes bibliographical references (p.) and index.
ISBN 0-312-08964-3
1. United States—Military policy. 2. Nuclear warfare.
I. Rearden, Steven L. II. Title. III. Title: Origins of US nuclear
strategy, 1945-1953. IV. Series.

UA23.W4593 1993
355.02'17—dc20   92-26597
                                                             CIP

For Joan and Pamela

CONTENTS

PREFACE

For more than four decades after World War II, the threat of nuclear war represented an ever-present danger in international politics. The collapse of communism in the late 1980s, followed shortly by the ending of the cold war and the breakup of the Soviet Union, removed much of the immediacy of that threat. Yet the underlying peril posed by the advent of nuclear weapons remains. Indeed, although a nuclear confrontation between the erstwhile superpowers may no longer be the dread possibility it once was, the spread of nuclear technologies to other countries raises the grim prospect that someday, somewhere, someone may make use of these enormously destructive devices.

Throughout the nuclear era, the United States often took the lead in developing and refining defense policies dependent, to one degree or another, on the use of nuclear weapons. As a reflection of this dependence, from 1945 on, the United States began to stockpile nuclear weapons, reaching an all-time high of around 30,000 bombs and warheads in the 1980s. As the stockpile grew, its components became increasingly more potent and sophisticated, far surpassing the relatively primitive devices that made up the nuclear arsenal in the 1940s. Their strategy and stated purpose, however, have remained fairly constant—to deter any would-be aggressor from attacking the United States and its allies or, in the event of war, to provide US and Allied armed forces with effective means of retaliation.

Given this potential for waging war at an unprecedented level of intensity and violence, questions naturally arise. How did the United States arrive at this situation? Why did the United States stockpile grow so large? Was reliance on nuclear weapons after World War II inevitable, or could it have been avoided? Were there other options and, if so, were they given serious consideration? In short, could the nuclear juggernaut have been avoided? There are, to be sure, no easy or simple answers, but with the gradual opening of previously classified official records, a clearer picture of what happened—and why—is finally beginning to emerge.

In recent years, the argument over the bomb's significance and influence has received almost unprecedented attention. What has emerged is a whole new discipline devoted in the broadest sense to nuclear history, a unique field of study that combines policy, diplomacy, technology, and military affairs, with the focus on the role and impact of nuclear weapons. Recent studies by John Lewis Gaddis, McGeorge Bundy, Melvyn P. Leffler, Robert Jervis, Lawrence Freedman, David Alan Rosenberg, and others have shed much new light on the problems raised by the advent of nuclear weapons, especially the political-military implications of the bomb and the complications it has posed in such areas as strategic planning, arms control, inter-allied relations, and basic national security policy. But even while scholars generally agree that nuclear weapons have had a profound influence on the postwar international environment, they have yet to arrive at a consensus on the precise effects.[1]

Our purpose here is not to challenge or rebut any earlier interpretation, but rather to add what we see as a further, often overlooked dimension. This concerns the ambiguous attitude of American policymakers after World War II toward the bomb and their unwillingness to confront the probable consequences that reliance on it posed. The central problem, as we see it, was not so much a lack of options (though as time went on they did indeed narrow), but rather an almost unavoidable, involuntary, and growing dependence on nuclear weapons because of overriding concerns for other problems. An ill-defined nuclear weapons policy opened the way for the development of technological refinements and other innovations that would make reliance on the atomic bomb easier, more economical, and ultimately more appealing to senior officials. By 1949, with the added impetus of increasingly austere defense budgets and the discovery that the Soviet Union had also broken the atomic "secret," dependence on the bomb as the West's first line of defense was no longer at issue. It had become an accomplished fact and would gain additional emphasis with the onset of the Korean War. With Western Europe included under American protection via the 1949 North Atlantic Treaty, nuclear weapons acquired an added mission—to augment conventional capabilities that neither the United States nor its allies were willing to raise and sustain. In brief, Harry S. Truman may have initially hated the atomic bomb, but he grew to love it nonetheless.

What follows is a refined and expanded version of an earlier study done originally in 1975 for the US Department of Defense in support of a larger, more comprehensive examination of US-Soviet strategic arms competition since World War II. For the resources to conduct additional research and writing, we would like to thank the Paul H. Nitze School of Advanced International Studies and its Foreign Policy Institute, which sponsored a 1988 conference on Dean Acheson at which portions of this study were presented; the Nuclear History Program at the University of Maryland; and the John D. and Catherine T. MacArthur Foundation for their generous support. For taking the time and patience to read and comment on the manuscript during its various stages of development, we also need to thank Ambassador Paul H. Nitze, Robert Jervis, Robert H. Ferrell, John Lewis Gaddis, Robert Art, Alfred Goldberg, David MacIsaac, Lawrence S. Kaplan, and Walton S. Moody. Our mentor, Ernest R. May, introduced us to this subject and shared many keen insights. He remains a steadfast source of intellectual inspiration. To our friend and colleague Samuel F. Wells, Jr., of the Woodrow Wilson Center in Washington, D.C., we owe a special debt of gratitude. At St. Martin's Press Simon Winder, ably assisted by Laura Heymann, provided welcome and useful editorial help. Finally, to those for whom this book is dedicated, we owe far more than we can possibly express here.

Samuel R. Williamson, Jr.
Sewanee, Tennessee
Steven L. Rearden
Washington, D.C.

NOTES

1. For more detailed treatments, see John Lewis Gaddis, *Strategies of Containment* (New York: Oxford University Press, 1982), and *The Long Peace* (New York: Oxford University Press, 1987); McGeorge Bundy, *Danger and Survival: Choices About the Bomb in the First Fifty Years* (New York: Random House, 1988); Melvyn P. Leffler, *A Preponderance of Power: National Security, the Truman Administration, and the Cold War* (Stanford, Calif.: Stanford University Press, 1992); Lawrence Freedman, *The Evolution of Nuclear Strategy* (New York: St. Martin's Press, 1981; rev. ed. 1989); Robert Jervis, *The Illogic of American Nuclear Strategy* (Ithaca, N.Y.: Cornell University Press, 1984); and David Alan Rosenberg, "The Origins of Overkill: Nuclear Weapons and American Strategy, 1945-1960," *International Security* 7 (Spring 1983): 3-71.

I

Onset of the Nuclear Age

On August 6, 1945, the world entered the age of nuclear warfare when the United States dropped the first atomic bomb on the Japanese industrial city of Hiroshima. Three days later the United States followed up with a second atomic attack, this time against Nagasaki. The immediate effects—over 100,000 people killed, six square miles and over 50 percent of the built-up areas of the two cities destroyed—were indeed stunning. But compared with the incendiary raids against Tokyo and other Japanese cities a few months earlier, the damage was in fact no more devastating.[1] What was different about the bombs dropped on Hiroshima and Nagasaki was the power compressed into them, the swiftness of the destruction they caused, and, of course, their unique, unprecedented source of energy. As a shocked world absorbed the news that the secret of the atom had at last been broken, there also came the sobering reality that the ultimate weapon might well have been discovered. Armageddon, it seemed, had taken another fateful step closer.

The development of the bombs used against Japan culminated one of the most extraordinary undertakings in American history. Known as the Manhattan Project, the effort began in 1939 under the presidency of Franklin D. Roosevelt and came to fruition six years later under his successor, Harry S. Truman. Roosevelt, who died on April 12, 1945, never lived to know whether the atomic bomb would work. But he was confident enough in the possibility to make the Manhattan Project a top priority of World War II, investing over $2 billion and mobilizing the energy and talents of the world's leading scientists and engineers in what became one of the single largest (yet one of the most secret) operations of the war. The results of the Manhattan Project materialized too late to affect the course of the war to any significant degree; but they were destined to have a profound impact on the peace afterwards.

ORIGINS OF THE ATOMIC BOMB PROGRAM

In wartime the unexpected tends to become commonplace. Thus it is not surprising that an event as momentous as the decision to develop the atomic bomb had its origins in a brief, casual encounter between Roosevelt and New York financier Alexander Sachs on October 11, 1939, just one month after Germany invaded Poland. What occasioned their meeting was a growing concern among certain members of the scientific community, voiced most strongly by European refugees, that Nazi Germany was on the verge of achieving a significant edge in nuclear research, an edge that could prove decisive in the recently declared war in Europe. Less than a year earlier, two German physicists—Otto Hahn and Fritz Strassmann—had demonstrated a process known as "nuclear fission," in which they split a particle of uranium in half by bombarding it with neutrons. Although the Germans apparently were not fully aware of what they had achieved, scientists elsewhere in Europe and in the United States readily grasped the implications. They concluded that under properly controlled conditions nuclear fission could produce an enormous explosion. Among those especially alarmed by the German breakthrough were Leo Szilard, a Hungarian expatriate, and Enrico Fermi, a refugee from Mussolini's fascist Italy, both now living in the United States. Together they sought to interest the Navy Department in a program of stepped-up nuclear research. Failing this, they persuaded Albert Einstein, the celebrated mathematician, to send a letter (written by Szilard) to Roosevelt, which outlined the implications of the Germans' experiment and warned of the possible consequences. And, to make sure the letter reached the President, they arranged for Sachs, an occasional White House advisor, to hand deliver it.[2]

Whether Roosevelt wanted to build the bomb or not, Einstein's letter left him no choice but to explore the possibility. Although Einstein did not say that an atomic bomb was a certainty, he left the strong impression that the odds were in favor of one becoming a reality someday. Such a device, he said, if "carried by boat and exploded in port, might very well destroy the whole port together with some of the surrounding territory." This suggests that Einstein and his friends did not visualize a fully weaponized bomb dropped from the air; what they had in mind instead was probably a large, heavy reactor that could be sailed to an enemy's shores and exploded on command. But whatever form the threat took, Germany's apparent interest in nuclear research had menacing ramifications. As Einstein noted dryly but ominously in his final paragraph: "I understand Germany has actually stopped the sale of uranium from the Czechoslovakian mines which she has taken over."[3] Roosevelt, realizing the gravity of the situation should the United States become involved in the war, turned to his aide, Maj. Gen. Edwin "Pa" Watson. "Pa," he said, "this requires action."[4] The competition, starting now with Nazi Germany and serving in effect as a prelude to the much larger competition with the Soviet Union, was underway.

Despite the gravity surrounding it, the project materialized slowly and spasmodically. If any written orders were ever issued, they did not survive; and while Roosevelt may have recognized the serious implications of what the Germans were doing, he saw no urgency, a sentiment shared by Szilard and Fermi, whose purpose in approaching the President in the first place was to gain moral rather than material support.[5] Instead of launching a government-led "crash" program, Roosevelt appointed an ad hoc Uranium Committee, composed of military and civilian representatives under the chairmanship of Lyman J. Briggs, director of the National Bureau of Standards, to assess the prospects and make recommendations. The committee concurred that the potential of nuclear fission needed more study and, as a token gesture, arranged a grant of $6,000 to Columbia University for Fermi to conduct uranium-graphite experiments. But like the President, the committee operated under no sense of impending crisis. Rather, the group followed the lead of its chairman, Briggs, whose 39 years in the federal civil service had instilled a habit for utmost caution in reaching decisions. Distrustful of foreigners, the committee disliked working too closely with Fermi, Szilard, and other émigré scientists lest their ideas prove unworkable and embarrass the government. It was, all things considered, an awkward and somewhat unpromising beginning.[6]

With the collapse of France in June 1940, Roosevelt realized that ultimately the United States would be drawn into the war. As part of a precautionary, yet modest, mobilization effort, he appointed Vannevar Bush, president of the Carnegie Institution in Washington, to head a National Defense Research Committee (NDRC), with broad authority to explore new avenues of research in science and technology to meet wartime needs. The Uranium Committee now answered directly to the NDRC. A mathematician and electrical engineer by profession, Bush took a personal interest in the Uranium Committee's project. Nevertheless, he was dismayed—as were others in the scientific community—to find that few of those working on it, including even Fermi, took seriously its military applications so long as the United States was not at war. While acknowledging that a bomb was a theoretical possibility, many scientists questioned its feasibility on technical grounds. They chose instead to channel their efforts into nonmilitary applications such as power generation and biological and medical research. The net result, as Bush later characterized it at this stage, was "a careful, but not an elaborate or expensive program" to keep the United States abreast of ongoing research in other countries (mainly Germany) and to be in a position to respond should the need arise.[7]

Meanwhile, in the aftermath of the Nazi occupation of Belgium, British intelligence learned that German scientists had acquired access to the uranium oxide stockpile at the Union Minière at Oolen, the largest such supply in Europe. Then came further information that the Germans had occupied the Norsk Hydro in Vemork, Norway, and were planning to step up production there of heavy water, a material used to moderate a nuclear chain reaction. These revelations convinced the British that Germany was bent on manufacturing an atomic bomb, though there was as yet no hard evidence to confirm such suspicions.[8]

Nonetheless, Britain's interest in atomic energy grew appreciably. Like the United States, the British government had also initiated a modest atomic energy program, but had not shown much vigor in pursuing it because of the apparent technical difficulty. Then, in April 1940, two German refugees living in England—Otto Frisch and Rudolph Peierls—offered their ideas on how a "superbomb" could be made by separating fissionable uranium-235 from less fissionable, but more abundant, uranium-238.[9] Intrigued by these ideas, a special group known as the MAUD Committee, working under cover of the Air Ministry, launched an exhaustive examination to assess the validity of the Frisch-Peierls study. Forwarding its findings to Prime Minister Winston Churchill in July 1941, the MAUD Committee advised that a bomb capable of "an explosion of unprecedented violence," fueled by either U-235 or a by-product called plutonium, did indeed appear feasible; that it could be reduced in size to be accommodated aboard existing bombers; and that it might even be ready in as little as two years. But with the war then exacting a heavy toll on British manpower and industry, Britain could not afford to divert the resources needed to see the project through to completion. Not surprisingly, as in other areas of their wartime struggle for survival, the British turned to the United States.[10]

By means that are still shrouded in mystery, the MAUD Committee established liaison with Briggs and his group in the United States sometime in early 1941. There followed a succession of carefully orchestrated "leaks" of material to American scientists who were well connected in Washington. The most interesting information appeared in early July of that year, when the MAUD Committee slipped a draft of its report to the Prime Minister to the NDRC representative in London, who promptly forwarded it to Bush in Washington. Alerted in advance what to expect, Bush hurriedly inserted several new paragraphs on the MAUD Committee's findings into the NDRC's first annual report to President Roosevelt. Bush advised that the NDRC was re-examining its entire atomic bomb program and might soon recommend a more "extensive and expensive" effort. Judging from the new information he had just received, Bush said, "one thing is certain: if such an explosive were made it would be a thousand times more powerful than existing explosives and its use might be determining."[11]

More than even Einstein's letter, the MAUD report had an immediately galvanizing effect on official American thinking. Further, it caused Bush to see possibilities he had never before imagined. On October 9, 1941, he met with Roosevelt and Vice President Henry Wallace for an off-the-record discussion to sketch his plans for a program of enhanced research and analysis, a program that would possibly serve as a prelude to the production of actual weapons, involving the expenditure of millions of dollars where tens of thousands had been spent before. Roosevelt, it seems, needed no convincing. Having already endorsed the basic idea of developing an atomic bomb, he could hardly back out now, especially with the United States and Germany engaged in a de facto sea war in the North Atlantic and relations with Japan deteriorating rapidly. With Wallace seconding the proposal, Roosevelt readily concurred. According to Bush, Roosevelt believed "that since this weapon was bound to appear in the world we must push forward to be sure that it appeared in our hands at least as early as elsewhere."[12] The ensuing discussion dwelt on practical matters—the need for reliable and adequate supplies of raw materials (i.e., uranium ore); the status of the German atomic energy program, about which practically nothing new was known; the maintaining of avenues for exchange of information with the British; and the question of postwar controls, an issue still too speculative to deserve much serious attention. In sum, it was a low-keyed, businesslike session, with no second-guessing or speculation on what consequences might follow other than that the United States should press ahead with increased speed. Yet it was a meeting that yielded one of the most fateful decisions of Roosevelt's presidency.[13]

THE MANHATTAN PROJECT

As Bush expected, the effort he proposed would eventually consume enormous resources at a time when other war work would also be clamoring for materials, facilities, and personnel. To underscore the urgency and high priority of the atomic program, Roosevelt, at Bush's suggestion, vested technical supervision of the project in a new body designated the Top Policy Group. As time went on, this unit came to function as Section 1 (or S-1) of the Office of Scientific Research and Development (OSRD), the organization in charge of coordinating defense-related applications of science and technology since the summer of 1941. To assure utmost secrecy, S-1 membership was confined to a select handful, including Bush, who was now head of the OSRD; President James B. Conant of Harvard University, one of the country's leading chemists and Bush's successor as chairman of the NDRC; Secretary of War Henry L. Stimson; Army Chief of Staff Gen. George C. Marshall; and Vice President Wallace, who acted as liaison with the White House. The inclusion of Stimson and Marshall served two important functions: it removed any lingering doubt among reluctant scientists as to the project's military purpose, and at the same time it assured the program's managers a convenient administrative mechanism through the War Department.[14] After Pearl Harbor there was no longer any question about the military's predominant interest in the program, as the Army assumed overall management responsibility under a headquarters organization known as the Manhattan Engineer District (MED), with Brig. Gen. (later Major General) Leslie R. Groves of the Corps of Engineers as its head.[15]

The Manhattan Project represented the first extended experience in American history of civilian scientists working closely with and taking directions from the military. In many respects, it heralded the far-flung system of defense-oriented laboratories and think tanks that sprang up in the United States after World War II to service an increasingly technology-dependent military establishment. But it was not the unalloyed success in civil-military relations nor the happy model for later associations that its admirers have sometimes depicted it to be.[16] For those civilian scientists long accustomed to the freedom and intellectual creativity of an academic environment, the transition to taking orders from the Army was difficult and uncomfortable, especially with someone like Groves in the role of commanding officer. Although a capable engineer and administrator, Groves's overbearing manner and obsession with secrecy and security alienated many scientists. The more frustrated and irritated they became because of Groves's policies and practices, the more convinced they were that postwar control of atomic energy should rest firmly in civilian, not military, hands.

All the same, progress went forward, in large part because of the presumed threat posed by Germany's atomic energy program, but for other reasons as well. For one thing, the Manhattan Project presented these same scientists with an extraordinary opportunity to test their theories and to develop new ones while working side-by-side with the top people in their fields. "It was a heroic period of our lives, full of the most exciting problems and achievements," recalled one participant. "We worked within an international community of the best and most productive scientists of the world, facing a stupendous task fraught with many unknown ramifications."[17] Those involved included not only distinguished scholar-administrators like Bush and Conant, but also such prominent figures as Fermi, I. I. Rabi, Hans Bethe, Ernest O. Lawrence, Arthur Compton, Harold Urey, and rising new talents like Edward Teller and J. Robert Oppenheimer, the brilliant director of the Los Alamos, New Mexico, laboratory where the bombs were finally designed and fabricated. From these men and others working on the project would come the inspiration and ideas that would shape nuclear research in the West for decades to come. Despite occasional personal friction, some bruised egos, and unexpected setbacks along the way, the Manhattan Project remained from first to last a highly professional and eminently productive enterprise.

As part of this effort, Roosevelt proposed to Prime Minister Churchill in October 1941 that the United States and Britain continue to collaborate on atomic energy.[18] Like others, including Bush, Roosevelt initially assumed that the British were further ahead of the United States and that their assistance would be invaluable in expediting progress. At a meeting at Roosevelt's home in Hyde Park, New York, in June 1942, he and Churchill reached an informal understanding, as Churchill later described it, to "pool all our information, work together on equal terms, and share the results."[19] This was apparently more than Roosevelt had in mind, and certainly more than the S-1 committee deemed prudent or practical. Indeed, as the American program developed, the research branched out into areas such as electromagnetic isotope separation, where the British had done no work at all and were therefore in no position to contribute. With the United States shouldering 90 percent of the financial burden, Bush and Conant thought it pointless—perhaps even counterproductive—to reveal to the British any more information than absolutely necessary. If the British wanted to participate, it would be as adjuncts, not as full partners.[20]

This change in the American attitude was a setback, but not entirely a surprise, to senior British policymakers, who had ruefully concluded that their investment in atomic energy would become a "dwindling asset" as the American program gathered momentum.[21] Yet the alternative of Britain's going it alone was utterly impractical, as estimates completed in January 1943 amply demonstrated. Startup construction and procurement costs alone would run well over £20 million ($80 million at the wartime rate of exchange). Nor was there any assurance that necessary facilities would be finished before war's end, considering the competing demands for resources.[22] At this stage, the British (as well as the Canadians, who had a lesser stake in the bomb project) might have been frozen out altogether had it not been for Roosevelt's overriding interest in keeping the Anglo-American alliance intact. Thus, despite reservations expressed by Bush and Conant, Roosevelt, while meeting with Churchill at Quebec in August 1943, concluded a formal secret agreement that assured continued wartime collaboration on "tube alloys" (the codename for the atomic project) and regular consultation through an Anglo-American-Canadian Combined Policy Committee. A year later, while conferring at Roosevelt's home in Hyde Park, the President and the Prime Minister initialed an *aide-mémoire* which signaled their intention to extend collaboration into the postwar period.[23]

These agreements eased, but did not entirely eliminate, the strain on Anglo-American relations caused by both countries' growing interest and investment in atomic energy. As historian John Morton Blum has observed, "The British accepted those terms because they could obtain none better."[24] Despite the appearance of equality, the United States throughout the war retained the dominant voice in the program, primarily because it had the most invested, but also because of suspicions in Washington that Britain's main interest in atomic energy was to exploit it for postwar commercial and political gains. Roosevelt knew that atomic energy could have enormous postwar consequences, but his central concern remained the war effort. For this reason, he saw no conflict in making concessions to the British, on the one hand, and, at the same time, limiting their access to information and participation in the program. A worthwhile cause could be served all around.

Yet if atomic collaboration with Britain was less than total and open, it was officially nonexistent with America's other major ally, the Soviet Union. Despite Roosevelt's repeated overtures promoting Soviet-American solidarity against Nazi Germany and postwar cooperation, he could not overcome the decades of mutual suspicion and strained relations between Washington and Moscow that had followed the 1917 Bolshevik Revolution. As a result, Soviet-American collaboration during the war remained limited and never extended into an area as sensitive as sharing atomic energy information. Roosevelt at times seemed uncomfortable with this policy, as it threatened to undercut his larger objectives with respect to establishing a working postwar partnership with Russia. But it was Churchill's view that atomic energy information should be as closely held as possible and not shared with anyone, least of all the Soviets. Roosevelt generally went along with this view.[25]

Critics of this policy, including Bush and Niels Bohr, the celebrated Danish physicist, labeled it a serious mistake. Such a stance, as Bush saw it, would simply fuel the Soviets' innate paranoia and suspicion of the West. It could also, he warned, cause them to initiate a crash program to develop their own bomb, thus provoking an atomic arms race that might culminate in a catastrophic East-West conflict in 20 years or so. Bohr's concerns were similar. Through his acquaintance with Supreme Court Justice Felix Frankfurter, one of Roosevelt's closest confidants, he was able to bring his views to the President's personal attention. Bohr worried that, unless the Soviets were made aware of the Manhattan Project before the war ended, they might conclude that it was part of an Anglo-American conspiracy to dominate the postwar world.[26]

What appears to have been a missed opportunity by the United States to remove a major source of postwar friction with the Soviets probably made little difference. Despite Groves's painstaking efforts to protect the secret, the Soviets had been well aware of the Manhattan Project almost from its inception. Groves knew as early as August 1943 that Soviet agents were active, and dutifully notified his superiors, including Roosevelt. Whether the President simply discounted the potential danger, or whether he tolerated Soviet espionage as a surreptitious means of circumventing Churchill's ardent opposition to sharing information, is unclear. In any case, despite awareness of the spying, it was Secretary of War Stimson's belief, which he conveyed to Roosevelt during a meeting on December 31, 1944, that Soviet espionage had not yet acquired any "real knowledge" of the program.[27]

Contrary to Stimson's estimate, the damage was substantial. Disclosures in 1992 by the Russian Intelligence Service (the successor to the KGB following the breakup of the Soviet Union) indicate that Soviet agents, including some never detected, succeeded in penetrating the Manhattan Project's most sensitive and secret areas.[28] One agent who was found out after the war was Klaus Fuchs, a German physicist who had joined the anti-Nazi communist underground in the 1930s before going to live in England.[29] In mid-1942, while working with Peierls in Birmingham, Fuchs began supplying the Soviets with information on the British program and continued to transmit sensitive material through the Rosenberg spy ring after joining the Manhattan Project the next year. Although the full extent of Fuchs's espionage remains classified, Fuchs stated in his 1950 confession that the data he gave the Soviets dealt only with the principles involved in making an atomic bomb, not with the industrial technology needed for construction. Fuchs apparently did not regard the material he passed on as particularly injurious to the West or vital to the Soviets, because he thought they were sufficiently advanced scientifically to design their own bomb. Hence the danger posed by a Soviet Union armed with nuclear weapons would have arisen one way or another. What surprised Fuchs was their industrial capacity to embark on production, in view of the damage the Soviet Union suffered as a consequence of World War II.[30] Yet Fuchs was not alone in underestimating the Soviets. As World War II ended, US and British intelligence likewise rated the prospects of a Soviet atomic bomb as exceedingly remote for similar reasons, with the result that it was all the more a surprise and shock when the Soviet atomic test came as it did in 1949, years ahead of most expectations.

ENTERING THE NEW ERA OF ATOMIC WAR

From the outset of the Manhattan Project, the chief motivating factor of all involved, from Roosevelt on down, was the status of nuclear research in Nazi Germany. With as much as an 18-month lead, the Germans were presumably well ahead of the United States in the "race" for the atomic bomb and would pose an unthinkable threat to Western civilization if they succeeded in developing it first. Although the Japanese were also known to have an atomic energy program, there was nothing to indicate that theirs was anywhere nearly as advanced as either the German or Anglo-American efforts. But by late 1944, a special US-led intelligence unit known as the *Alsos* ("grove" in Greek) Mission, operating on the front lines in Europe, had uncovered the first solid evidence confirming what scientists in Britain and the United States had suspected for some time: that the German program had barely progressed beyond the research stage. Based on interviews, records of production at the recently liberated Union Minière plant in Belgium, and files from the physics labs at the University of Strasbourg, the investigation concluded that the German program had remained research-oriented since 1940, and that it would be months, if not years, before Germany had a bomb.[31] "As far as the German scientists were concerned," recalled the US scientific head of *Alsos,* "the whole thing was still on an academic scale."[32]

Such revelations might well have slowed or even ended the Manhattan Project. Indeed, some scientists, especially those who had moral qualms about their involvement, saw no constructive purpose in continuing. They elected instead to channel their energies in other directions on the assumption that an atomic bomb was now likely to play little or no part in deciding the outcome of the war against Germany.[33] Japan, of course, was another matter. But for the majority of those recruited into the Manhattan Project—many of whom were Jewish and/or refugees from Hitler's Europe—it was the threat posed by Nazi Germany that had provided the stimulus for their work. Not surprisingly, the discovery that Germany had not in fact vigorously pursued development of the bomb drained some of the enthusiasm.

Even so, the Manhattan Project had now reached the point where, with or without German competition, the momentum behind it was more than enough to see it through to completion. Although the production of fissionable materials proved more difficult than originally expected, there were few doubts by the eve of Roosevelt's death in April 1945 that weapons, as Secretary of War Stimson put it, were "99% assured," and that they would be in production in four to five months' time.[34] Two types were undergoing final development: a gun projectile bomb using U-235, with an estimated yield of 5,000 tons of TNT, which scientists and engineers considered such a certainty that it would need no field testing; and an implosion-type bomb with a plutonium core, a more experimental device theoretically capable of much greater power. Confirmation that the latter design was indeed feasible came on July 16, 1945, with the TRINITY test at Alamagordo, New Mexico, which produced an explosion of 19 kilotons, nearly double the most optimistic predictions.[35]

For the scientists in the Manhattan Project, TRINITY culminated years of agonizing effort. It validated their theories and gave concrete proof that, despite the sneers and doubts of some, the money, time, and resources invested in the project had not been wasted. But for the military, TRINITY marked merely the end of the beginning—the jumping-off point for the climactic final phase of World War II. Heretofore, because of the many uncertainties surrounding the Manhattan Project, the atomic bomb had played no part in wartime strategy, despite numerous preparations for its eventual use. As early as the summer of 1944, the Army Air Forces (AAF) began to organize and train a special unit of B-29 heavy bombers—the 509th Composite Group—for air-atomic operations. From bomb designs "frozen" in the fall of 1944, the AAF proceeded to modify these aircraft to accommodate the unusually bulky dimensions and estimated payload of 10,000 pounds. When it became apparent that nuclear weapons would not be ready in time for use against Germany, the Air Force in February 1945 began preparing for their use against Japan, with the island of Tinian designated as the 509th's staging base in the Pacific. Deployment of the 509th began in early May and was completed around the end of July. By then, scientists on the Manhattan Project had verified the feasibility of the implosion design and were readying components for final delivery to the military.[36]

Few issues in recent American history have evoked as much comment and controversy as the atomic attacks on Hiroshima and Nagasaki in August 1945. The decision to launch those strikes was, as it turned out, not Roosevelt's to make. Rather, his successor, Harry S Truman, inherited the responsibility. In this, as in so many other areas, Truman found that Roosevelt had left behind no clear-cut policy concerning either the immediate or future use of atomic energy.[37] But even if Roosevelt had lived, he would in all probability have authorized the attacks. "At no time, from 1941 to 1945," recalled Stimson, "did I ever hear it suggested by the President, or by any other responsible member of the government, that atomic energy should not be used in the war. . . . it was our common objective, throughout the war, to be the first to produce an atomic weapon and use it." Truman, in other words, was merely following in Roosevelt's footsteps.[38]

Although Stimson overstated the consensus among high-level opinion, his point was well taken: it was part of Roosevelt's legacy, reflected in the mindset of those involved in running the program, that the bomb should be used. Indeed, so much had been invested in the Manhattan Project by 1945 that a different outcome was almost inconceivable. Truman accepted, in a sense, what he and most of those around him perceived to be the inevitable. "I regarded the bomb," he stated simply in his memoirs, "as a military weapon and never had any doubt that it should be used."[39] Some years later, as we shall see, when the question of building the H-bomb came before him, Truman would adopt a similar rationale.

Almost from the moment Truman became president, any other course of action was most improbable. On April 25, 1945, he got his first detailed briefing on the bomb during a meeting with Stimson and Groves. Rather than present the bomb as an option for possible consideration, Stimson and Groves discussed it as though it were a virtual fait accompli, even though, as Stimson acknowledged, an actual weapon was still four months or so away. All the same, Truman recalled, Stimson argued that "the atomic bomb would be certain to have a decisive influence on our relations with other countries. And if it worked, the bomb, in all probability, would shorten the war."[40] Accordingly, Stimson wanted not only to proceed with plans to use the bomb, but also to explore matters of broader political and diplomatic importance, including the question of possible postwar controls and information-sharing with other countries, i.e., the Soviet Union. Inexperienced and overwhelmed by the duties of his new job, Truman accepted Stimson's recommendation that these issues be placed before a special advisory body, the Interim Committee, organized under the War Department.[41] At the time this seemed a reasonable enough thing to do. But as Leon V. Sigal has pointed out, it also "left the choice of options in the hands of subordinate officials with the greatest stake in showing off the bomb to maximum effect—those responsible for building it and delivering it on target."[42]

From this point on, Truman lost effective control over the decision to use the bomb. His options shrank steadily, as the Interim Committee—dominated by Stimson, with Groves never far removed from the scene of action—seized the initiative to become the guiding voice in policy. The other members of the committee were Bush, Conant, and Karl T. Compton, president of MIT, all of whom had vested interests in seeing the S-1 project through to completion; and a group of somewhat bewildered civilian officials, including George L. Harrison, a life insurance executive and consultant to the War Department, who served as acting chairman in Stimson's absence; James F. Byrnes, soon to become secretary of state, who acted as Truman's representative; Under Secretary of the Navy Ralph A. Bard; and Assistant Secretary of State William L. Clayton. All of the latter group were able men, to be sure, but none, except perhaps Byrnes, who had been close to Roosevelt, had more than a rudimentary knowledge of the bomb or an awareness of the problems it posed.[43] For technical advice, the committee formed a scientific panel composed of Robert Oppenheimer, Arthur H. Compton (Karl's more celebrated brother), Ernest O. Lawrence, and Enrico Fermi.[44] No one, it seems, felt it necessary to include military advisors as well, possibly because Groves was already in close consultation with the AAF and had, at Marshall's direction, set up a target committee in late April to advise on the selection of aim points.[45]

Stimson later claimed that, in keeping with the understanding he had with Truman, the Interim Committee's work "ranged over the whole field of atomic energy, in its political, military, and scientific aspects."[46] Strictly speaking, the Interim Committee's function was to advise on matters of policy only, not strategy or tactics; so the question of using the bomb never formally appeared on the committee's agenda. Stimson, however, had his own agenda, and it involved nothing less than reconfirming in Truman's mind, as strongly as possible, that the bomb should be used on Japan when ready. "I felt that to extract a genuine surrender from the Emperor and his military advisors," Stimson later wrote as the reasoning behind his position, "there must be administered a tremendous shock which would carry convincing proof of our power to destroy the Empire."[47] And for this purpose Stimson believed that the atomic bomb was the only readily available, reliable weapon. "Stimson didn't want advice," recalled R. Gordon Arneson, an Army second lieutenant at the time, serving as the committee's notetaker. "The operation was in train and no one wanted to stop it. As-soon-as-possible was the overriding consideration. Probably no weapon in history went into operation so soon after being tested."[48]

On June 1, 1945, the Interim Committee unanimously approved tentative recommendations which Byrnes immediately conveyed to Truman. The bomb should definitely be used against Japan as soon as possible, the committee advised; it should be used against a "military target" surrounded by other buildings; and it should be used without prior warning.[49] Five days later, Stimson called on Truman in an apparent effort to elicit a formal decision, only to come away empty-handed. Nonetheless, there was no indication that Truman might reject the committee's recommendations or that he would entertain adopting a different course of action.[50] Relieved to find the President in such a frame of mind, Stimson and Groves proceeded as though they had his blessing anyway. "As far as I was concerned," Groves later said of Truman, "his decision was one of non-interference—basically, a decision not to upset the existing plans."[51]

In fact, the Interim Committee report settled less than either Stimson or Groves imagined. For in the following weeks the committee consensus began to unravel. Despite his initial concurrence with the other members, Bard had second thoughts about using the bomb without warning. He concluded that he could not, in good conscience, let his endorsement of this part of the report stand. On June 27 he registered a formal protest, citing "humanitarian" considerations and his growing sense that use of the bomb might not even be necessary in view of intelligence reports of Japanese peace-feelers. "Ever since I have been in touch with this program," he told his colleagues on the committee,

> I have had a feeling that before the bomb is actually used against Japan that Japan should have some preliminary warning for say two or three days in advance of use. The position of the United States as a great humanitarian nation and the fair play attitude of our people generally is responsible in the main for this feeling.
>
> During recent weeks I have also had the feeling very definitely that the Japanese government may be searching for some opportunity which they could use as a medium for surrender.... It seems quite possible to me that this presents the opportunity which the Japanese are looking for.
>
> I don't see that we have anything in particular to lose in following such a program.[52]

While doubtless sincere, Bard's protest bore traces of other worries as well. Indeed, it was in many respects an early sign of the Navy's uneasiness over its postwar prospects in the face of growing congressional interest in service unification and the emerging political power and prestige of the Army Air Forces. Having been largely excluded from the atomic program up to this point, Navy leaders generally held one of two opinions. Either they doubted any overt military need for the bomb, citing Japan's waning capacity to resist (owing, of course, to the Navy's success in subduing Japan's military power); or they believed the bomb would help the advocates of strategic bombing and accelerate the Air Force's efforts to stake a postwar claim as the dominant service. In either case, the Navy benefited from raising doubts about the bomb and urging caution in its use.

Concerns of a different sort prompted a group of scientists from the Metallurgical Laboratory of the University of Chicago to file a separate protest. A key contributor to basic research during the Manhattan Project's early days, the Met Lab, from 1943 on, had been steadily eclipsed in importance by the manufacturing and production work being done at Oak Ridge, Tennessee, and Hanford, Washington. Morale among the Met Lab's scientists had suffered accordingly, resulting in a general mood of dissatisfaction and discontent by 1945.[53] As a concession to those with moral doubts about the bomb, the Met Lab's director, Arthur Compton, had authorized a committee under the chairmanship of James Franck, a German refugee and highly regarded physicist, to examine the bomb's potential social and political implications.[54] In their subsequent report, Franck and his colleagues criticized the use of the bomb without prior warning as politically inexpedient and potentially damaging to the reputation, prestige, and security of the United States. "If the United States were to be the first to release this new means of indiscriminate destruction upon mankind," the scientists held, "she would sacrifice public support throughout the world, precipitate the race for armaments, and prejudice the possibility of reaching an international agreement on the future control of such weapons." As an alternative, they advocated a demonstration shot in some remote part of Japan so as to avoid any mass slaughter yet convince the Japanese of the bomb's superior power.[55]

Suspecting that Groves might try to exercise censorship, Franck arranged to go to Washington and hand-deliver the committee's report to Stimson personally. On June 12, 1945—nearly two weeks after the Interim Committee had offered its tentative recommendations—Franck and Compton went to the War Department but found Stimson unavailable and had to settle for leaving the report with Harrison. Feeling that it was not worth the Interim Committee's time or trouble at this point, Harrison turned the report over to the scientific panel, with vague instructions to study its contents and recommendations. Assembling in Alamagordo on or about

June 16, the panel found itself sympathetic to the scientists' concerns but unconvinced that a demonstration shot would have sufficient impact on Japanese thinking to end the war. The Interim Committee, meeting in executive session less than a week later to review the panel's evaluation, readily concurred.[56]

Though the Franck report came to naught, the Met Lab protest continued, led now by Leo Szilard, the lab's chief scientist and one of the bomb project's initial advocates. Earlier, in the spring of 1945, Szilard had tried to schedule a meeting with Roosevelt to discuss deferring use of the bomb (in effect, keeping it a secret) pending exploratory talks with the Soviets and the British on a system of controls. Roosevelt died before they could meet and Truman, busy with other matters, referred Szilard to Byrnes, who was then at his home in South Carolina. There they discussed the implications of the bomb at some length. According to Szilard's retrospective account, Byrnes argued that once Congress learned of the bomb (and already the secret was beginning to leak out on Capitol Hill), legislators would start asking questions about "what we got for the money spent." Byrnes also thought that the war would be over in six months and that, by that time, the United States would need all the military power at its disposal in order to deal with the Soviet Union, especially over questions concerning the political future of Eastern Europe. "I shared Byrnes's concern about Russia's throwing around her weight in the postwar period," Szilard said, "but I was completely flabbergasted by the assumption that rattling the bomb might make Russia more manageable."[57]

Increasingly disenchanted with the new administration's policies and attitude toward atomic energy, Szilard in early July circulated a petition among his colleagues. In it he denounced the bomb as morally indefensible, suitable only for "the ruthless annihilation of cities," and called on President Truman to withhold its use "in the present phase of the war" in order to give Japan a chance to surrender first.[58] Fifty-nine of Szilard's colleagues signed the petition. (A slightly toned-down version, dated July 17, 1945, collected even more signatures.) Szilard, mindful of the short shrift the War Department had given the Franck report, wanted to take the petition to Truman directly. But for reasons of security, since he had no authority to carry or transmit information on the bomb, his colleagues persuaded him (against his better judgment) to send the petition through channels. It reached Groves's headquarters in Washington on July 25 and remained there until Groves forwarded it to Stimson's office on August 1, by which time plans for the attack on Hiroshima were in their final stages.[59] Truman never saw the petition, nor did Groves believe he should. Groves dismissed the scientists' protest as nothing more than a movement inspired by German-Jewish refugees who had no further use for the bomb, now that the war in Europe was over. "To them," Groves thought, "Hitler was the supreme enemy and, once he had been destroyed, they apparently found themselves unable to generate the same degree of enthusiasm for destroying Japan's military power."[60]

Despite efforts by Groves and Stimson to isolate and contain the protests, Truman knew, from talks with Bard and others, that there were those with strong reservations to using the bomb. He also knew that the attacks being prepared by the Air Force on Japan's cities were not his only option. That he chose to proceed as planned, apparently unmoved by these concerns, supports his contention that he intended to use the bomb all along and that he never entertained serious doubts. Less clear, though, is why he adopted such a seemingly closed mind or what he hoped to achieve by adhering to such a rigid, fixed course.

The explanation apparently rests with Truman's perception of the bomb as an unproven weapon. This in turn caused him to discount its power until the TRINITY test in mid-July 1945, which confirmed not only its awesome destructiveness but also its potential, as Byrnes saw it, to gain certain political as well as military advantages. In contrast to Stimson, Groves, and even many of the scientists like Franck and Szilard, Truman resisted the temptation to view the bomb as the ultimate weapon. He knew the bomb would probably be exceedingly powerful, surpassing any other explosive in the arsenal, but he had no way of being sure that it would live up to predictions, like Stimson's declaration at their meeting on April 25, that it would be "the most terrible weapon ever known in human history."[61] Offsetting such estimates were those of others, such as Adm. William D. Leahy, Truman's liaison with the Joint Chiefs of Staff. Leahy thought the bomb would turn out to be a dud. "The bomb will never go off," he told Truman, "and I speak as an expert in explosives."[62]

Events showed Leahy to be wrong. But until Truman had confirmation of the bomb's capability, he dared not risk placing too much reliance on its use, either to end the war or to strengthen America's diplomatic posture. Nor did he have anything to lose by allowing plans to proceed for what would become the attacks on Hiroshima and Nagasaki. Thus, as the summer of 1945 progressed, Truman, always a cautious gambler, hedged his bets. While authorizing Stimson and Groves to work out the details of the atomic bombings (including the selection of suitable targets), he also told the Joint Chiefs on June 18 to proceed with the massing of troops and equipment for an autumn invasion of Japan.[63] One way or another, Truman's first concern was to bring the war to as early an end as possible. If the bomb contributed to that objective and lessened American casualties in the process, so much the better.

Nothing more concretely demonstrates Truman's cautious appreciation of the bomb than his determination that Stalin should fulfill his February pledge to Roosevelt at Yalta to enter the war against Japan three months after the surrender of Germany. This Soviet obligation, along with disagreements over the makeup of governments in Eastern Europe and territorial changes in the postwar Far East, had formed the crux of recurring disputes that had dogged Soviet-American relations since shortly before Roosevelt's death. As a sign of Stalin's general interest in continued cooperation and collaboration, if nothing else, Truman wanted firm guarantees that the Soviets would honor their commitment to enter the Pacific war. Having the bomb available may have been reassuring, but, unlike Soviet troops, the bomb was as yet an untested and untried commodity.

The Joint Chiefs, citing Japan's weakening strategic posture, now doubted the need for Soviet intervention, irrespective of the atomic bomb, and had so advised Truman at their meeting on June 18. But the President, whose daily intelligence briefings included a growing number of ULTRA intercepts showing a large and steady buildup of Japanese defenses against an invasion, persisted in wanting the Soviets in the war.[64] Indeed, this topped his agenda when, in mid-July 1945, he joined Stalin and Churchill at Potsdam for the last Big Three meeting of the war.[65] Shortly after arriving, he received the first sketchy news of TRINITY, an impressive success perhaps, but not one of such apparent magnitude as to dissuade Truman from pressing the Soviets to confirm that they would enter the war as promised. On July 17, during a meeting with Stalin, Truman finally got from the Soviet leader the promise he wanted. "He'll be in the Jap War on August 15th," Truman wrote with satisfaction in his diary afterwards. And, as if to leave no doubt about his feelings as to what Soviet intervention would mean, he added: "Fini Japs when that comes about."[66]

But within a few days, as more details of the TRINITY test arrived, Truman's attitude changed. "An experiment in the New Mexico desert was startling—to put it mildly," he noted. Indeed, so vast was the area affected by the blast that Truman thought it might be "the fire destruction prophesied in the Euphrates Valley Era"—a sign that the day of judgment might be at hand.[67] Sober reflection, however, produced a more practical outlook on Truman's part, one that, in his eyes, enormously enhanced the bomb's value, not just as a weapon that could now bring Japan to its knees in matter of days rather than weeks or months, but also as a confidence-builder and source of diplomatic strength in negotiations with the Soviets. An amazed Stimson, who had come to Potsdam to hand-deliver the final results of the TRINITY test, could barely contain his excitement over the "differences of psychology which now exist since the successful test."[68] The bomb, it seemed, had more than lived up to its proponents' expectations, giving Truman options he scarcely knew how to manage.

In the light of these new realities, Truman and Secretary of State Byrnes now sought to exploit whatever diplomatic leverage they thought the bomb afforded. They even explored whether it might now be possible to undo the recently reaffirmed agreement concerning Soviet entry into the Pacific war.[69] But their ensuing efforts at "atomic diplomacy," as some historians have characterized it, were awkward, poorly timed and coordinated, and, in the end, blatantly ineffective. Byrnes, who never doubted that the bomb would make all the difference in the world, must have been especially frustrated to find the Soviets standing firm on such matters as demands for German reparations and their claims to territorial concessions from Nationalist China—issues on which Byrnes thought the Soviets would now feel compelled to back down.[70] That the Soviets were unmoved by, or indifferent to, the pressures of atomic diplomacy suggests either that (1) they still had much to learn about the bomb's power, or (2) their espionage was so thorough and enlightening that Truman's revelation of the bomb's existence to Stalin (during a brief encounter on July 24) came as no surprise. Stalin appeared to take the news in stride, leaving Truman and Byrnes wondering whether the Soviet dictator had fully grasped the nature and importance of the disclosure.[71] The atomic bomb was indeed destined to play a major role in East-West relations. But these initial failures at Potsdam to sway Soviet behavior could only cast doubt on its credibility as a tool of American diplomacy.

As a source of military power, however, the advent of the atomic bomb represented a revolutionary, unprecedented expansion and extension of one nation's capacity to inflict death and destruction on another. For this reason alone, the attacks on Hiroshima and Nagasaki immediately thrust the atomic bomb into a class by itself. Whether they were decisive in ending the war remains a matter of conjecture. Nevertheless, the atomic bomb constituted the most intimidating, awe-inspiring weapon ever invented. The debate over whether Truman acted correctly in using the bomb—whether dropping it was necessary to win the war, whether he should have given other options more of a chance, and what exactly motivated his actions—will doubtless never be settled. On the other hand, having relied on the bomb once, Truman would be inclined to do so again. Indeed, he would turn to it repeatedly during his presidency when faced with difficult problems—not through direct use as against Japan, of course, but by exploiting its menacing nature in other ways in order to shore up his position elsewhere and to compensate for apparent weaknesses in conventional forces.

The atomic bomb, by its seemingly omnipotent, all-encompassing nature, thus contributed greatly to a false sense of American security as World War II drew to a close. Wartime science and technology had accomplished a virtual miracle: they had bestowed upon the United States a monopoly on the most powerful weapon in existence, a weapon that other countries might not be able to duplicate for years or maybe even decades. In these circumstances, the opportunities, from Truman's standpoint, must have seemed practically endless. Though he may have been initially skeptical of the bomb's power, Truman quickly realized that what he had in his hands was not only a devastating means of waging war but an asset of unrivaled potential for preserving peace as well.

NOTES

1. For a comparison of the effects, see U.S. Strategic Bombing Survey, *Summary Report (Pacific War)* (Washington, D.C.: G.P.O., 1946), 15-17, 22-25.
2. Leo Szilard, "Reminiscences," in *Perspectives in American History* II (1968): 94-114. The best account of the origins and development of the atomic bomb is Richard Rhodes, *The Making of the Atomic Bomb* (New York: Simon and Schuster, 1986). Also see Robert Jungk, *Brighter Than a Thousand Suns* (New York: Harcourt, Brace, 1958); Leslie R. Groves, *Now It Can Be Told* (New York: Harper and Brothers, 1962); and Richard G. Hewlett and Oscar E. Anderson, Jr., *A History of the United States Atomic Energy Commission,* vol. I, *The New World, 1939-1946* (Washington, D.C.: U.S. Atomic Energy Commission, 1962; reprinted 1972).
3. Ltr, Einstein to Roosevelt, Aug. 2, 1939, reprinted in Vincent C. Jones, *Manhattan: The Army and the Atomic Bomb* (Washington, D.C.: Center of Military History, Department of the Army, 1985), 609-610.
4. Quoted in James MacGregor Burns, *Roosevelt: The Soldier of Freedom, 1940-1945* (New York: Harcourt Brace Jovanovich, 1970), 250.
5. According to Szilard: "It was our general intention not to ask the government for money, but to ask only for the blessing of the government, so that then, with that blessing, we would go to foundations, raise the funds, and get some coordinated effort going." Szilard, "Reminiscences," 115.
6. Hewlett and Anderson, *The New World,* 20-21; Martin J. Sherwin, *A World Destroyed: The Atomic Bomb and the Grand Alliance* (New York: Vintage Books, 1977), 29-30.
7. Hewlett and Anderson, *The New World,* 24-41, 43; Bush quoted in McGeorge Bundy, *Danger and Survival* (New York: Random House, 1988), 44.
8. F. H. Hinsley, et al., *British Intelligence in the Second World War: Its Influence on Strategy and Operations* (3 vols.; London: HMSO, 1981-1988), II, 123-124.
9. Appendix 1, "The Frisch-Peierls Memorandum," in Margaret Gowing, *Britain and Atomic Energy, 1939-1945* (New York: St. Martin's, 1964), 389-393.

10. *Ibid.,* 45-89, and Appendix 2, "The Maud Reports," 394-436.

11. "Report of the National Defense Research Committee for the First Year of Operation, June 27, 1940, to June 28, 1941," quoted in Bundy, *Danger and Survival,* 44.

12. Ltr, Bush to Conant, Mar. 29, 1954, box 27, Conant file no. 2, Bush Papers, Library of Congress (hereafter L.C.).

13. Hewlett and Anderson, *The New World,* 45-46.

14. During his meeting with Roosevelt on October 9, 1941, Bush recommended that one of the military departments should assume management responsibility for the atomic program. Bush favored the War Department and encountered no objection from Roosevelt, who lacked confidence in the Navy's ability to provide effective administration. According to Hewlett and Anderson, *The New World,* 71-72, Roosevelt "was quite out of patience with the Navy for its lack of initiative and enterprise in the Pacific and with Secretary [of the Navy Frank] Knox for failing to control the intransigence of some of his officers."

15. Jones, *Manhattan,* 30-31, 73-77.

16. See for example James Phinney Baxter 3rd, *Scientists Against Time* (Cambridge, Mass.: M.I.T. Press, 1952; originally published 1946).

17. Victor F. Weisskopf, "Looking back on Los Alamos," *Bulletin of the Atomic Scientists* 41 (Aug. 1985): 20.

18. Roosevelt to Churchill, Oct. 11, 1941, doc. no. 78, in Francis L. Loewenheim, Harold D. Langley, and Manfred Jonas (eds.), *Roosevelt and Churchill: Their Secret Wartime Correspondence* (New York: Saturday Review Press, 1975), 161-162.

19. Winston S. Churchill, *The Hinge of Fate* (Boston: Houghton Mifflin, 1950), 380.

20. Jones, *Manhattan,* 239; Hewlett and Anderson, *The New World,* 263-270.

21. Sir John Anderson to Churchill, July 30, 1942, quoted in Martin Gilbert, *Winston S. Churchill,* vol. VII, *Road to Victory, 1941-1945* (Boston: Houghton, Mifflin), 1986), 415.

22. Gowing, *Independence and Deterrence,* I, 123, 162-163.

23. "Agreement Governing Collaboration Between the Authorities of the U.S.A. and the U.K. in the Matter of Tube Alloys," Aug. 19, 1943, U.S. Dept. of State, *Foreign Relations of the United States: The Conferences at Washington and Quebec, 1943* (Washington, D.C.: G.P.O., 1970), 1117-1119; "Aide-Mémoire of Conversation Between the President and the Prime Minister at Hyde Park," Sept. 18, 1944, U.S. Dept. of State, *Foreign Relations of the United States: The Conference at Quebec, 1944* (Washington, D.C.: G.P.O., 1972), 492-493.

24. John Morton Blum, *V Was For Victory: Politics and American Culture During World War II* (New York: Harcourt Brace Jovanovich, 1976), 319.

25. Sherwin, *A World Destroyed,* 76-89, 107-114.

26. Hewlett and Anderson, *The New World,* 325-329; Sherwin, *A World Destroyed,* 91-98.

27. Groves, *Now It Can Be Told,* 138-148; entry, Dec. 31, 1944, Henry L. Stimson Diary, Stimson Papers, Yale University Library, New Haven, Conn.

28. See *Washington Post,* Oct. 4, 1992.

29. There was some speculation, mostly on the British side, that Niels Bohr was a Soviet agent. While on a trip to London in 1944 Bohr was approached by an old Russian scientific friend, Peter Kapitza, who invited him to come to work in Moscow. Churchill apparently concluded from Bohr's continuing contacts with Soviet scientists that he was leaking information and persuaded Roosevelt during their Hyde Park meeting in September 1944 that Bohr was not to be trusted. See Burns, *Roosevelt: The Soldier of Freedom,* 457-458.

30. Robert Chadwell Williams, *Klaus Fuchs, Atom Spy* (Cambridge, Mass.: Harvard University Press, 1987). For Fuchs' confession, see Norman Moss, *Klaus Fuchs: The Man Who Stole the Atom Bomb* (New York: St. Martin's Press, 1987), 195-203.

31. Hinsley, *British Intelligence in the Second World War,* III, Pt. 2, 583-591, and Appendix 29, "Excerpts from the Joint Anglo-US Report to the Chancellor of the Exchequer and Major General Groves," Nov. 28, 1944, *ibid.,* 931-944. For a fuller account, see the memoirs of the security agent in charge of the mission, Boris T. Pash, *The Alsos Mission* (New York: Award House, 1969); and Leo J. Mahoney, "A History of the War Department Scientific Intelligence Mission (Alsos), 1943-1945," (Ph.D. diss., Kent State University, 1981).

32. Samuel Goudsmit, *Alsos* (New York: Henry Schuman, 1947), 70.

33. See for example Joseph Rotblat, "Leaving the Bomb Project," *Bulletin of the Atomic Scientists* 41 (Aug. 1985): 16-19.

34. Diary entry, Apr. 6-11, 1945, Stimson Papers.

35. Hewlett and Anderson, *The New World,* 320-321.

36. Wesley Frank Craven and James Lea Cate, *The Army Air Forces in World War II,* vol. 5, *The Pacific: Matterhorn to Nagasaki, June 1944 to August 1945* (Washington, D.C.: Office of Air Force History, 1983; new imprint), 705-707; Jones, *Manhattan,* 519-528.

37. See Leffler, *A Preponderance of Power,* 26-27.

38. Henry L. Stimson, "The Decision to Use the Atomic Bomb," reprinted in Robert A. Divine (ed.), *Causes and Consequences of World War II* (Chicago: Quadrangle Books, 1969), 310. For an overview of the historiographical controversy surrounding the bomb's use, see J. Samuel Walker, "The Decision to Use the Bomb: A Historiographical Update," *Diplomatic History* 14 (Winter 1990): 97-114.

39. Harry S. Truman, *Memoirs,* vol. I, *Year of Decisions* (Garden City, N.Y.: Doubleday, 1955), 419.

40. *Ibid.,* 87.

41. Diary entry, Apr. 25, 1945, Stimson Papers; Stimson, "The Decision to Use the Bomb," 312-314; and memo for the Files by Groves, Apr. 25, 1945, sub: Report of Meeting with the President, Apr. 25, 1945, reprinted as Appendix J in Sherwin, *A World Destroyed,* 293-294.

42. Leon V. Sigal, *Fighting to a Finish: The Politics of War Termination in the United States and Japan, 1945* (Ithaca, N.Y.: Cornell University Press, 1988), 176.

43. Diary entries, May 2 and 9, 1945, Stimson Papers; Stimson, "Decision to Use the Bomb," 314; and James F. Byrnes, *Speaking Frankly* (New York: Harper and Bros., 1947), 259.

44. Ltr, George L. Harrison to Oppenheimer, May 16, 1945, box 190, Scientific Panel folder, J. Robert Oppenheimer Papers, L.C.

45. Jones, *Manhattan,* 528-530.

46. Stimson, "Decision to Use the Bomb," 314.

47. Henry L. Stimson and McGeorge Bundy, *On Active Service in Peace and War* (New York: Harper and Bros., 1947), 617.

48. Quoted from an interview with Arneson, Dec. 11, 1986, in John Newhouse, *War and Peace in the Nuclear Age* (New York: Knopf, 1989), 44.

49. Stimson, "Decision to Use the Bomb," 314-315.

50. See diary entry, June 6, 1945, Stimson Papers.

51. Groves, *Now It Can Be Told,* 265.

52. Memo by Ralph Bard, June 27, 1945, sub: Use of S-1 Bomb, reprinted as Appendix O in Sherwin, *A World Destroyed,* 307-308.

53. Hewlett and Anderson, *The New World,* 198-199.

54. Hewlett and Anderson, *The New World,* 365-366; Szilard, "Reminiscences," 128-129.

55. "Report of the Committee on Social and Political Implications," June 11, 1945, in *Bulletin of the Atomic Scientists* 1 (May 1, 1946): 2-4, 16.

56. Hewlett and Anderson, *The New World,* 366-368.

57. Szilard, "Reminiscences," 123-128. A memo prepared by Szilard for Roosevelt on the subject of exploratory talks with the British and Soviets, dated Mar. 25, 1945, appears as Appendix II, *ibid.,* 146-148.

58. "A Petition to the President of the United States," July 3, 1945, *ibid.,* 150-151.

59. *Ibid.,* 130-132. Also see Fletcher Knebel and Charles W. Bailey, "The Fight Over the A-Bomb; Secret Revealed after 18 Years," *Look* (Aug. 13, 1963): 22-23.

60. Groves, *Now It Can Be Told,* 266.

61. Diary entry, Apr. 25, 1945, Stimson Papers.

62. Truman, *Year of Decisions,* 11.

63. Herbert Feis, *The Atomic Bomb and the End of World War II* (Princeton, N.J.: Princeton University Press, 1966), 9-11.

64. Edward J. Drea, *MacArthur's ULTRA: Codebreaking and the War Against Japan, 1942-1945* (Lawrence, Kan.: University Press of Kansas, 1992), 202-225.

65. See Truman's letters to his wife, Bess, from Potsdam, July 18 and 20, 1945, in Robert H. Ferrell, (ed.), *Dear Bess: The Letters from Harry to Bess Truman, 1910-1959* (New York: W. W. Norton, 1983), 520.

66. Robert H. Ferrell, (ed.), *Off the Record: The Private Papers of Harry S. Truman* (New York: Harper and Row, 1980), 53.

67. Diary entry, July 25, 1945, *ibid.,* 55.

68. Diary, July 30, 1945, Stimson Papers.

69. Diary, July 20-24, 1945, Stimson Papers; Leffler, *Preponderance of Power,* 37-38.

70. Sherwin, *A World Destroyed,* 224-225; Gregg Herken, *The Winning Weapon: The Atomic Bomb in the Cold War, 1945-1950* (New York: Knopf, 1980), 44-45.

71. Margaret Truman, *Harry S. Truman* (New York: Morrow, 1973), 276; Byrnes, *Speaking Frankly,* 263.

II

The Search for Controls: Foreign and Domestic

Within days of the attacks on Hiroshima and Nagasaki, Japan announced its surrender. The last act in a great drama had ended. What lay ahead for the victorious Grand Alliance of Great Britain, the United States, and the Soviet Union would be a peacemaking process as trying and difficult as any in history, one that would ultimately produce the disintegration of that alliance and help foment tensions, sometimes to the brink of war, that would persist for two generations. But the movement to that break, which became conclusive in the 1948 crisis over Berlin, would be slow and erratic. Despite differences that had arisen between East and West before the end of the war over the composition of the government in Poland, the status of lend-lease aid, the postwar treatment of Germany, and frontier adjustments in Eastern Europe and the Far East, among other issues, Truman remained hopeful through 1945, and indeed well into 1946, that an acceptable working relationship with the Soviet Union could be forged. Concurrently, however, Truman also had to cope with another problem—what to do about the atomic bomb.

Truman's interest in preserving the Grand Alliance was understandable. By September 1945, with the war finally over, the President's concerns were no longer just strategic and diplomatic. They also encompassed long neglected domestic problems, all with heavy political ramifications. As he put it in a press conference on August 16, "politics is open and free now." Demobilizing the armed forces, as quickly and equitably as possible, constituted a paramount consideration. So, too, did converting the wartime economy back into domestic, peacetime pursuits without producing the dislocations experienced after World War I or lurching back into the awful depression of the previous decade. In the background loomed the question of how organized labor, strengthened considerably by the New Deal legislation of the 1930s, would react to this transition program, and how both big labor and big business would behave without a variety of wartime economic controls. The specter of inflation, just as much as that of depression, would never be far from Truman's preoccupations. Further, there was the prospect of shaping a federal budget that balanced peacetime expenditures and receipts, and, if possible, had a surplus to help erase the wartime debt.

Another of Truman's major concerns centered on the staffing of his administration with reliable advisors. Broadly speaking, Truman had inherited a tired administration, worn from the rigors of war and the prolonged bureaucratic rivalry and infighting that had been rife during Roosevelt's 12 years in office. Having already appointed a new secretary of state (James F. Byrnes), Truman would soon find himself working with a new secretary of war (Robert Patterson), a new chief of staff (General of the Army Dwight D. Eisenhower), a new chief of naval operations (Fleet Admiral Chester Nimitz), a new commanding general of the AAF (Gen. Carl Spaatz), a new ambassador to the Soviet Union (Walter Bedell Smith), and four new members of the cabinet. In short, new faces soon abounded, giving the administration an altogether new appearance and new perspective on domestic and global affairs.

Preoccupations with government at home did not, of course, permit neglect of the kaleidoscopic international scene. Occupation policies in Germany and Japan, the return and demobilization of US troops, preparations for the projected peace conferences, arrangements for reparations, the immediate relief of millions of displaced persons, the continuation of Selective Service and the merits of Universal Military Training (UMT), and the forthcoming inauguration of the United Nations—each of these issues commanded attention. For some US policymakers, like Secretary of the Navy James Forrestal, the future of Soviet-American relations was paramount. But for others, including the President, that issue was simply one of many troubles that had to be addressed and processed.

One priority issue—the control of atomic energy—would, however, tie the international and domestic agenda together. This issue would influence both the immediate and long-range development of US-Soviet relations and, at the same time, affect the tenor of US-British relations as well. The domestic and international struggles over control of atomic energy were, at times and in many respects, so closely connected as to be nearly indistinguishable. From the start, Truman saw them as interconnected, in part because he believed that Congress—which had remained largely ignorant of the Manhattan Project during the war—would now demand a voice in controlling this remarkable new source of energy. At the same press conference, on August 16, 1945, Truman put his expectation succinctly when he insisted that Congress had to decide whether atomic energy would "be used for the welfare and benefit of the world instead of its destruction; and if Congress is willing to go along, we will continue the experiments to show how we can use that for peace instead of war."[1] That imposing challenge represented the immediate agenda.

EARLY THOUGHTS ON THE ATOMIC BOMB'S IMPACT

As Truman's depiction of the problem suggests, the United States entered the atomic age in 1945 almost totally unprepared for what would follow. Roosevelt had been reluctant to make plans for atomic energy beyond its use in the war; his foremost concern was to make a bomb, though he realized that, if successful, the program would have profound and far-reaching political, military, strategic, and even economic implications. Yet he also realized that the development of a comprehensive policy in advance for such a complex set of problems was next to impossible. One could only guess what the bomb would mean for the future security of the United States or the fate of mankind. The uncertainty and apprehension generated by the bomb's advent extended throughout large and important segments of the American public. Within the scientific and intellectual community emerged a growing consensus that the unprecedented destructiveness of nuclear weapons and the absence of any effective defense against them could only lead to their being outlawed or to the creation of totally new rules governing conflicts between nations. The release by the War Department in August 1945 of the Smyth report, an exceptionally detailed scientific and technical history of the bomb's origins, further encouraged this view.[2] The conclusion drawn by Bernard Brodie, one of the first to probe the bomb's potential impact in any depth, was that it came close to being the "absolute weapon" and therefore compelled a total rethinking of military doctrine. Brodie based his conclusion on the assumption that any future use of these devices would be impractical and that their only conceivable function was one of deterrence. "Thus far," he argued, "the chief purpose of our military establishment has been to win wars. From now on its chief purpose must be to avert them. It can have almost no other useful purpose."[3]

Members of the military establishment generally agreed that the atomic bomb's potency set it apart from other weapons. Its potential for deterrence—for making a future enemy think twice and decide not to attack after all—no less than its capacity for destruction, was obvious. Of more immediate significance, the weapon appeared to confirm the predictions of air power enthusiasts, dating from the 1920s, about the supremacy of bombardment from the air. Overall, as the US Strategic Bombing Survey had found, the air campaigns against Germany and Japan had produced mixed results at best and certainly had not lived up to some people's expectations that strategic bombing would decide the outcome of the war. But the advent of the atomic bomb recast the entire debate about the efficacy of strategic bombing, as it opened whole new possibilities for air warfare. Put another way, the bomb rescued the doctrine of strategic bombing at a time when its fundamental principles were open to serious question and criticism. Pictures of Hiroshima and Nagasaki spoke for themselves. While they did not totally silence criticism of strategic bombing, they certainly helped to mute it. "With the atomic bomb," as one historian has noted, "airpower could be said to have come of age."[4]

Yet, as awesome and revolutionary as nuclear weapons appeared to be, they also had serious limitations, virtually hidden to all but a few, who were privy to the secrets of the program. While powerful, the bombs were exceedingly few in number and were likely to remain so for some time to come. Although the size of the stockpile was (and still is, for the most part) a closely guarded secret, the Smyth report clearly revealed that the manufacture of atomic weapons was a complex and costly process requiring enormous amounts of uranium ore to produce just a few ounces of explosive. In fact, by the end of the war, the United States had in operation three graphite reactor piles at Hanford, Washington, capable of yielding a combined output of four to six kilograms of plutonium per year—or about enough fissionable material for the fabrication of 10 to 12 bomb cores annually.[5] Whether this would be enough weapons to have the impact that Brodie and others imagined was a matter of conjecture.

Nonetheless, the very existence of the bomb raised awkward questions about whether a large postwar defense establishment was, as American military planners believed, really necessary. In the wake of the near-total disaster of Pearl Harbor and the American defeats that had followed early in World War II, mobilization potential seemed less important than capabilities in-being that could absorb a future enemy attack and respond effectively. Service planners, looking ahead to the postwar period, emphasized the need for a sizable permanent peacetime military establishment—something on the order of a 25-division army, a two-ocean navy with over 300 major combat ships and 3,600 aircraft, and a 70-group air force, with heavy emphasis on strategic bombardment. Now, with the possibility of so much destructive power in a single weapon, a much smaller postwar force might suffice.[6]

No group was more concerned than the AAF, which in September 1945 hastily convened a panel of senior officers, headed by General Carl Spaatz, architect of the recent strategic air campaign against Germany, to study the bomb's likely impact.[7] Completed in less than a month, the Spaatz report roundly endorsed the full exploitation of atomic technology. Yet, as a precursor to later force-level demands, the board saw no reason why the existence of nuclear weapons should alter the AAF's plans concerning its postwar size, composition, or organization. The board reasoned that while atomic weapons were indeed an important breakthrough, the limited number of bombs would probably confine their use to only the highest priority targets for some time to come. In other words, the advent of nuclear weapons did not necessarily signal a new era in strategic air warfare or require drastic doctrinal changes. "The atomic bomb," the board concluded, "has not altered our basic concept of the strategic air offensive but has given us an additional weapon."[8]

Put succinctly, as they entered the postwar era, neither the military nor the civilian leadership was sure what exactly to make of the atomic bomb. Most probably agreed with Brig. Gen. Alfred R. Maxwell's assessment that the atomic bomb fell in the category of an "experimental weapon."[9] So long as the stockpile of bombs remained small, military planners were reluctant to place too high a premium on their use, despite their immense deterrent value and military potential. And, like many civilians, they were not at all sure how wars of the future, should any occur, would be affected.

THE STRUGGLE OVER DOMESTIC CONTROL

For many, a further reason for uncertainty about the atomic bomb centered on the belief—indeed, in some quarters, the expectation—that ultimately these weapons would be outlawed or placed under strict international control, much like poison gas was after World War I. Indeed, as World War II ended, it was far from clear that the United States would, in fact, keep and develop an atomic arsenal. A more likely scenario, given the tenor of the times and public and congressional opinion, focused on harnessing this new source of power and making it subject to rigorous domestic and international controls.

Of the two areas of control, the most notable and enduring achievements turned out to be on the domestic front. Discussion of the need for postwar controls dated from as early as October 1941, when Bush had outlined to Roosevelt an accelerated program of nuclear research aimed definitely at developing an atomic bomb. Not until 1944, however, as scientists became fairly certain that the uranium bomb design would work, did Bush again address the subject. His immediate concerns were not so much postwar policy per se as the need to quell rumors at the Chicago Metallurgical Laboratory that the War Department would close the lab after the war. In August 1944, in an effort to boost the lab's sagging morale, Bush and Conant persuaded Groves to appoint an investigatory committee on postwar policy headed by his scientific advisor, Dr. Richard C. Tolman. After interviewing dozens of scientists connected with the Manhattan Project, the committee concluded that atomic energy research should continue to receive high priority after the war. The committee recommended the creation of a national authority similar to Bush's wartime Office of Scientific Research and Development, which would be in charge of distributing funds and promoting research.[10]

In September 1944, eager that the matter of postwar controls should receive attention at the highest level, Bush and Conant sent Secretary of War Stimson two papers that they hoped would find their way to the President. Both dealt with the future international handling of atomic energy, one in more detail than the other. Arguing that the secret behind the bomb could not be protected forever, they favored an international clearing house for information under the auspices of whatever association of nations emerged after the war. They also recommended creation of an advisory committee on domestic uses. Stimson took the matter under advisement and agreed to discuss it with the State Department. Beyond this he was noncommittal, confiding to aides that arriving at a policy on controls would demand enormous care.[11]

But as the Manhattan Project neared completion, Stimson began to realize that postwar planning could not wait indefinitely. On March 15, 1945, while briefing Roosevelt on the progress of the S-1 program, he also mentioned the growing interest in some circles in postwar controls. Broadly speaking, he said, he had thus far detected two schools of thought on the subject. One group, which he described as the "close-in" school, favored keeping an American monopoly on atomic energy as long as possible; the other wanted some form of international supervision and control. Although Stimson expressed no preference for either, he believed it advisable that the United States have a definite policy, set forth in a public statement, at the time of the first use of the bomb. Roosevelt agreed that this should be done, but he apparently did not regard the matter as urgent enough to require immediate action.[12]

As a result, no systematic preparations for control—either at the international or domestic level—had been developed by May 1945, when President Truman approved Stimson's proposal of the Interim Committee to advise on atomic energy policy. As part of the committee's charter, he gave it the task of drafting postwar legislation on atomic energy.[13] Preoccupied with wartime concerns, especially the question of whether or not to use the bomb, the Interim Committee gave infrequent attention to this part of its mission, so that the eventual drafting fell to two War Department lawyers—Brig. Gen. Kenneth C. Royall and William L. Marbury. Not surprisingly, their product, submitted to the committee in July 1945, carefully delineated a set of control mechanisms that matched military practices used in the wartime Manhattan Project. The plan included a supervisory commission of nine members (four with service connections), four advisory boards with sweeping powers, and a full-time administrator with authority similar to that Groves had exercised. Bush and Conant objected, arguing that these measures were overly deferential to military, as opposed to civilian, uses of atomic energy, and predicting (correctly) that they would encounter strong resistance from the scientific community. Subsequently, in a lame effort to broaden support, the War Department offered token changes. But the proposal that went to Congress that autumn, known as the May-Johnson bill, essentially took the form of the original Royall-Marbury Plan.[14]

Although Truman associated himself with the May-Johnson bill, he never directly endorsed it. Instead, on October 3, 1945, he sent Congress a special message outlining his own desires. The message included, as did the May-Johnson bill, a request for a supervisory commission with broad powers and authority over the acquisition of minerals and ores, production of fissionable materials, plant operations, and research and development.[15] Two weeks later, when asked by a reporter how he felt about the May-Johnson bill in the light of his own proposals, Truman hedged. "I don't know," he replied, "because I haven't studied it [the May-Johnson bill] carefully." But, he added, "It is substantially in line with the suggestions in the message, I think."[16]

From this point on, Truman found himself in the midst of a controversy over domestic control he probably never anticipated. Congressional ambitions and jurisdictional fights, Bush's and Conant's lobbying against the May-Johnson bill, and some moral self-flagellation by members of the scientific community about the actual use of the A-bomb enlivened the debate. The ensuing furor left it clear that many of the scientists connected with the Manhattan Project, still smarting from Groves's dictatorial methods, abhorred the prospect of continued military control of atomic energy; and that most in Congress shared their sentiments. Truman, an expert at measuring congressional opinion, saw the change and edged steadily away from the original bill. By late November 1945, he wrote the secretaries of war and navy to object to the proposal, especially its provision that military men could sit on the commission. Truman now sided with those arguing for full civilian control and expressed a strong preference for a commission of three members, serving at his pleasure and establishing policies approved by him.[17]

The final legislative product was not so much Truman's as it was Senator Brien McMahon's. McMahon, an ambitious Democrat from Connecticut, consciously sought to become the leading authority in Congress on atomic energy. On December 20, he introduced S. 1717, which would provide for a full-time, civilian dominated, five-member commission to control atomic energy. Supported by Truman (though not to the point of receiving precise information about the bomb), McMahon gradually won adherents to his cause, which resulted in the Atomic Energy Act of 1946. According to opinion polls, the American public initially favored leaving control of atomic energy in the hands of the military. But as the debate in Congress unfolded, popular sentiment shifted in the other direction.[18] Even so, McMahon and the White House still wound up having to make several important concessions to offset persistent complaints from the War Department that its interests were not being sufficiently protected.[19] The upshot was an amendment, sponsored by Republican Senator Arthur H. Vandenberg, creating a Military Liaison Committee. The MLC would be controlled by the armed services and would have the specific function of coordinating distinctly military applications of atomic energy with the new commission. Additionally, the President, not the commission, would have the final word on transferring nuclear weapons from the custody of the civilian agency to the armed forces. And, following the discovery of a Soviet atomic spy ring operating in Canada, Congress insisted on strict safeguards over the handling and transfer of atomic energy information, giving it the special appellation of "restricted data." Some of these changes would, as it happened, harbor the potential for continuing civil-military friction over weapons custody, weapons development, and the production of fissionable material. But on the big issues, especially the principle of civilian control, Truman and McMahon won when, in late July 1946, the law cleared Congress for the President's signature.[20]

The new law, regrettably, contained some unintended side-effects. First, it cast a chill over the prospects for future Anglo-American collaboration in atomic energy. Throughout the debate, despite repeated requests for information, most members of Congress remained largely in the dark about the various understandings and agreements reached between Roosevelt and Churchill during the war and the implied—sometimes explicit—provisions in their discussions of postwar cooperation. As early as the spring of 1945, the British had begun to send out feelers, mentioning two documents in particular—the 1943 Quebec Agreement, summarizing wartime obligations to one another; and the September 1944 Hyde Park *aide-mémoire,* which had called for "full collaboration" after the war.[21] Truman, acting on the advice of Bush and others, held that these accords were obsolete after V-J Day; but the British persisted and received assurances, at a November 1945 meeting in Washington between Truman and British Prime Minister Clement Attlee, that new arrangements would be forthcoming. Still, as far as Whitehall was concerned, passage of the 1946 Atomic Energy Act—with its severe restrictions on sharing information—was tantamount to a "death blow" to future US-UK collaboration. Even though subsequent negotiations leading to the 1948 US-UK *modus vivendi* undid much of the actual damage, the feeling on the part of the British was still that the United States had behaved in bad faith, in all likelihood to protect its monopoly on the bomb.[22]

These suspicions were essentially correct. Looking back, Truman acknowledged as much and regretted that collaboration had to be curtailed; but he maintained at the same time that he had had no other choice. "The McMahon Act," he explained,

> was the statutory expression of the American mood at that time to retain sole custody of the atomic bomb secrets in the United States. Since Britain had been a partner with us in the initiation of the atomic bomb and a close ally during two world wars, I, for one, felt that Canada and Great Britain should be allowed a closer association with us in this field. But for all practical purposes at that time, Canada and Britain were in no economic position to manufacture the bomb. Both had reason to expect that American possession of the bomb would safeguard their security as well as our own.[23]

Exactly why Congress was not better informed is still something of a mystery. Certainly, as Dean Acheson, Under Secretary of State from 1945 to 1947, later wrote, the whole episode was unfortunate, the British having been "ungenerously, if not unfairly, treated."[24] But with knowledge of the Quebec and Hyde Park agreements so closely held for so long, a breakdown of communication between the executive and legislative branches is hardly surprising. In any case, Acheson, who learned belatedly of the wartime accords, did in fact try to brief several key members of the Senate. Although McMahon does not seem to have been among that group, he had been involved in other consultations that bore on the status of US-UK atomic collaboration. Indeed, he had learned from Bush as early as November 1945 "some of the facts of British-American scientific collaboration" during the war.[25] But the effect of these disclosures, as Acheson discovered, was to harden, not soften, congressional resistance to the sharing of information and technology.[26] Several years later, though, McMahon apparently told British Defence Minister A. V. Alexander that had he known the full story of Anglo-American wartime agreements, the Atomic Energy Act would have incorporated quite different wording.[27] Whether his congressional colleagues would have agreed, however, is questionable.

As if British annoyance over the McMahon Act were not enough, Truman soon found himself embroiled with Congress in a further controversy over appointment of the Atomic Energy Commission members. In the selection of David Lilienthal, former head of the Tennessee Valley Authority, to chair the commission, Truman chose an individual with humane instincts, proven bureaucratic and managerial skills, and a liberal conscience that reinforced his commitment to the peaceful use of nuclear energy. But Lilienthal also brought distinct liabilities, chiefly the rancorous hostility of Democratic Senator Kenneth McKellar of Tennessee, who accused him of being a communist, a charge for which he offered no proof. The ensuing hearings were nonetheless exceedingly unpleasant and effectively delayed what should have been an easy confirmation process. Although the appointment of the commissioners was announced on October 28, 1946, the final confirmation of Lilienthal and his colleagues (Sumner Pike, Lewis Strauss, William Waymack, and Robert Bacher) did not occur until April 1947.[28]

As a practical matter, however, the transition from military to civilian control occurred as scheduled. On December 31, 1946, as mandated by Congress, the Manhattan Engineer District ceased to exist and the commissioners, yet unconfirmed, took charge. What they found was a program in utter disarray. With the emergency that had brought them together long over, the highly trained staffs of scientists and technicians assembled to build the bomb had practically melted away. Some had returned to campuses, others to industry or private research. Budget appropriations also reflected the slide, falling from $610 million in 1945 to $281 million by December 1946. The morale of those employees who chose to remain, often working in facilities at Los Alamos, New Mexico, and Hanford, Washington, that were rapidly deteriorating, was understandably low. "Without the wartime sense of urgency," recalled one Army administrator, "development and production of weapons practically stopped."[29]

This lag in activity roughly coincided with the CROSSROADS tests on Bikini atoll in the Pacific in the summer of 1946, which saw the detonation of two atomic bombs against naval targets. (A third test explosion had also been planned, but concern over the shortage of fissionable material caused it to be called off.) In terms of raw destructive power, no one could doubt the bomb's potency after the tests. So awesome were the results that, according to the group of observers representing the Joint Chiefs of Staff, atomic weapons, if "used in numbers," could "nullify any nation's military effort" and "demolish its social and economic structures and prevent their reestablishment for long periods of time."[30]

Other observers were less impressed. The first test—an air-dropped bomb—had such poor ballistics that it missed its target by some 1,500 yards and failed to cause the immediate sinking of any ship in the targeted area. In the view of Alexander P. De Seversky, the Russian-born aircraft designer serving as an advisor to the War Department, the bomb's numerous design flaws and demonstrated shortcomings reconfirmed his earlier suspicion that it was "a force of measurable dimensions, with known potentials and known limitations." "As sheer panic subsides," Seversky believed, "the American people are beginning to recognize that fact."[31]

In short, CROSSROADS was inconclusive, the results ambiguous. Not only did the exercise uncover numerous technical flaws in bomb design, but also, in doing so, it raised new questions about the bomb's military utility. The overall effect was to reinforce the ambivalent attitude, evidenced by the President and others, toward the production and stockpile of nuclear weapons. Thus, by the second half of 1946, Truman reckoned that he had at his disposal an arsenal of not "over a half dozen" nuclear cores, a modest number to be sure, but still, he felt, "enough to win a war."[32] Yet, at a time when Soviet-American relations were perceptibly chilling and when the posthaste demobilization of US armed forces had reduced the American military presence in Europe to one and one-third understrength divisions, the American capacity for mounting military operations—either by atomic or conventional means—was by no means overwhelming. In these circumstances, international control and cooperation, not bickering and conflict, seemed the more reasonable and advisable path to follow.

THE DEBATE OVER INTERNATIONAL CONTROLS

Like the efforts made to achieve domestic control of the atom, those aimed at establishing international control can be seen as either quixotic or deliberately insincere. Even before nuclear weapons were a reality, American leaders, from Truman on down, recognized the political as well as military value of this new source of power. The idea of using the bomb for diplomatic leverage purposes—implicit in many of Truman's actions at the Potsdam Conference in July-August 1945, explicit (or nearly so) in Byrnes's behavior there and at the first meeting of the Council of Foreign Ministers in London that autumn—needs no further elaboration.[33] Cynics might argue from this the illogic of expecting the Soviet Union, or any other power for that matter, to forego the development of their own bomb. Others, less charitably, might hold that the United States never made a genuine effort at international control, that the attempts were window dressing at best and self-serving at worst. Critics might also charge that the Baruch Plan, which became the cornerstone of American policy on international control, retained all the most important powers for Washington until Moscow agreed to a set of political and inspection conditions that would have altered the fundamental character of the Soviet regime. But the partial truths in these views should not obscure the more fundamental reality: that Truman and his senior advisors were genuinely anxious to find a way to curb the international spread of atomic destructiveness.

As comforting and reassuring as the American monopoly on the bomb may have been, it had its disquieting aspects also. Based on everything they heard from the scientists and technicians who had worked on the Manhattan Project, American policymakers had good reason to assume that the US monopoly on the bomb would not continue indefinitely, and that at some future point other countries—most likely the Soviet Union, first of all—would possess the industrial and engineering capacity to exploit the relatively simple scientific principles involved in constructing atomic weapons. For proliferation on a worldwide scale to be avoided, some form of international control appeared essential, maybe even imperative.

In these circumstances, the question became: how could the United States attain the goal of suppressing the spread of nuclear technology while preserving its security? Truman approached the problem with ambivalence. On the one hand, as he stated in his special message to Congress on October 3, 1945, a "satisfactory arrangement" for the control of atomic energy, both at home and abroad, constituted his ultimate hope and desire.[34] But just a few days later, on October 8, he assured Americans that the United States would never divulge how to make atomic weapons and that it would, moreover, continue to make them for experimental purposes.[35]

The President reiterated these themes in New York City before a Navy Day audience on October 27. The development of the atomic bomb, he said, "means we must be prepared to approach international problems with greater speed, with greater determination, with greater ingenuity, in order to meet a situation for which there is no precedent." Insisting that the bomb was "no threat to any nation," he held that it was "the highest hope of the American people . . . that world cooperation for peace will soon reach a state of perfection that atomic methods of destruction can be definitely and effectively outlawed forever. We have sought, and we will continue to seek, the attainment of that objective." And he concluded, "We shall pursue that cause with all the wisdom, patience, and determination that the God of Peace can bestow upon a people who are trying to follow His path."[36]

The American drive for international control of atomic energy proceeded from the same realism that propelled American policy in other related areas: the worry that another power would achieve an atomic capability. At first, during the war, it had been Hitler, but as Germany's defeat grew certain, attention shifted to the Soviet Union. The leading concern, of course, was how long it would take Soviet scientists to duplicate the American success, a question that the Interim Committee took up in May 1945, even before the United States had tested its first atomic device. At the time, Groves speculated that the Russians would need 20 years to emulate American achievements. But Conant, with far more accuracy, said four years would be enough. In June, the Interim Committee returned to the subject, this time reviewing estimates by the various managers of the Manhattan Project who put the prospects of a Soviet A-bomb in the five-to-six years-plus bracket. But there was also a disposition to think the Russians could do it sooner with German scientific help. At best, in other words, the U.S. lead was temporary. This fact made the control issue all the more urgent, the temptations to use American knowledge as a bargaining lever all the greater.[37]

On the eve of the TRINITY test, three separate avenues for dealing with the Soviets and atomic energy were emerging, each dependent on a form of effective international control: (1) offering the Soviets information in the hope of winning their gratitude and trust; (2) offering this information on a *quid pro quo* basis in return for the settlement of outstanding diplomatic issues; and (3) moving directly into the international arena and seeking a broad international accord there.[38] A fourth option—letting events take their course—would also surface and would, in the long run, be the one adopted by default. Initially, the first two approaches were the ones most actively discussed, although a thorough canvassing of them at the highest levels of government did not occur until September 1945, well after the Potsdam summit conference and the bombing of Hiroshima and Nagasaki.

Secretary of War Stimson, who had once been an ardent advocate of the *quid pro quo* approach, now found himself tending toward a policy of openness. Pressed steadily by Conant and Bush since late the previous year to weigh the merits of an open move, Stimson had hesitated. He continued to do so even in June and July, inclining to favor something he and Truman had discussed at one point: a trade-off between Soviet concessions and

American information.[39] But the use of the bomb and his own instincts convinced him that, despite the risks, the scientists were right. Acting on this, he persuaded Truman to hold a high-level discussion on the matter in mid-September. "To put the matter concisely," he wrote Truman before the meeting, "I consider the problem of our satisfactory relations with Russia as not merely connected with but as virtually dominated by the problem of the atomic bomb." Stimson believed that it was well within the Soviets' capacity to build bombs of their own, so that sharing information would be of little consequence in the long run. The alternative, as he saw it, was for the United States to attempt to protect its monopoly and continue to negotiate, in which case "having this weapon rather ostentatiously on our hip, their suspicions and their distrust of our purposes and motives will increase."[40]

Stimson's request for a high-level discussion produced a meeting of the full cabinet on September 21, a forum that Stimson found larger than expected and inappropriate for a candid discussion of an issue as sensitive as atomic energy and its impact on Soviet-American relations. As Bush, who accompanied Stimson to the meeting, later described the situation, "we both pulled our punches a bit in discussion, and it is just as well that we did," because of news leaks afterwards.[41] Among those at the meeting who endorsed Stimson's position were Dean Acheson, representing the State Department in Byrnes's absence, Secretary of Commerce Henry A. Wallace, Labor Secretary Lewis B. Schwellenbach, and Acting Secretary of War Robert Patterson. Expressing a view he would later totally reverse, Acheson explained that he could "not conceive of a world in which we were hoarders of military secrets from our Allies, particularly this great Ally upon our cooperation with whom rests the future peace of the world." But others, including Secretary of the Navy Forrestal, Attorney General Tom Clark, Secretary of Agriculture Clinton Anderson, and the President's close personal friend, Secretary of the Treasury Fred Vinson, were dubious about the proposal. "If we give this one advantage of war," said Vinson, "it necessarily follows that we have to give *all others* and not only to Russia but to all nations." Forrestal concurred and suggested instead that the United States keep control of the bomb and act as its trustee on behalf of the United Nations, limiting the manufacture of weapons to those for such missions as the UN should direct. A middle position, advanced by Julius Krug, chairman of the War Production Board, and supported by John Snyder, Leo Crowley, and Senator Kenneth D. McKellar, was to wait and see how Soviet-American relations unfolded. If things improved, then one might decide to offer Moscow information after all. A modest *quid pro quo* approach, this would emerge as a leading theme of subsequent American policies.[42]

Though hardly decisive in carving out an American policy, the cabinet meeting of September 21 seems to have swayed Truman toward a more guarded posture on sharing atomic secrets, not only with the Soviets but with anyone. Basic information on how to make the bomb, he told members of his White House staff afterwards, verged on common knowledge within the scientific community; but under no condition would he "turn over the plants and equipment to do it."[43] His military advisors, he soon found, were of a similar mind. After meeting informally with the President to air their views, the Joint Chiefs followed up with a memorandum on October 23 detailing their position. While concurring that the scientific "secret" of the bomb could not be protected indefinitely, they pointed out that many of the technical procedures and manufacturing processes used for atomic weapons were still highly classified. Any disclosure of this information, they argued, particularly in the absence of agreement among the great powers on a range of fundamental international issues, could promote an atomic arms race. Rather than expose the United States to this danger, the Chiefs urged prompt action of a "political nature" leading to international controls that would restrict or outlaw nuclear weapons.[44]

The return of Secretary of State Byrnes from the recent London meeting of the Council of Foreign Ministers added another voice to those of the doubters. Disappointed by his lack of success in London, especially in trying to use the bomb as a bargaining lever to bring the Soviets around, Byrnes was increasingly pessimistic about being able to work with the Russians. He now resolved to take a tougher line, reiterating views he had expressed earlier that international control "was not practical."[45] Reversing the position expressed by Acheson at the cabinet meeting, he declared that he wanted to "see whether we can work out a decent peace" with the Russians before making any concessions on atomic energy. He dismissed Stimson's offer to share information with the Soviets as being unduly influenced by scientists who did not know "the facts" or have "the responsibility for the handling of international affairs."[46] Whatever lingering questions may have remained in Truman's mind, Byrnes's return seems to have settled them.

From this point on, Truman decided to forego the *à deux* approach recommended by Stimson. He sought instead to place the control of atomic energy within a broader international framework in which the Soviets might or might not choose to participate. This would, of course, as Stimson correctly predicted, eventually render the entire effort at control nugatory. But it was the only approach that Truman could possibly have comfortably adopted without feeling that he was compromising American security.

THE RISE AND DEMISE OF THE BARUCH PLAN

By the end of 1945, it was clear that the United States would press ahead for some form of international control, though the details of the American position remained wholly unformed. As a preparatory step, Byrnes went to Moscow in December to discuss, among other things, a possible forum for future international controls. What emerged was uncommonly swift Soviet endorsement of a US-British proposal to establish a United Nations commission on atomic energy, which would operate under the UN Security Council and be made up of the council's member states. From Byrnes's standpoint, Soviet acceptance of the commission concept was a major breakthrough, a sign that cooperation between East and West might yet be possible. Still to be decided, however, as Byrnes well knew, were the more sensitive and basic issues of what authority the commission would exercise and how intrusive international controls should be.[47]

Then, in February 1946, Byrnes turned the entire matter over to Under Secretary of State Acheson. With no prior experience in the atomic energy field, Acheson sought help from recognized scientific experts and proceeded to assemble a board of consultants, chaired by David Lilienthal, to develop recommendations. Most of the ideas that emerged owed their inspiration to J. Robert Oppenheimer, the former head of Los Alamos, whose "informal notes" on the subject of international control formed the core of the group's report.[48] Presented to Truman in mid-March, the so-called Acheson-Lilienthal report called for creation of an international agency to control access to raw materials, to monitor the production of fissionable materials, to license nuclear facilities, and, ultimately, to have custody of atomic bombs if any were allowed to remain in existence. Under no illusions about the problems posed by Russian participation, the consultants carefully linked the progressive release of US knowledge, material, and weapons to demonstrated Soviet cooperation.[49]

The next step was to convert these recommendations into a workable package for presentation to the United Nations, a task that fell to sometime presidential advisor Bernard Baruch. What is surprising throughout the unfolding of this process is the comparatively modest part played by the American military, doubtless the result of Baruch's lack of interest in the actual military applications of atomic energy. By and large, he seems to have preferred the advice of scientists over that of the military.[50] In fact, Baruch was never briefed on the size or condition of the US nuclear stockpile, nor is there any evidence that he ever requested such information. As David Alan

Rosenberg has observed, Baruch's "knowledge of atomic weapons or how they would be used in war was minimal."[51]

Groves, never one to be reticent, had already made known his views in a memorandum dated January 2, 1946. Although he favored international control, he also felt that: "If there are to be atomic weapons in the world, we must have the best, the biggest and the most."[52] Later, the Joint Chiefs of Staff, responding individually, commented in much the same vein. But their answers only arrived on (or perhaps after) the eve of Baruch's presentation to the United Nations. In general, as they had told Truman the previous September, the Chiefs backed the move toward international control but stressed the need to assure American security. They made clear their opposition to war but doubted the United States could achieve lasting peace. Nor were they enthusiastic about the chances of enforcing any accord. Adm. William D. Leahy, the President's chief of staff to the JCS, and Adm. Nimitz added a further proposition as well: they would link the UN discussions with a variation of atomic diplomacy, making US concessions dependent upon a satisfactory completion of the European peace treaties.[53]

Baruch's efforts did not, in the long run, alter the basic shape of the Acheson-Lilienthal report, but they did add refinements that gave greater weight to protecting American security interests. Baruch also insisted that the American plan have a clause forbidding permanent members of the Security Council from exercising their veto power in any international enforcement system. The scheme made clear, moreover, that an immediate ban on nuclear weapons—soon to become a major Russian theme—would not be acceptable to the United States.[54] The Baruch Plan, with its obvious dependence upon inspections and international controls, certainly contained provisions that Moscow could not help but find distasteful. An American willingness to renounce the first-use or even the use of atomic weapons except under UN auspices might have been a more balanced approach. Yet, given the intensity of Soviet efforts to develop the bomb at this time, there is little room for doubt that any American initiative, short of actually delivering weapons into the hands of the United Nations, would have only met with Soviet disapproval. In any event, the proposals reached the international organization on June 14, 1946, with Baruch's famous introduction: "We are here to make a choice between the quick and the dead. That is our business."[55]

For the remainder of 1946, these proposals constituted one of the United Nations' main agenda items, with repercussions not only for American diplomacy but for American domestic politics as well. On September 12, Secretary of Commerce Henry A. Wallace, the lone liberal hold-over in the cabinet from Roosevelt's day, delivered a controversial speech at New York's Madison Square Garden calling for greater flexibility and patience in dealing with Moscow. Five days later, as a further gesture of his differences with the administration, Wallace released a letter he had written to Truman in July in which he attacked the step-by-step approach to international control of atomic energy and urged greater American generosity toward the Soviets. Worried that the continued presence of the atomic bomb and "other revolutionary new weapons" like poison gases and biological warfare capabilities were inherently destabilizing to the international order, Wallace cautioned that "a peace maintained by a predominance of [military] forces is no longer possible." It followed, in Wallace's view, that the only way out of this awful situation was for the United States to agree to a total ban on such devices and be prepared to destroy its entire stockpile of nuclear weapons. "If we are willing to negotiate on this basis," he contended, "I believe the Russians will also negotiate seriously with a view to reaching an agreement."[56]

As sincere and well meant as Wallace's suggestions may have been, they did not strike Truman as particularly helpful or realistic. The ensuing uproar made Wallace's departure from the cabinet certain, which in turn prompted an outpouring of criticism of Truman in the liberal press.[57] Wallace's dramatic exit, though possibly a reflection of Truman's growing impatience with the Soviets, seems more likely to have been the logical outcome of what for some time had been an awkward and tenuous relationship. Wallace had been Roosevelt's vice president in 1944, and would in all probability have been president had Roosevelt not chosen to dump him as his running mate that year. As one thing led to another, a split between Truman and Wallace became all the more probable, and when it came it must have been a surprise to neither. In any event, it failed either to alter American policy or to enhance the prospects for international control at the United Nations.

By late September, the prognosis for Truman's goal of international control was bleak. Although a UN special committee overwhelmingly endorsed the Baruch Plan (including the veto provisions), the Soviet Union and communist-controlled Poland balked. The committee's vote on the final report, adopting the American position, on December 30, 1946, was anticlimactic: ten "ayes" and two abstentions. Long before, the Russians, by introducing their plan for complete and general disarmament, had effectively side-tracked any conceivable chance to control atomic energy through the United Nations.[58] Later, as the cold war deepened in 1947 and 1948, the United States would consider withdrawing the Baruch Plan altogether, fearful that the Soviets might suddenly accept it and force the United States to give up its most powerful military weapon.

As 1946 neared a close, Soviet behavior in the UN and elsewhere ensured that ultimately the United States would opt for "the best, the biggest, and the most" atomic weapons. The effort for international control was not succeeding. Even Stimson, who had earlier supported the idea, now evinced deep misgivings. The attempt to abort a Soviet-American arms race, seen as a viable, plausible policy option in the autumn of 1945, had come to nothing. Neither the offer to give over atomic energy to international control nor the implicit threat to withhold it had influenced Soviet behavior. Paradoxically, as the UN efforts appeared increasingly illusionary, the urgency behind the control effort also eased. In part, this may have stemmed from revised estimates by the JCS intelligence staff that now placed a Soviet atomic weapon in the three- to ten-year range. Or it may have come from Conant's amended prediction that it would be 5 to 15 years before the Soviets could engage in the production of atomic bombs in "considerable quantity—say 25 to 500 a year."[59] Moreover, as 1946 progressed, the urgency of reaching agreement on atomic energy became overshadowed by a panoply of other Soviet-American issues, including a now-forgotten war scare in Europe that summer and troubles over Iran, China, and treaties with the Axis satellite countries. Despite a few dissenters like Henry Wallace, Truman and those around him were gradually reaching the conclusion that an improvement in political relations would have to precede any arms control accord.

Such thinking led to other implications. Parallel to American efforts at international control of atomic energy was the opposite tendency to hedge and to make the bomb more readily available for use again should the need arise. Thus, in July 1946, Spaatz, now commanding general of the AAF, visited England and elicited from Air Chief Marshal Sir Arthur Tedder an oral agreement that the Royal Air Force (RAF) would provide "certain physical facilities" on two British airfields adequate for handling "some very special purpose" long-range aircraft. Included under the list of facilities were such items as runways, hoists, and other gear required for air-atomic operations, with construction to be handled as a routine matter so as not to attract undue attention.[60] Whether Spaatz and Tedder immediately notified their superiors of these arrangements (or whether they were apprised in advance) is unclear. What is known is that shortly after the Spaatz-Tedder meeting, Col. Elmer E. Kirkpatrick, Jr., the officer who had supervised the digging of the A-bomb loading pits on Tinian in World War II, arrived in England to discuss similar construction with the British.[61]

Despite portents of worsening Soviet-American relations and certain precautionary measures like the Spaatz-Tedder agreement, the United States did not immediately accelerate the buildup of its nuclear capabilities. On the contrary, it dawdled. Progress in implementing the Spaatz-Tedder agreement, perhaps because of the restrictions in the McMahon Act, was almost nil. By the time of 1948 Berlin crisis, in fact, none of the planned work had even yet begun. Meanwhile, by September 1946, the Air Force had an operational inventory of only 17 atomic-modified B-29s, all part of the 509th Bombardment Group, compared with 46 a year earlier. The 509th had one loading pit at its base at Roswell Field, New Mexico, but it had no bomb assembly teams and no practice bombs because of security considerations.[62] Failure to win Soviet acceptance of the control scheme had not led, however much Forrestal and others among the emerging group of Washington "hardliners" may have been inclined, to a heavier emphasis on cultivating military options. Diplomacy, economic aid, and limited military assistance continued instead to constitute the American response to the chilling of Soviet-American relations during 1946 and 1947.

NOTES

1. "President's News Conference of August 16, 1945," *Public Papers of the Presidents of the United States: Harry S. Truman, 1945* (Washington, D.C.: G.P.O., 1961), 224.
2. See Henry D. Smyth, *Atomic Energy for Military Purposes: The Official Report on the Development of the Atomic Bomb Under the Auspices of the United States Government, 1940-1945* (Princeton, N.J.: Princeton University Press, 1946).
3. Bernard Brodie (ed.), *The Absolute Weapon: Atomic Power and World Order* (New York: Harcourt, Brace, and World, 1946), 76.
4. The quote is from Lawrence Freedman, *The Evolution of Nuclear Strategy* (New York: St. Martin's Press, 1981), 22. On the controversy surrounding strategic bombing in World War II, see especially Michael S. Sherry, *The Rise of American Air Power* (New Haven: Yale University Press, 1987); David MacIsaac, *Strategic Bombing in World War Two: The Story of the United States Strategic Bombing Survey* (New York: Garland Publishing, 1976); and Kenneth P. Werrell, "The Strategic Bombing of Germany in World War II: Costs and Accomplishments," *Journal of American History* 73 (Dec. 1986): 702-713.
5. David Alan Rosenberg, "Toward Armageddon: The Foundations of United States Nuclear Strategy, 1945-1961," (Ph.D. diss., University of Chicago, 1981), 11-12.
6. On the origins and development of service plans for postwar forces, see Michael S. Sherry, *Preparing for the Next War: American Plans for Postwar Defense, 1941-1945* (New Haven: Yale University Press, 1977); Vincent

Davis, *Postwar Defense Policy and the U.S. Navy, 1943-1946* (Chapel Hill: University of North Carolina Press, 1966); and Perry McCoy Smith, *The Air Force Plans for Peace, 1943-1945* (Baltimore: Johns Hopkins University Press, 1970).

7. Herman S. Wolk, *Planning and Organizing the Postwar Air Force, 1943-1947* (Washington, D.C.: Office of Air Force History, 1984), 121.

8. Spaatz Board Rpt, "Effect of the Atomic Bomb on Employment, Size, Organization, and Composition of the Postwar Air Force," Oct. 23, 1945, Record Group (RG) 341 (HQ, USAF) OPD 384.3 Atomic (17 Aug 45), sec. 1, Military Reference Branch, National Archives and Records Administration (NARA).

9. Memo, Maxwell to Lt. Gen. H.S. Vandenberg, Dec. 13, 1945, sub: Publicity on the Atomic Bomb, RG 341, OPD 384.3 Atomic (17 Aug 45), sec. 1.

10. Richard G. Hewlett and Oscar E. Anderson, Jr. *A History of the United States Atomic Energy Commission*, vol. I, *The New World, 1939-1946* (Washington, D.C.: U.S. Atomic Energy Commission, 1972), 324-325; Vincent C. Jones, *Manhattan: The Army and the Atomic Bomb* (Washington, D.C.: Center of Military History, 1985), 563-564.

11. Hewlett and Anderson, *The New World*, 329-331.

12. Diary entry, Mar. 15, 1945, Stimson Papers.

13. Hewlett and Anderson, *The New World*, 344-346; Henry L. Stimson and McGeorge Bundy, *On Active Service in Peace and War* (New York: Harper and Bros., 1947), 616.

14. Hewlett and Anderson, *The New World*, 415-433; Jones, *Manhattan*, 568-569.

15. "Special Message to the Congress on Atomic Energy," Oct. 3, 1945, *Truman Public Papers, 1945*, 362-366.

16. *Ibid.*, 403.

17. Ltr, Truman to Patterson and Forrestal, Nov. 28, 1945, George Elsey Papers, box 88, Harry S. Truman Library (HSTL), Independence, Mo.; Truman, *Year of Decisions*, 533-534.

18. Hazel Gaudet Erskine, "The Polls: Atomic Weapons and Nuclear Energy," *Public Opinion Quarterly* 27 (Summer 1963): 170-171.

19. See ltr, Patterson to McMahon, [Feb. 6, 1946], Byron S. Miller Papers, box 2, S. 1717-Military Role folder, Library of Congress (L.C.).

20. For the struggle over the Atomic Energy Act, see Hewlett and Anderson, *The New World*, ch. 14.

21. Articles of Agreement Governing Collaboration . . . in the Matter of Tube Alloys, Aug. 19, 1943, U.S. Dept. of State, *Foreign Relations of the United States: The Conferences at Washington and Quebec, 1943* (Washington, D.C.: G.P.O., 1970), 1117-1119; and Aide-Mémoire Initialed by President Roosevelt and Prime Minister Churchill, Sep. 19, 1944, U.S. Dept. of State, *Foreign Relations of the United States: The Conference at Quebec, 1944* (Washington, D.C.: G.P.O., 1972), 492-493.

22. Gowing, *Independence and Deterrence*, 105-108.

23. Harry S. Truman, *Mr. Citizen* (New York: Bernard Geis Associates, 1960), 294.

24. Dean Acheson, *Present at the Creation* (New York: W. W. Norton, 1969), 168.

25. Ltr, Bush to Conant, Nov. 10, 1945, Bush Papers, box 27, Conant folder no. 1, L.C. For additional evidence of McMahon's inclusion in consultations, see: memo for the Files by John M. Hancock, May 1, 1946, [sub: Consultations on Atomic Energy], U.S. Dept. of State, *Foreign Relations of the United States, 1946* (Washington, D.C.: G.P.O., 1972), I, 780-783, 1242-1243 (hereafter cited as *FRUS* with year and volume).

26. Acheson, *Present at the Creation,* 167.

27. Gowing, *Independence and Deterrence,* I, 107-108.

28. The fight over the confirmation can best be followed in *The Journals of David Lilienthal,* vol. I, *The Atomic Energy Years, 1945-1950* (New York: Harper and Row, 1964), 88-166; Richard G. Hewlett and Francis Duncan, *A History of the United States Atomic Energy Commission,* vol. II, *Atomic Shield, 1947-1952* (Washington, D.C.: U.S. Atomic Energy Commission, 1972), 1-53; and Leslie R. Groves, *Now It Can Be Told* (New York: Harper and Bros., 1962), 373-400.

29. K.D. Nichols, *The Road to Trinity* (New York: William Morrow, 1987), 225.

30. JCS Evaluation Board for Operation Crossroads, Final Rpt, June 30, 1947, RG 330 (Office of the Secretary of Defense), CD 25-1-12.

31. Ltr, Alexander P. De Seversky to Robert P. Patterson, Oct. 4, 1946, Spaatz Papers, box 264, SecWar folder, L.C.

32. Diary entry, Oct. 14, 1946, in Robert H. Ferrell (ed.), *Truman in the White House: The Diary of Eban A. Ayers* (Columbia: University of Missouri Press, 1991), 161. Truman's estimate may have been on the low side. Retrospective figures compiled by the Department of Energy show a stockpile by mid-1946 of nine nuclear cores. See David Alan Rosenberg, "U.S. Nuclear Stockpile, 1945 to 1950," *Bulletin of the Atomic Scientists* 38 (May 1982): 25-30.

33. For a sampling of the literature in this regard, see Gar Alperovitz, *Atomic Diplomacy: Hiroshima and Potsdam* (New York: Random House, 1977); Martin J. Sherwin, *A World Destroyed: The Atomic Bomb and the Grand Alliance* (New York: Random House, 1977); Robert L. Messer, *The End of an Alliance* (Chapel Hill: University of North Carolina Press, 1982); and Barton J. Bernstein, "Roosevelt, Truman, and the Atomic Bomb, 1941-1945," *Political Science Quarterly* 90 (Spring 1975).

34. "Special Message to the Congress on Atomic Energy," Oct. 3, 1945, *Truman Public Papers, 1945,* 362-366.

35. "Presidential Press Conference," Oct. 8, 1945, *ibid.,* 382-383.

36. *Ibid.,* 437-438.

37. Hewlett and Anderson, *The New World,* 354-359.

38. See for example Stimson's comments at the meeting of the Combined Policy Committee, July 4, 1945, *FRUS, 1945,* II, 13.

39. See diary entry, June 6, 1945, Stimson Papers.

40. Memo, Stimson to Truman, Sep. 11, 1945, sub: Proposed Action for Control of Atomic Bombs, *FRUS, 1945,* II, 41-44. Also see Stimson and Bundy, *On Active Service,* 642-646.

41. Ltr, Bush to Conant, Sep. 24, 1945, Bush Papers, box 27, Conant folder no. 1, L.C.

42. This summary draws mainly on Forrestal's notes, labeled "Atomic Bomb Cabinet," Sep. 21, 1945, retyped on White House stationery and filed in the President's Secretary's File (PSF), Subject File, box 157, Defense—Forrestal Special Letters folder, HSTL. Also see Walter Millis, with E.S. Duffield (eds.), *The Forrestal Diaries* (New York: Viking Press, 1951), 94-96; and Truman, *Year of Decisions*, 525-527.

43. Diary entry, Sep. 24, 1945, in Ferrell (ed.), *Ayers Diary*, 84.

44. Truman, *Year of Decisions*, 527-528; James F. Schnabel, *The Joint Chiefs of Staff and National Policy, 1945-1947* (Wilmington, Del.: Michael Glazer, 1979), 256-261.

45. Quoted from Oppenheimer to Stimson, Aug. 17, 1945, in Hewlett and Anderson, *New World*, 417.

46. Daniel Yergin, *Shattered Peace* (Boston: Houghton, Mifflin, 1977), 133-134; Mins, Mtg Secs of State, War, and Navy, Oct. 10, 1945, *FRUS 1945*, II, 56; Mins, Mtg Secs State, War, and Navy, Oct. 23, 1945, *ibid.*, 62.

47. McGeorge Bundy, *Danger and Survival* (New York: Random House, 1988), 145-158; Messer, *End of an Alliance*, 137-155.

48. Informal notes, Dr. J. R. Oppenheimer to Mr. D. E. Lilienthal, Feb. 2, 1946, J. Robert Oppenheimer Papers, box 46, David E. Lilienthal folder, L.C.

49. U.S., Secretary of State's Committee on Atomic Energy, *A Report on the International Control of Atomic Energy* (Washington, D.C.: Dept. of State, Mar. 16, 1946), copy in W. Averell Harriman Papers, box 220, Atomic Energy folder, L.C.

50. See Bernard Baruch, *The Public Years* (New York: Holt, Rinehart and Winston, 1960), 365.

51. Rosenberg, "Toward Armageddon," 57.

52. Memo by Groves, Jan. 2, 1946, *FRUS 1946*, I, 1197-1203.

53. Leahy to Baruch, June 11, 1946, *ibid.*, 851-853; Nimitz to Baruch, June 11, 1946, *ibid.*, 853-854; Eisenhower to Baruch, June 14, 1946, *ibid.*, 854-856; Spaatz to Baruch, n.d. (ca. June 7, 1946), RG 218 (Records of the Joint Chiefs of Staff), CCS 471.6 (8-15-45), sec. 3.

54. Memo, Baruch to Truman, June 6, 1946, *FRUS 1946*, I, 838-839; "Statement of United States Policy," June 7, 1946, *ibid.*, 846-851.

55. Quoted in Baruch, *Public Years*, 369.

56. Ltr, Wallace to Truman, July 23, 1946, in John Morton Blum (ed.), *The Price of Vision: The Diary of Henry A. Wallace, 1942-1946* (Boston: Houghton, Mifflin, 1973), 589-601.

57. Alonzo Hamby, *Beyond the New Deal: Harry S. Truman and American Liberalism* (New York: Columbia University Press, 1973), 126-133.

58. On the fate of the UN proposals, see Hewlett and Anderson, *New World*, 582-597; and Joseph I. Lieberman, *The Scorpion and the Tarantula: The Struggle to Control Atomic Weapons, 1945-1949* (Boston: Houghton, Mifflin, 1970), 303-396.

59. Joint Intelligence Committee Rpt 250/8, Feb. 8, 1946, DoD History of Strategic Arms Competition Collection, OSD Historian; ltr, Conant to Grenville Clark, Oct. 5, 1945, Bush Papers, box 27, Conant folder no. 1, L.C.

60. The only evidence in the United States of the Spaatz-Tedder agreement is in memo, Maj. Gen. Clayton Bissell to Spaatz, July 6, 1946, sub: Reminder on decisions taken during London visit July 4 to 6, 1946, RG 341, entry 337, box 7, TS AAG file 23. Neither the British Air Ministry nor Chiefs of Staff Committee files at the Public Record Office in London contain any reference to the agreement.

61. Simon Duke, *US Defence Bases in the United Kingdom: A Matter for Joint Decision?* (New York: St. Martin's Press, 1987), 21.

62. R. D. Little, *The History of Air Force Participation in the Atomic Energy Program, 1943-1953,* vol. II, *Foundations of an Atomic Air Force and Operation Sandstone, 1946-1948* (MS, USAF Historical Division, n.d.), 216, 391. Sanitized copy available at the Center of Air Force History, Bolling AFB, Washington, D.C.

III

Policy in Transition

The months that witnessed American efforts to control atomic energy also saw the simultaneous erosion of US-Soviet relations, a process that would eventually give rise to a more militant American policy involving greater reliance on nuclear weapons. Growing suspicions about Soviet intentions in Eastern Europe and Manchuria, alarm over the Soviet failure to leave Iran, new fears about Russian ambitions in the Turkish Straits, and the Soviet Union's obstructionist behavior in the United Nations all contributed to reinforcing the harder, more "realistic" assessments being offered around Washington of long-range Soviet ambitions. So too did Stalin's provocative speech of February 9, 1946, announcing three or more new five-year industrial development plans to guarantee the Soviet Union against "all contingencies," a statement that Justice William O. Douglas at the time called "The Declaration of World War III."[1] Meanwhile, in Western Europe, the Italian and French communist parties grew increasingly strident. In these months of transition, roughly from September 1946 through December 1947, the public rupture of Soviet-American relations slowly evolved. During this period, new initiatives, including the Truman Doctrine and the Marshall Plan, and new institutions created by passage of the 1947 National Security Act would also appear, adding in their own ways, sometimes directly, sometimes indirectly, to the rapidly changing face of relations between Washington and Moscow and, eventually, to American perceptions of the role nuclear weapons should play in that relationship.

THE PRESIDENT'S PERSPECTIVE

Throughout the first year-and-a-half of his presidency, Truman handled the Soviet question with deliberate circumspection, sometimes even appearing to vacillate over what to do. Throughout 1945 and on into 1946, despite mounting stresses and strains on US-Soviet relations and his earlier talk of getting "tough" with the Russians, he still spoke publicly and often privately of his hopes for improved ties with Moscow. He saw the Soviets, as he saw politicians he had known in Kansas City, as "direct-action fellows" who knew what they wanted and were prepared to bargain for it. If the United States adopted a similar attitude, he thought, "we would get along all right with them."[2] While he may have shared Winston Churchill's views about Soviet behavior as expressed in the famous "iron curtain" speech at Fulton, Missouri, Truman studiously kept an arm's length from the former British Prime Minister.[3] Writing his mother on March 11, 1946, just after returning from Fulton, he said: "I'm glad you enjoyed Fulton. So did I. And I think it did some good, although I am not yet ready to endorse Mr. Churchill's speech."[4] Such caution on Truman's part was typical of his entire approach to Soviet-American differences throughout this period and did not give way easily.

All the same, warnings of an impending rupture were hard to ignore. On top of the problems of 1945 came new US-Soviet differences in 1946, including a controversy over the continuing presence of Soviet troops in northern Iran and apparent Soviet support of a communist-led separatist movement in the Iranian province of Azerbaijan. In an effort to put matters in perspective, the US chargé d'affaires in Moscow, George F. Kennan, cabled Washington in February his own detailed analysis of what he believed lay behind Soviet actions. In a measured, precise essay running to some 8,000 words, Kennan endeavored to sort out for his superiors the historic and ideological reasons behind Soviet behavior and methods, the implications for the West, and the prospects for the future—ideas he would later condense in his celebrated article, "The Sources of Soviet Conduct," published the following year in *Foreign Affairs*. "At bottom of Kremlin's neurotic view of world affairs," Kennan argued, "is traditional and instinctive Russian sense of insecurity." Although Kennan did not predict war, he foresaw, at best, a period of almost indefinite tensions and ideological conflict. "In summary," he observed, "we have here [in the Soviet Union] a political force committed fanatically to the belief that with US there can be no permanent modus vivendi."[5] It was not an encouraging or optimistic assessment.

The effect Kennan's "long telegram" (as it came to be known) had on some Washington officials was as if a thunderbolt had struck, leaving in its trail revelations that would change the thinking of many. So struck was Forrestal when he saw a copy of the telegram that he made it required reading for his staff and had it reprinted for distribution to many senior military officers. Shortly thereafter, Forrestal also arranged with the State Department to have Kennan reassigned to Washington, where he would be closer at hand, as deputy commandant of the War College, to offer advice.[6] Truman also looked at the cable, but was apparently less impressed. "Essentially," recalled George Elsey, one of the President's administrative aides, "it didn't tell us anything we didn't already know."[7] But as easily as some in the White House may have dismissed Kennan's warnings, it was impossible to ignore them.

Then, in September 1946, the President received White House special counsel Clark Clifford's private report (done at the President's request) on the state of US-Soviet relations. Compiled with Elsey's help, the Clifford report was essentially a distillation of views collected randomly from senior administration officials and the military service chiefs. While recounting in detail repeated Soviet failures to keep treaty commitments and other agreements, the report also ominously noted ongoing Soviet military research, especially in electronics, guided missiles, and atomic weapons. One possible explanation for such activities—certainly the most readily apparent now that Germany no longer posed a danger—was that the Soviets were preparing to threaten or to use force to realize their foreign policy objectives. But as Clifford saw the situation, it would become obvious to the Soviets that they would have no choice other than to "work out with us a fair and equitable settlement when they realize that we are too strong to be beaten and too determined to be frightened." Barring such an accord, it was Clifford's view that the "United States must be prepared to wage atomic and biological war" should an East-West confrontation become unavoidable. In preparation for possible hard times ahead, Clifford called for a campaign to solicit public support for a policy of resistance to Moscow, a recommendation also made in Kennan's long telegram.[8]

All of this, however, struck Truman, at least at the time, as too extreme. Indeed, the morning after he read the report, he told Clifford that his paper would—if it became public—"have an exceedingly unfortunate impact" on relations with the Soviet Union. Thus, at roughly the same time that Henry Wallace was leaving the cabinet in pique over the administration's policies, Truman was locking all the copies (apparently save one) of the Clifford report in his safe.[9] Although Truman did not rule out eventual recourse to military options, American responses to Soviet moves remained diplomatic and political.

The reasons for Truman's caution appear to have been several. One, no doubt, was his desire to avoid doing anything that might torpedo the Baruch proposal then before the United Nations. Although the President may have harbored doubts about the feasibility of an international control agreement involving the Russians, he had to let the UN session run its course. Moreover, he could not ignore the domestic political mood. To move too quickly to a tougher stance might alarm the left wing of the Democratic party, which was still vocal and strident in its pleas for trust and cooperation with the Soviet Union. To move too slowly might expose him to still further attacks, already vitriolic and ill-tempered, from Republic conservatives.[10] More crucially, perhaps, public attention remained fixed on domestic problems, including rising prices and shortages of many consumer goods. The year 1946 also saw unpleasant, intensified labor strife, culminating in nearly 5,000 strikes with a loss of 116,000,000 working days, a number virtually without precedent in the American experience.[11] Given these concerns, it was less than certain that Americans would long sustain a continuing, active international burden. The prospect of isolationism, though on the wane, could not be totally ruled out.

A further reason for Truman's public reticence may have been his confidence in America's ability to deter Stalin from a precipitate military move, despite the ongoing demobilization of US forces. "With the U.S. holding a nuclear monopoly," Clifford recalled, "he [Truman] felt there was no direct or immediate danger to the nation."[12] Having the bomb, in other words, was Truman's backup insurance policy, one that he still judged he could use, implicitly if not explicitly, to influence Soviet behavior. Though American attempts at atomic diplomacy may have failed in 1945, the mere existence of the bomb made it an ever present factor in US-Soviet relations. If worse came to worse, Truman could be reasonably confident that his fall-back options included a most powerful form of retaliation.

For their part, however, the Soviets continued to give no sign that they felt intimidated either by the bomb or by any other form of American power. Rather, as they had since the end of the war, they seemed intent on testing and probing in a manner apparently designed to expose the West's weak points. In early June 1946, for example, Western intelligence reported unusual Soviet troop movements in eastern Germany, an obvious escalation in the ongoing war of nerves between East and West and soon the object of speculation in Washington that the Soviets might be planning a military move. These alarms, which coincided with Secretary Byrnes's impending departure for another conference in Paris, were the occasion for a major White House review of the situation on June 11. At the meeting, Truman heard his advisors—military and civilian—survey the situation. Forrestal and Eisenhower, while agreeing that "the Reds desire to dominate the world," differed significantly over whether a move was imminent. Eisenhower believed an effort would only come when the Soviets had an adequate logistical base. Since they did not, he doubted whether the Soviets would move, either in central Europe or in the Near East. War, in Byrnes's opinion, was likely only if there were some "impulsive act by hot-heads" in an area such as Trieste. The President appears to have accepted the more optimistic assessments of the situation. But he reminded his subordinates that internal politics in Russia might trigger something. "If Stalin should die," Truman speculated, "we would probably see a considerable internal upheaval. Under such conditions the Reds might look to a war as a means of gearing the nation to meet the new situation and of thus solving the internal problems." Yet even this possibility seemed only that—a possibility.

All in all, the meeting minimized both the chances and dangers of war. Eisenhower did not believe "for a minute that we could be wiped off the face of this earth in Germany by anything like the Russian forces now located there." While there were admitted American weaknesses because of demobilization, Truman could be reasonably assured that, with millions of highly trained servicemen only recently discharged, the US could respond effectively to a Soviet aggression by conventional means. At no point during the meeting were atomic weapons even mentioned, though no doubt they crossed some minds.[13] Nonetheless, the June crisis eased quickly, followed by renewed concerns elsewhere: Soviet pressures on Turkey, the civil war in Greece, and the problems of the Marshall mission in China. Despite the repeated tensions, there were apparently no further White House reviews of the strategic situation during the remainder of 1946.

During these months Truman was not immune from entreaties by his subordinates about the need for stronger actions and forces. Secretary of War Patterson strongly urged the President, in a report on July 27, to continue a policy of US vigilance and determination against the Soviet Union, with military forces adequate to meet the challenge. Secretary of the Navy Forrestal, perhaps the most strident critic in the cabinet of Soviet actions, offered similar advice. But the results were mixed. In addition to sending the battleship USS *Missouri* into the Mediterranean as an obvious show of force, Truman authorized a regular naval deployment there in late September.[14] But at the same time he steadfastly adhered to a tough budget policy, announcing in May 1946 that military spending would be limited to one-third of the funds left after all fixed charges had been met. The result for Fiscal Year (FY) 1948 was a ceiling of just over $10 billion based on the so-called "remainder method" of calculating security expenditures, which would become a familiar feature of Truman's budget policies until the Korean War.[15] Whatever other steps he may have been prepared to take in the face of worsening US-Soviet relations, an abandonment of fiscal prudence was not among them. Ironically, it was this same policy of fiscal conservatism that would eventually help drive Truman into greater reliance on nuclear weapons as the West's first line of defense.

UMT AND UNIFICATION

During these months of transition emerged two other issues: UMT and the unification of the armed services. Truman, buttressed by the strong convictions of former army chief of staff General George C. Marshall, believed that Universal Military Training offered a preferred means of strengthening American security. It would create a pool of trained manpower for mobilization, abort the need for a large standing army, and act as a reminder to all, including the Soviet Union, that the United States took its security needs seriously. Repeated administration proposals to Congress, strong support from distinguished citizens, and a blue-ribbon advisory commission headed by MIT's president Karl T. Compton, were part of the effort. Meanwhile, pending congressional approval of UMT, the administration relied on Selective Service to provide manpower until the draft law became too expensive to administer and was allowed to lapse in 1947.[16]

Despite the administration's concerted effort on behalf of UMT, the President could not overcome congressional resistance, even though public support of the program seems to have been generally favorable.[17] What may have offered a viable alternative to reliance on nuclear weapons, i.e., a large, readily available conventional force, failed to materialize chiefly because of its lack of appeal to lawmakers. And with the loss of Selective Service as well, it was only a matter of time before the military—the Army especially—would begin to experience shortages of enlisted personnel. Yet even before these shortages became apparent, the controversy over UMT and the futile effort to enact legislation had probably damaged America's security position more than anyone then realized, sending the wrong signal to the Soviets at precisely the wrong time.

The emotions displayed over UMT, intense though they may have been, did not begin to compare with those expended over the question of service unification. As World War II had amply demonstrated, unified direction and control of military forces and of resources had proved indispensable in achieving victory, so much so that when the war ended Congress readily turned its attention to reorganizing the nation's armed services. With the advent of atomic weapons, this issue became all the more important. But despite widespread agreement on the need for reform, it took nearly two years to work out an acceptable compromise.

By and large, the unification debate hinged on the merits of two competing plans—one drawn up by the War Department, the other by the Navy. The War Department's plan had many variants and appeared under several guises, but all followed essentially the same theme, calling for a single military department, a single secretary of defense, a single military commander or chief of staff, a single military high command, and functionally unified services for air, sea, and ground warfare. The Navy, fearing loss of its air component and possible absorption of the Marine Corps into the Army, consistently took exception. In the fall of 1945 Secretary of the Navy Forrestal offered an alternative plan, developed from recommendations by his close friend, Ferdinand Eberstadt, that stressed increased coordination, as opposed to outright unification, not only for the military but on a government-wide basis.[18]

The ensuing struggle was one of the most bitter and divisive bureaucratic quarrels in American history, leaving scars that would take decades to heal.[19] Truman initially supported the War Department plan and so advised Congress in a special message on December 19, 1945. Not only did he believe that centralized authority would be more effective; he also saw it as more economical, a view that most in Congress also shared.[20] But with the Navy and its die-hard Capitol Hill supporters stubbornly resisting, he reluctantly accepted Clark Clifford's advice that, even though the Army's position might be preferable, it was politically out of reach.[21] On June 15, 1946, Truman reaffirmed his support of a single military department and three coordinate services—an army, a navy, and an air force. But he also endorsed in principle the retention of land-based air by the Navy (such as that used in antisubmarine warfare) and continuation of a separate Marine Corps with its own air support.[22] While these decisions helped to settle some of the more contentious issues, important details remained, especially in sorting out service roles and missions and, by extension, overall service responsibilities.

For the remainder of 1946, Forrestal and Secretary of War Patterson sought to settle, where they could, the sharp differences over service functions. Eventually, in a deal formalized on January 16, 1947, they were able to reach a modicum of agreement on the questions of unification, while, in effect, agreeing to disagree over roles and missions.[23] The latter issue, because of its importance in determining budget shares, would continue to corrode service relationships long after unification became a reality.[24] Confronted with the Patterson-Forrestal agreement, Truman gave in even further to the Navy's viewpoint, accepting not only a secretary of defense with limited powers but also the various bits and pieces of coordinating machinery that Forrestal wanted. Even so, Truman was determined to defend his presidential prerogatives and not allow the National Security Council—the centerpiece of Forrestal's coordinating system—to impinge on his authority or turn his administration into a British cabinet-style government.[25] As for the rest of the new defense organization, its flaws and weaknesses would become apparent on their own, with the ironic result that Forrestal would be the one to suffer and make the recommendation that the secretary of defense needed stronger, clearer authority.

The final stages of the unification debate were handled, to ensure adherence to Truman's wishes, by Clifford and members of his White House staff. The basic measure went to Congress on February 26, 1947, and finally passed both houses on July 25, some 20 months after Truman's initial proposals. At length, a step toward improved management of military resources and national policy had been taken. But as other events were demonstrating, the completion of this leisurely pace came none too soon in the face of worsening Soviet-American relations and mounting resolve on the part of the administration to combat Soviet expansionism. A turning point was at hand, and from it would flow both a new era in East-West relations and a gradual reordering of military priorities that would lead to increased reliance on nuclear weapons.

THE TRUMAN DOCTRINE AND THE MARSHALL PLAN

The winter of 1946-1947 brought with it the final phase in the transition of the United States and the Soviet Union from wartime allies to postwar antagonists. Bitterly cold winter weather, economic instability, political unrest, and mounting despair typified conditions throughout much of Europe. The wartime preparations for economic reconstruction and development plans were proving inadequate and ineffective. In France and Italy, especially, the prospect of communist takeovers loomed dangerously large. On the periphery the situation was even less encouraging. Although Soviet forces had finally withdrawn from Iran, Soviet pressure on Turkey continued, as did the communist-led insurrection in Greece. Palestine verged on open Arab-Jewish conflict, a result that could yield numerous opportunities for Soviet penetration of the Middle East. In East Asia little remained of the herculean efforts of the Marshall mission to propitiate Mao Tse-tung and Chiang Kai-shek. Everywhere, it seemed, the tide was turning against the West and the United States. A time for fresh approaches that departed from the old shibboleths had come. Something more was required to restore Europe, thwart further Soviet expansion, and turn chaos into order.

Although historians still disagree over the origins of the cold war and, in particular, who was responsible, almost all concur that the enunciation of the Truman Doctrine and the Marshall Plan was a major milestone in a tougher American policy toward the Soviet Union. Taken together, as John Lewis Gaddis has observed, these two major initiatives delivered the "shock therapy" to an American public increasingly disturbed by Soviet behavior but unsure about an appropriate American response.[26] These calls-to-action came, moreover, at a time when Britain's capacity to act was rapidly declining, when the elections of November 1946 had given the Republican opposition a majority in Congress, and when growing inflation at home threatened to wreak havoc on the administration's fiscal policies. At the same time, America's prestige and influence abroad seemed at an all-time postwar low, most notably in countries increasingly dependent on American power and support. As viewed by the British Foreign Office in a January 1947 "stocktaking" paper: "The Americans are a mercurial people, unduly swayed by sentiment and prejudice rather than by reason or even consideration of their own long term interests."[27] The United States, in other words, might not prove the most reliable of partners if times got any tougher.

In these circumstances, Truman might well have opted for one of several courses of action. To be sure, as the British worried he might, he could have eschewed any further commitments abroad, letting events take their course, while the United States conserved its resources. Or, alternatively, he might have called for a military buildup, including an acceleration of the nuclear program, in an effort to divert attention from domestic problems and rally the country behind him. In fact, he chose none of these, but decided instead to deal with the country's difficulties abroad by political and economic means fueled by more rhetoric and a judicious allocation of money. Only in Greece and China would the response have military implications, and then within strict limits.

Truman's continuing adherence to a political response vis-à-vis Moscow was almost certainly buttressed by his confidence in the new team at the State Department. Increasingly dissatisfied with and distrustful of Byrnes, Truman in January 1947 replaced him as secretary of state with former army chief of staff General George C. Marshall. Reputation, experience, good sense, Truman's acknowledged esteem—all combined to strengthen Marshall's position and provide him with the crucial voice on many security and policy issues. The importunings of Forrestal would now be frequently balanced by the clear ascendancy of the new secretary, and Marshall's initial disposition, unlike Forrestal's, was that patient political and economic pressure might make the Soviets more tractable. But this pressure, given the European situation and Britain's growing weakness, required prompt American initiatives.[28]

The event precipitating the change in American policy was the delivery in late February 1947 of the British *aides-mémoire* concerning Greece and Turkey. With their resources stretched to the limit, the British could no longer afford the subsidies and other support they had been giving these countries.[29] Although it was clear that conditions in the Near East had been deteriorating for some time, the British announcement seems to have caught Washington wholly off guard, leaving the United States no choice but to take some kind of action or risk a political vacuum in the area that the Soviet Union appeared all too ready and eager to fill. The decision was to intervene with economic and military aid, in effect taking over Britain's responsibilities in the eastern Mediterranean. Faced with a newly elected Republican Congress that was preparing to do battle with the White House on a variety of domestic issues, the administration endeavored to rally support for its proposed aid program by stressing the importance of bipartisanship in foreign policy and by playing on known congressional fears of communism.[30] Yet as Under Secretary of State Dean Acheson described it at a cabinet meeting on March 7, the seriousness of the situation could not be minimized: ". . . if Greece fell within the Russian orbit," Acheson argued, "not only Turkey would be affected but also Italy, France, and the whole of western Europe."[31]

Acheson's radically altered view of the Soviets mirrored similar changes that had been evolving in Truman's thinking. His hand having been forced by the British, Truman acted quickly and with outwardly firm resolve, though privately he continued to harbor worries that the initiative he had approved might provoke a resurgence of isolationism.[32] Addressing Congress on March 12, 1947, the President made a clear public break with past taciturnity about Soviet activities. In asking Congress for $400 million in economic and military aid for Greece and Turkey, he stressed a new American determination to prevent free institutions and democratic governments from being captured by totalitarian regimes. "I believe," he declared, "that we must assist free people to work out their own destinies in their own way."[33] A broad, sweeping statement, it seemed especially ill-fitting for the oligarchy that ran Greece, but it was the kind of rhetoric that Senator Arthur H. Vandenberg of Michigan, chairman of the Foreign Relations Committee, deemed vital to sway Congress.[34] The ploy worked. Moving with unusual alacrity, Congress provided an aid bill for the President's signature by May 22.

The chaotic economic and political conditions in Western Europe and the apparent strength of the communist parties there, especially in Italy and France, made the next move self-evident. If one believed, as Acheson contended, that the whole of Western Europe could be in jeopardy, then "Band-Aid" help such as the Greek-Turkish aid program or the 1946 American loan to Britain would not suffice in the long run; the proper American response had to be some form of broader economic assistance, buttressed by direct US involvement, to counter communist pressures and restore local confidence. To launch this commitment would necessarily involve issues such as reparations, the fate of Germany, and the investment of American resources on an unprecedented scale. Above all, it would mean political steps that could result in the division of Europe into two competing coalitions, one in the East, the other in the West, with the United States committed to the protection and welfare of the latter.

With these implications before him, Secretary of State Marshall, in late April 1947, gave George F. Kennan the task of setting up a long-range planning body, known as the Policy Planning Staff (PPS), to develop recommendations.[35] The upshot was the European Recovery Program, first outlined publicly in the secretary's Harvard graduation speech of June 5, 1947. In sharp contrast to the announcement of the Truman Doctrine, however, Marshall's offer of assistance singled out "hunger, poverty, desperation and chaos"—not unspecified opposing political forces—as the main enemies.[36] "It seemed to General Marshall and to me," recalled Charles "Chip" Bohlen, who helped draft the secretary's commencement address, "that there was a little too much flamboyant anti-Communism in the [Greek-Turkish aid] speech."[37] Others in the State Department, including Kennan, concurred, so that the final product was a nearly open-ended proposal: even Soviet participation was possible. The administration was now committed to an active role in a postwar Europe. Russia could be either a partner (or possibly a recipient) or an antagonist.

While the western European governments were drafting their shopping lists for recovery, Stalin (after momentary hesitation) decided not to participate. Thus another move was made toward the division of Europe into two distinct blocs—a division that would endure for more than two generations. At home, the American people recognized still more vividly that America's wartime partner had become its peacetime adversary. Gallup polls, for example, now showed a substantial majority of Americans believing that the Soviets wanted to dominate the world and that American policy toward them was too soft. Relations with the Soviet Union, the public believed, constituted America's foremost international problem.[38]

Still, the alienation of US-Soviet relations was not yet complete. Henry Wallace, after all, remained a potent political figure, one whose further ambitions and allies could not be entirely ignored by a Democratic president.

Moreover, despite the clarion calls from Truman and Marshall for sacrifices to meet the Soviet challenge, economic aid for Europe did not come easily. As promptly as Congress may have acted on the Greek-Turkish aid bill, the Republican majority—many with isolationist leanings that Truman rightly feared—was less than eager to embrace larger commitments. As it happened, Truman had to reconvene Congress just to get a first installment of $580 million in late 1947, and his December plea for an authorization of up to $17 billion would only be acted upon in April 1948, in the aftermath of the communist coup d'etat that drew Czechoslovakia behind the iron curtain.

Nor did the call for a more active American political and economic policy bring an upsurge of defense expenditures. In fact, the trade-offs went precisely in the other direction. Truman was at heart a fiscal conservative. His memories of his own financial setbacks after World War I, when the haberdashery he co-owned had gone broke, were vivid reminders of where imprudent business deals could lead. And, as a shrewd, knowledgeable politician, he sensed the depth of the public's adverse reaction to any mention of either inflation or the reimposition of "warlike" economic controls. Further, there was sound political appeal in a balanced budget after years of war-induced deficit spending. In these circumstances, Truman looked at the most elastic item in the federal budget—defense—as the area for economies. If something gave, it would be the military services. In fact, during 1947-1948, the President had it both ways. While he was able to report an expected surplus in his FY 1948 budget, he did so partly on the strength of cuts in defense expenditures, which fell from $13.2 billion the previous year to $10.1 billion in FY 1948. Yet he did not have to face the full impact of paying for the European Recovery Program (ERP) until FY 1949. Into this rosy scenario, however, the Republican-controlled Congress inserted one slight complication: after failing twice in 1947 to override the President's veto, it finally voted a tax cut in 1948.[39]

These short-term fiscal advantages thus had long-term limitations. The tax cut meant that federal receipts would be lowered by at least $4 billion. On the other hand, the payments for ERP and other economic aid would jump from $4.5 billion in FY 1949 to $6 billion in FY 1950. In addition, military assistance programs such as those for Greece, Turkey, and China and a broad, multilateral effort launched in 1948 would reinforce the constraints initially imposed by ERP. Given these competing demands, the feasibility of a larger defense effort was limited, as Forrestal would discover during deliberations over the FY 1950 defense budget. What emerges, budget requests and appropriations aside, is a relative plateau of defense expenditures from FY 1948 through FY 1950 when measured in current dollars, and a sizable drop (possibly as much as 7 to 8 percent) if measured in constant dollars.[40] Though there is no assurance that Truman would have turned these funds over to the military had ERP never become a reality, defense nonetheless experienced cutbacks that might otherwise have been avoidable. Barring recourse of deficit financing, the massive economic response that Truman adopted to contain communism left fewer dollars in the till for discretionary spending, including defense.

There were, however, several ancillary benefits of a strategic nature from the Marshall Plan that were probably unanticipated. One involved base rights, a subject on which service planners since before the end of the war had repeatedly expressed themselves, only to be greeted by lukewarm responses from the State Department, which wanted to avoid giving the Soviets a pretext for making similar demands.[41] Meanwhile, the progressive liquidation of wartime basing privileges continued. Regular access to Japan, Germany, and Italy (all occupied areas) posed no urgent problem; but if access routes across the Atlantic via Iceland, Greenland, the Azores, or even Britain ended, the strategic picture would be significantly altered. This was particularly true in view of the increasing importance that postwar US defense planning attached to forward bases overseas for a possible strategic air offensive against the Soviet Union. Prudent strategic planning thus called for a resolution as early as possible of the base-rights issue, preferably with long-term leases guaranteeing unhindered US access.[42]

Then came the Marshall Plan, and, with it, a clear set of economic inducements to assist in negotiating base rights. Indeed, as the aid program was taking shape, the Joint Chiefs in May 1947 again pointed to their need for base rights from Portugal, France, Spain, and other countries bordering the Atlantic, suggesting that American assistance ought to be doled out in such a way as to "enhance our possibilities of receiving the base rights desired from these countries."[43] Although the ensuing pressure on the Europeans to make these and other concessions was never as strong as it might have been, the operating assumption in Washington was, for the most part, that American aid should elicit some reciprocal benefits or at least generate movement in that direction. The Europeans, on the other hand, took a decidedly different view, with the result that concessions were few and far between.[44]

The other unforeseen benefits of ERP concerned the British. During 1947, congressional ire and high-level concern about Anglo-American atomic relations intensified. British requests for weapons information, London's decision to produce plutonium and to develop its own nuclear arsenal, and British rights (under the wartime Combined Trust arrangements) to 50 percent of the Congo's uranium ore fueled the growing controversy that passage of the McMahon Act had helped touch off. Congressional sentiment, as expressed by Senators Vandenberg and Bourke Hickenlooper, chairman of the Joint Committee on Atomic Energy, favored using the leverage of economic loans and ERP to extract British concessions. Careful efforts by Robert A. Lovett, Acheson's successor as under secretary of state, and subtle hints to London, helped eventually to avert a confrontation. In early 1948 the administration, Congress, and the British arrived at a new *modus vivendi* arrangement covering exchanges of information, new allocations of uranium ore to the advantage of the United States, and the abrogation of the "trigger finger" clause in the 1943 Quebec Agreement.[45] American strategic planning, aided indirectly by the Marshall Plan, had overcome one more (even if admittedly fragile) obstacle.

ATOMIC MATTERS: CONTROL, PRODUCTION, AND INTELLIGENCE

While the administration in Washington took positive, public steps to meet the Soviet challenges in Europe and the Near East during the first half of 1947, it also faced a series of problems specifically related to atomic energy and its impact upon US-Soviet relations. Fading hopes for international control and grim reports on the status of American atomic progress were also part of the agenda. Here, too, the situation appeared, as did the diplomatic and economic dimensions, foreboding and worrisome. But with scant evidence that the Soviet Union would soon be a competitor in the nuclear arena, American superiority provided a margin of security that Truman and his advisors were increasingly loath to give up.

At the United Nations the United States officially stuck to its support of the Baruch Plan. But by early January 1947, misgivings had surfaced about the wisdom of continuing to press the scheme. Baruch's final report on his efforts, dated January 4, 1947, urged both a renewed attempt at international control as well as the development of more American weapons.[46] Later that same month Secretary Marshall and Secretary Forrestal, among others, expressed concern over the public impact of a failure to achieve control; they suspected a Soviet propaganda effort to blame the failure on American demands for certain security guarantees.[47] The President, though prepared to support further efforts at control, shared their anxieties. On January 30, 1947, he directed that American delegates make clear that the United States had had one tragic experience with unilateral disarmament (the scrapping of much of its navy after World War I) and would under no circumstances commit itself to a repetition of that experience. The

United States, Truman said, "must have definite concrete assurances as a basis for any agreement on disarmament."[48] With these cautions in mind, Washington left the Baruch Plan in the UN forum.

The Soviets did not disappoint the cynics. Indeed, they gave not one hint of responsiveness to the American offer. Nor did the entire second session of the UN General Assembly ever touch upon the matter of atomic energy. By the end of 1947, the issue of an international approach to the control of atomic energy was, for all practical purposes, finished. It had been that way since December 1946, but the fear of propaganda losses, plus a continuing long-shot hope that Moscow might reconsider, had kept it partly alive. That was no longer the case. Not until the fall of 1949, under entirely different circumstances, would high-ranking American officials again accord the control issue any further serious consideration.

The other dimension of the control problem—the domestic operation of the AEC—was not at first an unalloyed success. In fact, the confirmation controversy over the commissioners, principally aimed at Lilienthal, deprived the new agency of formal leadership until the spring of 1947. In the meantime, physical facilities continued to deteriorate, staff morale continued to decline, and all three of the reactors at Hanford, Washington, became increasingly unsafe and almost inoperable. In March 1946, scientists at Hanford had noticed dangerous swelling of the graphite reactor piles that, if not corrected, would have rendered them inoperable in a few years. In addition to producing plutonium for bomb cores, these piles also yielded a by-product called polonium, which was critical to the maintenance of the stockpile. Polonium initiators were used in atomic weapons to increase the neutron background of the core to insure that fission would occur on schedule. But because of its short half-life (138 days), polonium could not be stored. So production of polonium could not be interrupted without threatening the operability of the entire stockpile. Seeing no choice but to accept the risk, the Army ordered the oldest reactor (B) shut down and placed the other two on reduced power, with only one operating at a time.[49]

Moreover, practically no progress whatever on weapons development had taken place since 1945. Of the two types of bombs then available, very few, if any, of the LITTLE BOY gun-type used at Hiroshima entered the stockpile, apparently due to their less efficient use of scarce fissionable material.[50] Though more efficient, the other available weapon—the FAT MAN implosion-type, also called the MARK III, similar to the TRINITY test device and the bomb dropped on Nagasaki—also had serious flaws. As demonstrated in 1946 by the first CROSSROADS experiment, the poor accuracy inherent in the bulky shape of this bomb, coupled with weaknesses in the design and structure of the housing, made necessary an extensive training program for bomber crews. Each weapon had to be assembled by hand and, once assembled, had to be monitored constantly. The life span of batteries, once charged and installed, was nine days, during which time they had to be recharged twice. Further, the accumulation of heat around the nuclear capsule required its removal after ten days. Neither operation could be performed without a complete disassembly and reassembly of the bomb, a process requiring about 16 hours.[51]

In March 1947, the AEC's General Advisory Committee (GAC), composed of many of the country's leading physicists under the chairmanship of J. Robert Oppenheimer, reviewed and tendered its first report on the technical status of the U.S. atomic energy program.[52] It was abundantly clear, in the committee's view, that the nation's nuclear weapons program was in a woeful state, facing a major crisis. Los Alamos, where most of the design and research had centered during the war, needed to be revitalized; jurisdictions between the AEC's Division of Military Application and the Military Liaison Committee needed to be defined; the production of fissionable material had perforce to be increased; the problems of a hydrogen or thermonuclear "super bomb" should be more thoroughly explored; more assembly teams needed to be trained; and above all, the manufacture of atomic bombs had to be resumed.[53] While these were not policy recommendations per se, the implications were obvious. America's nuclear weapons program had reached a turning point. Would it be reinvigorated, or would it continue to decline?

As a corollary to the committee's last recommendation, the AEC realized that a new round of tests was necessary if there was to be any hope of improving the actual design of the weapons.[54] At a White House meeting on June 27, Secretary of State Marshall urged that the tests be delayed until early 1948; he wanted nothing to interfere with the forthcoming foreign ministers conference scheduled for November. On this he won. But he lost out on the question of where the tests would be held. He, along with Secretary of War Patterson, favored holding them within the United States; Lilienthal, backed by Army Chief of Staff General Dwight D. Eisenhower, preferred a remote Pacific location. All, including Lilienthal upon reflection, agreed to keep the tests secret and to have no advance publicity on the matter.[55] In these decisions, Truman gave his emphatic endorsement, paving the way for the momentous SANDSTONE series in the spring of 1948. Whatever certain Congressmen may have believed and charged later, Lilienthal and his fellow commissioners were not dragging their feet on the development of atomic weapons.

The AEC's decision on weapons production coincided with efforts to elicit views from the Joint Chiefs on the number of weapons needed. The result would be the first real decision by the military on the future size and composition of the stockpile. But in the course of reaching this point, the Chiefs became divided over how and by whom the bomb should be employed. Although the Navy initially resisted, it eventually acquiesced to Air Force proposals that nuclear weapons be included as a matter of course in US war plans.[56] In the end, though, it took the intercession of both the AEC and Senator Bourke B. Hickenlooper, chairman of the JCAE, to galvanize the military establishment into developing a statement of requirements. This information, which Forrestal, Patterson, and the JCS agreed to provide on July 10, 1947, did not reach the AEC until late fall and would be slightly amended in January 1948.[57] In their year-by-year statement of demands, the JCS noted the need for more delivery vehicles and set a requirement for a total stockpile of 400 Nagasaki-type implosion bombs by January 1, 1953.[58]

These requirements did not, surprisingly, necessitate any adjustment in the projected production schedule for fissionable materials. In fact, in April 1947, President Truman reaffirmed an earlier directive he had approved authorizing continuation of production at the current level. At the same time, the AEC submitted its first official inventory, showing a stockpile of about a dozen weapons, only half of which, probably, were operable. According to Lilienthal, the news came as "quite a shock" to Truman. But despite his uneasiness, the President saw no immediate reason to step up production as long as the Joint Chiefs were satisfied.[59] In short, the military, divided as it was by interservice rivalry over use of the bomb, was not initially a source of pressure on the AEC to increase weapons production capabilities. Rather, the effective military pressure on the AEC came—as will be shown later—from concerns, expressed by Forrestal and others, over the custody of completed weapons and from friction within the AEC itself.

At least one influential individual suspected that the military was not asking for enough. Though not privy to the actual numbers, Senator Hickenlooper wrote Forrestal early in 1948 inquiring whether the JCS requests reflected actual needs or merely an estimate of what the AEC could produce. Forrestal's evasive response stressed the interim nature of the JCS formulation, while offering assurances that the 1947 statement took into account all "the safe minimum strategic requirements and experimental needs through 1952" and had been "correlated with existing strategic plans for the security of the United States." Such assurances, to be sure, were neither wholly candid nor accurate. But under the circumstances, with the atomic energy program in a state of flux and with strategic planning in disarray, they were probably the best he could offer.[60]

Thus, by the end of 1947, the AEC could consider that its efforts, despite the handicaps it inherited, were on the whole moving ahead. With weapons production up to nearly four nuclear cores per month, the American edge in bomb production—a monopoly since TRINITY—appeared to hold. At the same time, intelligence reports continued to minimize the imminent danger that that monopoly would soon be lost, despite growing suspicions among some that the Soviets might be progressing faster than expected. In late July 1947, Karl T. Compton sent Forrestal (as the recently named first secretary of defense) a letter expressing concern that earlier estimates, dating from 1945, that it would take the Soviets at least five years to develop a bomb might be wrong. On thinking it over, with the knowledge that the Russians now had the help of German scientists, engineers, and manufacturing capabilities, Compton brought the estimate to the minimum of "Potsdam plus three years," or the summer of 1948. Requesting quick action, Forrestal referred Compton's letter to Rear Adm. Roscoe H. Hillenkoetter, director of the Central Intelligence Group. Hillenkoetter replied on August 18. Reminding Forrestal that the available information was scanty and of doubtful merit, Hillenkoetter advised that the intelligence community could find no new evidence that would cause it to alter its earlier estimate. Thus, the prediction of 1950 went unchanged.[61]

Likewise, for delivery capabilities, the Soviet threat seemed remote. Air Force intelligence estimated that as of September 1947, the Soviet Union probably had no more than 14 long-range aircraft (all copied from a US B-29 that had fallen into Russian hands during the war) with sufficient range to reach the United States.[62] If an emergency loomed sometime in the future, it was hardly apparent. Yet it was a danger that all recognized was likely to materialize sooner or later.

THE NATIONAL SECURITY SYSTEM

During the course of 1947, Congress and the Truman administration dealt with a variety of issues that influenced or impinged on the conduct of US-Soviet relations and on the nation's defense posture: the Greek-Turkish aid program, the Marshall Plan, the acceleration of atomic bomb production, and the international control of atomic energy. Concurrent with these developments were the efforts to streamline the structural process of national security policy. A major instrumental step in that direction came with the passage, in mid-summer 1947, of the National Security Act. Its passage signaled the end of the legislative phase of service unification, leaving the struggle over service roles and missions and related organizational issues to be settled within the new military structure. Its passage also created a new set of institutions that reflected not only the experience of World War II but also the emerging concept of "national security." New ways of planning, of coordinating, and of implementing policy—including nuclear weapons policy—rested on the new structural arrangements. And for some, especially James Forrestal, there were hopes that the new structure would herald more systematic reviews of American policy and a tougher stand toward the Soviets.[63]

The new law did not wholly revamp the national security system, but it did make significant modifications. Most importantly, it provided for a secretary of defense with "general direction, authority, and control" over a supposedly unified, bureaucratic hybrid known as the National Military Establishment (NME) and composed of three co-equal military departments—army, navy, and air force. (Amendments passed by Congress in 1949 replaced the NME with the present-day Department of Defense.) As one of his official responsibilities, the secretary of defense was also the presiding officer of a deliberative body within the Pentagon known as the War Council, composed of the service chiefs, the departmental secretaries, and other senior NME officials. Forrestal, whom Truman reluctantly named the first secretary of defense, immediately opted to create yet another such body, known as the Committee of Four (secretaries of defense, army, navy, and air force), mainly to iron out unification problems.

With coordination, rather than unification, as its motto, the law also for the first time gave statutory authority to the Joint Chiefs of Staff and to two other coordinating bodies—the Munitions Board, which was supposed to oversee interservice activities with respect to logistics, and the Research and Development Board, which had similar responsibilities in the areas of science and technology. Under the President's aegis came the National Security Council (NSC), the National Security Resources Board (NSRB), and the Central Intelligence Agency (CIA). The NSC's specific mandate was to act as a policy coordinating and advisory forum on behalf of the President; it had nine statutory members, an executive secretary, and a small staff, supplemented at first by personnel detailed from the services and the State Department.[64]

No one had higher hopes for this new organization than Forrestal. In particular he visualized the NSC as the panacea for coordination and policy-formulation, as the forum through which the machinery of government could be made to function more effectively on national security issues. An episode on the eve of the first NSC meeting reveals his ambitions for the new process. On September 25, 1947, he assembled in his office the service secretaries, other senior military officials, and Under Secretary of State Lovett for a "dry run" of their presentations and arguments for the NSC meeting the next day. He wanted to leave nothing to chance in his effort to convince Truman of the NSC's potential usefulness.[65]

Such preparations and Forrestal's own hopes for the NSC were soon stultified by the President's calculated distance from the new organization. Seldom in attendance at NSC meetings before the Korean War (unless there was a crisis as over Berlin), Truman sought to make clear that his prerogatives on national security matters remained intact. To the position of NSC executive secretary Truman named Rear Adm. Sidney Souers, a former naval intelligence officer whose role in the new apparatus Forrestal likened to that of a "buckle." Contrary to what Forrestal may have expected, Souers stayed scrupulously within the President's guidelines. Once the NSC got down to business, moreover, its members decided that their first task consisted not of presenting agreed positions on policy matters, but of outlining the pros and cons of each issue for the Chief Executive. In sum, a new forum existed, whose long-term worth remained to be decided by experience.[66]

Thus, the new NSC structure, as such, did not immediately transform the process by which senior policymakers addressed the momentous issues of nuclear weapons, defense policy, and Soviet-American relations. Except for the issue of strategic exports to the Soviet Union, relations with Moscow were not explicitly discussed in the NSC until May and June of 1948, at which time the NSC also took up the question of nuclear weapons-use policy for the first time. Instead, the initial NSC agenda items dealt with directives for the CIA, the communist threat to Italy, base rights, and the political situations in Greece, China, and Palestine. Despite Forrestal's constant prodding, it was not until March 1948 that the NSC staff prepared a paper (NSC 7) on US policy objectives toward the Soviet Union, a paper that proved inadequate and disappointing to all concerned.[67]

But if the NSC did not review Soviet-American relations or strategic plans until 1948, others did in the interim. Forrestal, for instance, chaired several discussions on US war plans in September 1947 and repeatedly pressed the Joint Chiefs to step up their work. As far as Forrestal was concerned, a basic outline war plan was a top priority, not only for strategic reasons but as a way of demonstrating defense budget needs before Congress. Maj. Gen. Alfred Gruenther, director of the JCS Joint Staff, where the work was being done, gave assurances that studies were underway. However, two major barriers stood in the way. One was the absence of political guidance concerning wartime objectives; the other, continuing discord over service functions and allocation of resources, reflected especially in the growing conflict between the Air Force and the Navy over who should have the mission of delivering the bomb. Progress, in these circumstances, was slow and intermittent.[68]

A full review of Soviet-American relations took place at a meeting of the cabinet on November 7, 1947. Only the day before had Soviet Foreign Minister Molotov stated publicly that "in expansionist circles of the U.S., a new, peculiar sort of illusion is widespread—faith is placed in the secret of the atomic bomb, although this secret has long ceased to exist." In the meeting, Marshall dominated the discussion, reading from a memorandum prepared by Kennan's Policy Planning Staff, which asserted that the Russian advance had been curbed and that Moscow would be forced to reassess its policy. Insisting that the danger of war with the Soviet Union was exaggerated, Marshall warned instead of renewed Soviet-directed pressure on Greece, Italy, France, and Tito's Yugoslavia. He conceded the possibility of a Soviet move against Czechoslovakia, without proposing what, if anything, the United States should do. In the presentation he laid special stress on Germany's role, especially the western zone's integration into Western Europe and its importance to the restoration of the European balance of power. While troubled about Palestine and China, Marshall concluded that the overall situation was such that there was "no reason to expect that we will be forced suddenly and violently into a major military clash with Soviet forces."[69] Although Harriman and Forrestal differed with Marshall on the question of export controls for goods going to Russia (Marshall favored a more flexible approach), they found—as did the rest of the Cabinet—much in the presentation to applaud. For the first time in months, the causes for optimism appeared to outweigh those for pessimism.[70]

A third forum that helped elucidate overall Soviet-American strategic policy was the President's Air Policy Commission, headed by Thomas K. Finletter. Appointed by Truman in the summer of 1947 to investigate and make recommendations on the role of aviation in American policy, the Finletter Commission heard testimony from ranking service officers, aviation experts, and defense officials. Not surprisingly, its final report emphatically endorsed the efficacy of air power in modern war, especially land-based air, and the need for a peacetime Air Force maintained at a "minimum" of 70 groups.[71] Among those who testified, Forrestal had perhaps the most sensitive understanding of the complexities of the issue under discussion. Appearing on November 3, 1947, in closed session, he asserted his disagreement with those who might favor a military showdown with the Soviet Union. "Conquering the Russians," he told the commission, "is one thing and finding what to do with them afterward is an entirely different problem." He also refused to profess too much alarm over the possibility that the United States lagged behind on military funding; a strong economy and a "somewhat understaffed military establishment" could do the job. Further, Forrestal urged caution about "supplanting existing models [of aircraft] with new types." And he told the committee that the United States might next time be faced with fighting a so-called "containing war," not the large-scale mobilization conflict it had experienced in World War II. Although perhaps uncomfortable to the American people, he added, it was a possibility that had to be faced.[72] Such realism about strategic problems would not always be replicated either by Forrestal or his fellow policymakers. Yet, in a way, it symbolized the growing awareness of the magnitude of the task facing the military in a period of long-term, global confrontation with the Soviet Union.

NOTES

1. For a summary of Stalin's speech, see *FRUS 1946*, VI, 694-696; Douglas's observations are in Millis and Duffield, *Forrestal Diaries*, 134.

2. Diary entry, Sep. 24, 1945, in Robert H. Ferrell (ed.), *Truman in the White House: The Diary of Eban A. Ayers* (Columbia: University of Missouri Press, 1991), 84.

3. See Truman's evasive answers to the press conference query about Churchill's visit, Feb. 21, 1946, *Public Papers of the Presidents of the United States: Harry S. Truman, 1946* (Washington, D.C.: G.P.O., 1962), 130.

4. Quoted in M. Truman, *Harry S. Truman* (New York: Morrow, 1973), 312.

5. Kennan to Byrnes, Feb. 22, 1946, *FRUS 1946*, VI, 696-709; excerpts in George F. Kennan, *Memoirs, 1925-1950* (Boston: Little, Brown, 1967), 547-559.

6. *Ibid.*, 294-295; Millis and Duffield, *Forrestal Diaries*, 135-140; Lloyd C. Gardner, *Architects of Illusion* (Chicago: Quadrangle Books, 1970), 277.

7. Quoted in M. Truman, *Harry S. Truman*, 309.

8. The Clifford-Elsey report appears in full in Arthur Krock, *Memoirs: Sixty Years on the Firing Line* (New York: Funk and Wagnalls, 1968), 417-482.

9. M. Truman, *Harry S. Truman*, 347-348.

10. See Henry W. Berger, "Bipartisanship, Senator Taft, and the Truman Administration," *Political Science Quarterly* 90 (Summer 1975): 221-237; and James T. Patterson, *Mr. Republican: A Biography of Robert A. Taft* (Boston: Houghton, Mifflin, 1972), chs. 20-23.

11. U.S. Bureau of the Census, *Historical Statistics of the United States: Colonial Times to 1957* (Washington, D.C.: G.P.O., 1960), 99.

12. Clark Clifford with Richard Holbrooke, *Counsel to the President: A Memoir* (New York: Random House, 1991), 110.

13. Memo for the Record, June 12, 1946, sub: White House Conference on Activities of the Soviet Union, June 11, 1946, RG 165 (Records of the War Department General and Special Staffs), Plans and Operations Division, P&O, 092 (1946-48), case 70/7, NARA. Also see notes dictated by George A. Lincoln, June 11, 1946, *ibid.*

14. Millis and Duffield, *Forrestal Diaries,* 141, 171, 211. Also see David Alan Rosenberg, "The U.S. Navy and the Problem of Oil in a Future War: The Outline of a Strategic Dilemma," *Naval War College Review* 29 (Summer 1976): 53-64.

15. Samuel P. Huntington, *The Common Defense* (New York: Columbia University Press, 1961), 42-43.

16. For Truman's endorsement of UMT, see "Address Before a Joint Session of the Congress on Universal Military Training," Oct. 23, 1945, *Truman Public Papers, 1945,* 404-413. Also see Truman, *Year of Decisions,* 510-512; Harry S. Truman, *Years of Trial and Hope* (Garden City, N.Y.: Doubleday, 1956), 53-55; and U.S. Congress, House, Committee on Military Affairs, *Hearings: Universal Military Training,* 79:1, Nov. 8, 1945—Feb. 21, 1946 (Washington, D.C.: G.P.O., 1946).

17. According to a Gallup Poll conducted in July 1947, fully 75 percent of those surveyed favored some form of military training for young men. Six months later, however, the figure had dropped to 65 percent, indicating that UMT was gradually losing popular support. See George H. Gallup, *The Gallup Poll: Public Opinion, 1935-1971* (New York: Random House, 1972), 661, 700.

18. Steven L. Rearden, *History of the Office of the Secretary of Defense: The Formative Years, 1947-1950* (Washington, D.C.: Historical Office, Office of the Secretary of Defense, 1984), 16-20.

19. The most vivid account of the unification controversy is to be found in Townsend Hoopes and Douglas Brinkley, *Driven Patriot: The Life and Times of James Forrestal* (New York: Knopf, 1992). Also see Demetrious Caraley, *The Politics of Military Unification* (New York: Columbia University Press, 1966), which looks mainly at the legislative side of the struggle; Lawrence Legere, Jr., "Unification of the Armed Forces" (Ph.D. Thesis, Harvard University, 1950), for the Army's viewpoint; and John C. Reis, *The Management of Defense* (Baltimore: Johns Hopkins University Press, 1964), for the Navy's perspective.

20. "Special Message to the Congress Recommending Establishment of a Department of National Defense," Dec. 19, 1945, *Truman Public Papers, 1945,* 546-560. For congressional views, see Steven L. Rearden, "Congress and National Defense, 1945-1950," in Richard H. Kohn (ed.), *The United States Military under the Constitution of the United States, 1789-1989* (New York: New York University Press,1991), 271-289.

21. Clifford, *Counsel to the President,* 150.

22. Ltr, Truman to Patterson and Forrestal, June 15, 1946, in Alice C. Cole, et al. (eds.), *The Department of Defense: Documents on Establishment and*

Organization, 1944-1978 (Washington, D.C.: Historical Office, Office of the Secretary of Defense, 1978), 26-28.

23. Ltr, Patterson and Forrestal to Truman, Jan. 16, 1947, *ibid.*, 31-33.

24. For an interesting analysis from the Navy's perspective of the impact the roles and missions controversy had, see Dean C. Allard, "Interservice Differences in the United States, 1945-1950: A Naval Perspective," *Airpower Journal* 3 (Winter 1989): 71-85.

25. Alfred D. Sander, "Truman and the National Security Council, 1945-1947," *Journal of American History* 59 (Sep. 1972): 369-388. One who especially disliked the NSC approach was George C. Marshall. See his memo to Truman, Feb. 7, 1947, *FRUS 1947*, I, 712-715.

26. John Lewis Gaddis, *The United States and the Origins of the Cold War, 1941-1947* (New York: Columbia University Press, 1972), 351.

27. Quoted in Victor Rothwell, *Britain and the Cold War, 1941-1947* (London: J. Cape, 1982), 434.

28. The most thorough treatment of Marshall's tenure as secretary of state is Forrest C. Pogue, *George C. Marshall: Statesman, 1945-1959* (New York: Viking Press, 1987). Also see Robert H. Ferrell, *George C. Marshall*, vol. XV in Robert H. Ferrell and Samuel Flagg Bemis (eds.), *The American Secretaries of State and Their Diplomacy* (New York: Cooper Square, 1966); and Alexander DeConde, "George Catlett Marshall," in Norman A. Graebner (ed.), *An Uncertain Tradition: American Secretaries of State in the Twentieth Century* (New York: McGraw-Hill, 1961), 245-266.

29. *FRUS 1947*, V, 32-37.

30. Diary entry, Feb. 27, 1947, William D. Leahy Papers, L.C. Also see Arthur H. Vandenberg, Jr., with Joe Alex Morris (eds.), *The Private Papers of Senator Vandenberg* (Boston: Houghton, Mifflin, 1952), 338-344; and Joseph Marion Jones, *The Fifteen Weeks* (New York: Viking, 1955).

31. Memo by Robert P. Patterson, Mar. 7, 1947, sub: Cabinet Mtg, Mar. 7, 1947, Robert P. Patterson Papers, box 19, Cabinet Meetings File, L.C.

32. The best analysis of the changes in Truman's thinking is Deborah Welch Larson, *Origins of Containment: A Psychological Explanation* (Princeton, N.J.: Princeton University Press, 1985), chs. 6-7.

33. "Special Message to the Congress on Greece and Turkey: The Truman Doctrine," Mar. 12, 1947, *Public Papers of the Presidents of the United States: Harry S. Truman 1947* (Washington, D.C.: G.P.O., 1963), 179f.

34. Acheson, *Present at the Creation*, 219.

35. Kennan, *Memoirs, 1925-1950*, 325-326; Wilson D. Miscamble, "George F. Kennan, the Policy Planning Staff and the Origins of the Marshall Plan," *Mid-America* 62 (April-July 1980): 75-89.

36. *FRUS 1947*, III, 237-239.

37. Charles E. Bohlen, *Witness to History, 1929-1969* (New York: Norton, 1973), 261.

38. George Gallup, *The Gallup Poll*, 664, 682.

39. Robert J. Donovan, *Conflict and Crisis: The Presidency of Harry S. Truman, 1945-1948* (New York: Norton, 1977), 260-261, 352. Defense expenditures

from U.S. Dept. of Defense, Office of the Assistant Secretary of Defense (Comptroller), "National Defense Budget Estimates for FY 1985" (Mar. 1984), 116.

40. These adjustments are based on increases in the consumer price index. Taking 1929 as the base year, the price index rose from 126 in 1946 to 152 in 1950. The most dramatic increase occurred between 1947 and 1948 when the index went up 8 points. See US Bureau of the Census, *Historical Statistics*, 139.

41. Memo, JCS to Byrnes, Nov. 7, 1945, *FRUS 1946*, I, 1112-1118; memo, JCS for SWNCC, Jan. 23, 1946, *ibid.*, 743-744; memo, JCS to SWNCC, Feb. 11, 1946, *ibid.*, 1142-1160; memo, Matthews to Byrnes, Jan. 17, 1947, *FRUS 1947*, I, 708-712.

42. Memo, JCS for SWNCC, Apr. 11, 1946, *FRUS 1946*, I, 1171-1174; Schnabel, *JCS and National Policy, 1945-47*, 310-321; Melvyn P. Leffler, "The American Conception of National Security and the Beginnings of the Cold War, 1945-1948," *American Historical Review* 89 (Apr. 1984): 349-353.

43. Memo, JCS to SWNCC, May 12, 1947, *FRUS 1947*, I, 747-748.

44. For a fuller discussion, see Alan S. Milward, *The Reconstruction of Western Europe, 1945-1951* (Berkeley, Calif.: University of California Press, 1984), 113-125.

45. For the U.S. side of the dispute, see Hewlett and Duncan, *Atomic Shield*, chs. 9-10; for the British perspective, see Gowing, *Independence and Deterrence*, 241-272.

46. Baruch to Truman, Jan. 4, 1947, *FRUS 1947*, I, 332-336.

47. Mins., Mtg of Secs of State, War, and Navy, Jan. 29, 1947, *ibid.*, 381-387.

48. Marshall relayed the President's comments in a note to Acheson, Jan. 30, 1947, *ibid.*, 387.

49. Rosenberg, "Toward Armageddon," 21-22; Hewlett and Duncan, *Atomic Shield*, 39-40; and Rearden, *Formative Years*, 439-440.

50. See Rosenberg, "U.S. Nuclear Stockpile, 1945 to 1950," 26; and Nichols, *Road to Trinity*, 228.

51. Little, *Foundations of an Atomic Air Force*, 473-474.

52. In addition to Oppenheimer, GAC membership at this time included James B. Conant of Harvard; Lee A. DuBridge, president of the California Institute of Technology; Enrico Fermi, now at the University of Chicago; Hood Worthington of the DuPont Company; Isidor I. Rabi, the Nobel laureate; Hartley Rowe, who had helped Conant direct the wartime NDRC; Cyril S. Smith, a British-born metallurgist who had played a key role in fabricating the first atomic weapons; and Glenn T. Seaborg, a chemist and one of discoverers of plutonium, who would go on in the 1960s to become chairman of the AEC.

53. Hewlett and Duncan, *Atomic Shield*, 42-46.

54. Leahy Diary, June 9, 1947, L.C.

55. Hewlett and Duncan, *Atomic Shield*, 84-85.

56. Rosenberg, "Toward Armageddon," 58-59.

57. Entry, July 10, 1947, Forrestal Diaries, vol. VIII, p. 1723, Forrestal Papers, Princeton. The fullest account of the problem of extracting a statement of JCS

requirements is in US Congress, Joint Committee on Atomic Energy, "The Scale and Scope of Atomic Production: A Chronology of Leading Events," Jan. 30, 1952 (galley proofs), RG 330, CD 471.6 (A-Bomb).

58. Draft memo, JCS to CAEC through CMLC, Dec. 17, 1947, enclosure to JCS 1745/5, Dec. 8, 1947, RG 218, CCS 471.6 (8-15-45) sec. 8. Also see David Alan Rosenberg, "American Atomic Strategy and the Hydrogen Bomb Decision," *Journal of American History* 66 (June 1979): 67-68.

59. Ltr, Lilienthal, Forrestal, and Patterson to Truman, Jan. 1, 1947, Confidential File (CF), box 4, A-Bomb 1945-49 folder, Truman Papers, HSTL; *Lilienthal Journals,* II, 165; Rosenberg, "U.S. Nuclear Stockpile," 27.

60. Ltr, Hickenlooper to Forrestal, Jan. 15, 1948; ltr, Forrestal to Hickenlooper, Feb. 6, 1948, both in RG 330, CD 16-1-4.

61. Arthur B. Darling, *The Central Intelligence Agency: An Instrument of Government, to 1950* (2 vols.; Washington, D.C.: Historical Staff, Central Intelligence Agency, 1953, released 1989), I, ch. IV, pp. 64-65.

62. AC/AS-2-ONI, "Special Report Covering New U.S.S.R. Aircraft," Sep. 25, 1947, NSC Records, box 19, Air Intelligence Division Study No. 178 folder, HSTL.

63. For a detailed analysis of Forrestal's views, see Cecilia Stiles Cornell, "James V. Forrestal and American National Security, 1940-1949" (Ph.D. diss., Vanderbilt University, 1987). Paul Y. Hammond, *Organizing for Defense: The American Military Establishment in the Twentieth Century* (Princeton: Princeton University Press, 1961) examines the development of the national security concept.

64. P.L. 80-253, The National Security Act of 1947, in Cole, et al., *Department of Defense,* 35-50. For a general history, see John Prados, *Keepers of the Keys: A History of the National Security Council from Truman to Bush* (New York: William Morrow, 1991).

65. Memo by Marx Leva, Sep. 25, 1947, sub: Mins of Mtg, RG 330, CD 9-1-10.

66. On the maneuvering over the NSC's functions, see Rearden, *Formative Years,* 118-123; and Anna Kasten Nelson, "President Truman and the Evolution of the National Security Council," *Journal of American History* 72 (Sept. 1985): 360-378. Also see Henry M. Jackson (ed.), *The National Security Council* (New York: Praeger, 1965); and the comments by James S. Lay, Jr., in Francis H. Heller (ed.), *The Truman White House* (Lawrence: Regents Press of Kansas, 1980).

67. NSC agenda items from "Record of Actions by the National Security Council, 1947-1948," RG 330, Records of the Office of the Under Secretary of Defense for Policy, Assistant Secretary of Defense (International Security Policy). Hereafter cited as OASD(ISP).

68. See the entries for Sep. 22, 25, Oct. 13, 28, 1947, sub: U.S. War Plans, in notebooks kept by John H. Ohly, OSD Historian. Hereafter cited as Ohly Notebooks.

69. See the Report by the PPS, Nov. 6, 1947, *FRUS 1947,* I, 770-777 and the footnote on p. 770.

70. Millis and Duffield, *Forrestal Diaries,* 340-341.

71. See U.S. President's Air Policy Commission, *Survival in the Air Age* (Washington, D.C.: The Commission, Jan. 1, 1948).
72. Felix Larkin's notes of Forrestal's Nov. 3, 1947, presentation to the Finletter Commission, "Files for 1947," Ohly Notebooks, OSD Historian.

IV

1948: Year of Crisis

In its early stages, for the two years or so immediately following the end of World War II, the developing cold war between Washington and Moscow was essentially a contest waged by economic and political means. Clearly, as both the Truman Doctrine and the Marshall Plan signaled, the United States was increasingly dedicated to offering resistance to what it saw as the threat of communist takeovers and Soviet expansion. But whether the United States would go so far as to intervene forcibly (going beyond limited military assistance as in Greece and China) in support of this policy, possibly risking a third world war, remained to be seen. No issue thus far in the growing East-West confrontation had posed such dire possibilities.

Then, on June 24, 1948, Soviet authorities sealed off all road, rail, and canal traffic into Berlin from western Germany, touching off the most severe Soviet-American confrontation up to that time. By denying surface access to Berlin from the west, Soviet authorities risked a variety of responses, including ones from the Western custodians of Berlin—the United States, Britain, and France—that they would use force to regain access to the city. From this situation came a host of spin-offs that would dramatically alter American perspectives. Military preparedness, the adequacy of the defense budget, manpower and equipment, the finalizing of war plans, and the articulation of an American posture to meet what now seemed a more serious and long-term Soviet challenge were all part of the crisis atmosphere generated in 1948.

Yet the struggle over Berlin and the ripples emanating from it are not the whole story of 1948. Indeed, the year saw a series of foreign policy jolts that converged to make Berlin appear as an even more decisive issue than one could have imagined possible at the start of the year. The Palestine question, the continuing deterioration of the Greek situation, new uncertainties about Italy, and intimations about trouble over Germany prompted successive degrees of alarm in Washington during the early part of 1948. Then came the communist coup d'état in Prague on February 24, followed by the mysterious death of Jan Masaryk in mid-March. Although the State Department had forecast trouble in Czechoslovakia the previous November, the dénouement came suddenly, swiftly. As it happened, the Soviet move triggered, as Berlin would later, a set of American responses. But this time, unlike the crises of 1947, the reactions would be not only political and economic; they would be military as well. The broad, interactive quality of Soviet-American relations that had quickened with the deterioration of relations in 1945-1946 and then with the Truman Doctrine now assumed a more precise, distinct quality. The Truman administration, having tried other remedies, now saw no choice but to consider—in a tentative and fiscally restrained fashion, to be sure—the military requirements of containing Soviet ambitions. Military containment began its lengthy journey of becoming more than a meager atomic arsenal.

THE ROOTS OF MILITARY CONTAINMENT

On January 12, 1948, President Truman sent Congress his budget for Fiscal Year 1949, in which he estimated defense expenditures of $11 billion and international expenditures, including foreign assistance, of $7 billion. In addition, he proposed to increase the AEC budget from $456 million in FY 1948 to $660 million in FY 1949. The overall national security budget thus called for outlays of $18.6 billion in a total budget of $39.6 billion. At the same time, Truman anticipated a budget surplus of almost $5 billion, although tax reductions, he noted, might erode some of the surplus.[1]

In the same message, the President reiterated his call for the enactment of "universal training" (the "military" part of the program having been dropped for publicity purposes) and implicitly argued for a "balanced forces" concept that would produce equally effective land, sea, and air capabilities. Nonetheless, he contemplated no real increase in the size of the military establishment. The Army would remain at 11 regular divisions (all understrength) and the Navy would maintain an active fleet of 277 major combatant vessels (destroyer escorts and larger), including 11 heavy attack carriers of the Essex and Midway classes. The Air Force, though given permission to expand from 48 to 55 groups, would have to do so with no increase in its budget.[2] The recommendations of the Finletter report, which Truman had only received a few days earlier, urging a fully equipped 70-group Air Force, were of course not reflected in the budget. This fact soon caused problems, for, by mid-February, congressional opponents of UMT and European recovery (still to be fully funded) were beginning to turn to the Finletter report as a simpler, more attractive—and less expensive—solution to the country's security problems than programs like ERP.[3]

All in all, though, the President's budget presented a reassuring picture, one that gave the outward appearance of coping with a wide range of security problems in an expeditious and economical fashion. Prudent, fiscally sound, politically shrewd, the budget purported to achieve a balance between security and economy, with a preponderance still toward the economic and political policies of containment, backed by viable military capabilities. But behind the facade of strength and stability was a military establishment of sagging effectiveness, racked with internal dissension and facing a growing list of critical shortages for which the President's budget made no allowance.

What is surprising, given more than two years of steadily worsening US-Soviet relations, is how ill-prepared the armed forces actually were by 1948 for a possible military showdown with the Soviet Union. The unification controversy, demobilization, and interservice rivalry all, of course, contributed to this situation. But basically the lack of military preparedness was the product of neglect on the part of senior policymakers, from the President on down. They had placed their faith in nonmilitary courses of action, knowing full well that, if a crisis spilled over, the United States still had other reserves to fall back on, not the least of which was a monopoly on the atomic bomb. As Forrestal confidently described the situation at one point: "As long as we can out-produce the world, can control the sea and can strike inland with the atomic bomb, we can assume certain risks otherwise unacceptable in an effort to restore world trade, to restore the balance of power—military power—and to eliminate some of the conditions that breed war."[4]

In these circumstances, military plans for a possible confrontation with the Soviet Union necessarily evolved slowly, paced by fiscal realities, to be sure, but also to some extent by developments in the nuclear program. Probably the most advanced and sophisticated planning studies by 1948 were those done by the Air Force, which, because of its longer reach and emphasis on strategic bombing, expected to operate in the forefront of any future war. Even so, the Air Force, crippled by demobilization, found preparing to do so difficult, despite efforts pointed in that direction since the end of the war. March 1946 saw the creation of a special organization for such purposes: the Strategic Air Command. SAC's assigned mission was "to conduct long range offensive operations in any part of the world either independently or in cooperation with land and Naval forces."[5] But during its early years of existence, due chiefly to budgetary cutbacks and a chronic shortage of technical personnel, SAC was barely more than a shell. Initially, the nucleus of its strike force consisted of seven bombardment groups, only one of which—the 509th—was capable of sustained combat operations.[6] Until 1948, the 509th, based at Roswell Field, New Mexico, near the Sandia nuclear storage facility, was the only bombardment group in the Air Force flying SILVERPLATE B-29s, each specially modified to carry a single Nagasaki-type atomic bomb weighing 10,000 pounds. As late as October 1, 1947, only 18 SILVERPLATE planes were operational; six more B-29s had also been modified, but they were designated for training purposes and were not considered suitable for combat use. To man these planes the 509th had 30 combat flight crews, 11 qualified commanders, and 6 weaponeers. Of the available crews, 20 were cleared for atomic activities, though only 11 were rated as fully qualified through practice drops of dummy bombs. No bomb assembly teams were as yet assigned to the Air Force, and the only ones available were two skeleton units attached to the 38th Engineer Battalion at Sandia.[7]

Within SAC itself and, indeed, throughout nearly the entire Air Force, the idea of air-atomic warfare took root slowly so long as the stockpile of weapons remained relatively small. Actual planning, therefore, as encompassed in an operational plan codenamed HARROW, assumed that in any future conflict strategic bombing would necessarily involve a combination of conventional and nuclear munitions.[8] In fact, it was not until January 1948, at the second series of meetings of the USAF Aircraft and Weapons Board, that senior Air Force planners began to pay serious attention to the problems of developing the full range of equipment and facilities that would be required for a comprehensive program of atomic warfare. "It is necessary," pleaded one of the organizers of the conference, "that the USAF Aircraft and Weapons Board make basic decisions regarding these atomic weapons, in the same manner that it does regarding aircraft, armament, communications, etc."[9]

Although the board concurred that more needed to be done, its acting chairman, Gen. Joseph T. McNarney, did not feel that it was "the job of the Weapons Board to develop the concepts of atomic warfare." During most of 1948, therefore, the development of an atomic operational capability within the Air Force proceeded according to a program agreed upon at Air Force Headquarters in December 1947. The ultimate goal, with a target date of January 1, 1951, was to be able to conduct a three-phase operation embodying the "Spaatz concept," according to which the first and decisive phase of any air offensive would be a paralyzing blow to the Soviet urban-industrial complex delivered in a minimum of time, preferably less than 48 hours. To support this concept, the Air Force envisioned six atomic bombardment wings at war strength, which would be 50 percent overstrength in personnel and aircraft. Assigned to the Eighth and Fifteenth Air Forces of SAC, they would have the support of two specialized Strategic Support Squadrons and would constitute the Atomic Striking Force. But because of personnel and equipment shortages in the various squadrons designated to make up this force, the 509th remained throughout 1948 the only complete atomic bombardment unit operational within 48 hours.[10]

The hesitant pace of planning in the Air Force was matched elsewhere, especially at the joint planning level. Here, service interests clashed repeatedly as the Joint Chiefs endeavored to agree on a unified plan of action, or joint outline war plan, in the event of an emergency. Broadly speaking, the problem was not so much what should be done as who should do it, with the Air Force and the Navy locked in a bitter contest (a legacy of the unification controversy) over their respective roles and missions. Based on available intelligence, sketchy though it may have been, it seemed clear that the Soviet Union could easily overrun and occupy most of Western Europe, the Middle East, and large parts of East Asia. US planners agreed that the immediate American response should take the form of the most readily available and potent means of retaliation—a strong air offensive—followed by general mobilization, a buildup of forces, and the gradual retaking of lost territory. Where opinions differed was over the use of air power—whether land-based or carrier-based air should spearhead the initial retaliatory effort—and whether naval air, operating mostly from carriers in the Mediterranean, should be included in that phase of the bombing offensive involving nuclear weapons.[11]

Another set of planning problems that concerned the Chiefs were composed of those problems with politico-military implications. The immediate foreign policy challenges, whether in Palestine, Greece, Italy, or possibly Czechoslovakia, suggested that what the American defense posture needed was more Army manpower, not more strategic bombers or aircraft carriers. This theme, sounded before the House Armed Services Committee in January 1948 by Lt. Gen. Albert Wedemeyer, director of Army Plans and Operations, would be reiterated throughout the year.[12] But the most dramatic revelations were those Truman received at a secret White House briefing held on February 18, 1948, by Maj. Gen. Alfred M. Gruenther, director of the JCS Joint Staff. Laying bare the stark realities, Gruenther pointed out that, for an emergency, there were less than two-and-a-half reserve divisions in the United States; with enlistments declining, the Army would be short 165,000 men by the end of 1948.[13] Gen. Omar Bradley, recently named Army chief of staff to succeed Eisenhower, reinforced these views in a March 11 report in which he said that the Army was unable to "back up our country's policies."[14] Subsequent studies would not be so pessimistic, although, in assessing manpower needs for a number of contingencies, the NSC staff and the JCS would repeatedly refer to "partial mobilization" as a distinct possibility.[15]

To buttress these evaluations, Forrestal supplied a private report of his own to the President on February 28, 1948. In it, he reviewed major defense shortcomings, including the Army's manpower shortage, the absence of an agreed joint emergency war plan, and the need for new equipment to replace the obsolescent World War II matériel. He also noted the slow progress on the B-52 intercontinental bomber (the planned successor to the problem-plagued B-36); advised that the country was "a very long way" from having usable long-range missiles; and warned that for the foreseeable future there was little chance of reductions in defense expenditures. Any savings from service unification would have to be reinvested and, he added, there were prospects for new funding requests just to maintain the current US level of preparedness. Although Forrestal personally discounted the threat of overt Soviet aggression, he saw the demands on the defense establishment increasing to such an extent that it would soon encounter serious trouble in meeting any new dangers. Between the lines, his message to Truman was crystal clear: like it or not, the time for stocktaking was at hand.[16]

THE MARCH CRISIS AND ITS AFTERMATH

Having alerted Truman to these impending difficulties, Forrestal meanwhile made a further attempt at a meeting with the Joint Chiefs in Key West, Florida, to resolve interservice differences, especially the vexing problem of service roles and missions, that were holding up final agreement on a joint emergency war plan. When he returned to Washington on March 13, it was with a newly-agreed-upon statement of service functions that seemed to assure the Navy access to the atomic bomb. He also brought back the unanimous recommendation of the Chiefs that the President seek restoration of selective service, turn over custody of nuclear weapons to the military, and ask Congress for supplemental defense appropriations.[17]

Truman, in the meantime, had decided on his own that the time for dalliance was over. The recent Soviet-directed coup d'état in Czechoslovakia and rumors of possible war in Europe, fueled by an alarming cable from Lt. Gen. Lucius D. Clay, the American military governor of Germany, required a firm presidential response. Otherwise, as Truman confided to members of his White House staff, the country would be "sunk."[18] Nor could the impending autumn presidential election (despite his disclaimers) have been far from Truman's considerations. Nonetheless, Truman's dramatic address to a joint session of Congress on March 17 indicated a new American zealousness in relations with the Soviet Union. Calling Moscow a "growing menace" with ambitions toward the rest of Western Europe, the President insisted that preparedness must be the watchword of the American position. In what sounded to many (including Forrestal) like a call for re-armament, Truman urged prompt action generally along the lines his military advisors had urged—full funding for the remaining European Recovery Program requests, passage of legislation for Universal Training, and temporary reinstatement of the draft. Implicit in all this was that Congress would soon also receive a supporting request for supplemental appropriations.[19]

Eight days later, on March 25, during an appearance before the Senate Armed Services Committee, Forrestal publicly backed calls for congressional action in a strident, ringing assessment of the dangers facing the free world. Indeed, an early draft of his prepared remarks (written by Boston attorney Robert Cutler) had prompted Marshall to chide Forrestal for proposing what sounded more like "a preliminary to war than a proposal for preparation to avoid war."[20] Marshall's admonitions brought only a few alterations in the Defense Secretary's presentation. Drawing historical comparisons, he assailed the lack of preparedness in 1939, arguing that weakness had created temptation for Mussolini and Hitler. To prevent this, the United States must now prepare itself for the long challenge ahead. In practical terms, asserted Forrestal, this meant 350,000 more men for the armed forces through the draft or UMT; balanced air, sea, and land forces; new aircraft procurement for a 55-group Air Force; and a $3 billion supplement (in addition to $11 billion previously requested) to the FY 1949 defense budget.[21] Except for UMT, Congress duly obliged, giving the administration everything it asked for, including an additional, unrequested appropriation of $822 million for air procurement.[22]

While Congress was in the process of acting, members of the administration fought among themselves over the nature of the supplemental and its projected consequences for future defense budgets. With unified budgeting still more a hope than a reality, the JCS came up with a figure of $9 billion merely by adding up individual service totals. Since this was clearly above what Truman preferred ($1.5 billion), Forrestal had no choice but to contemplate tough allocation decisions. Yet he had few guideposts, save an awareness that at least half of any supplemental would go to aircraft procurement and the rest to balancing the forces, especially the Army.

Into the void of expertise and practice moved the Bureau of the Budget (BoB). The bureau soon recognized that an increase in funding for one year, if extended into the next, would commit the administration, not to a continuation of linear budgets, but rather to budgets that might jump to $17.1 billion in FY 1951 and possibly $18 billion by FY 1952. This, Truman believed, would heat up inflation (then running at 8 percent a year) and require deficit financing, a prospect he regarded as wholly unacceptable.[23] Such tardy awareness about the fiscal ramifications of a defense buildup effectively checked any proclivity Truman might have had for a larger supplemental or even the desire to spend all that would in fact be appropriated. Hence his curious stance of agreeing to the new monies (pared, from Forrestal's original request of $3.5 billion, to $3.1), then his subsequent decision not to spend the funds earmarked by Congress for air procurement.

The struggle over the supplemental was also the beginning of the end of Forrestal's tenure as secretary of defense. Citing the defense secretary's inability to curb the military's appetite for money and his apparently all-too-close collaboration with Republicans in Congress, Truman declared at a meeting with White House staff that he was "getting damn sore" with Forrestal and might have to find a new head for the Pentagon.[24] But for the time being, as he announced at a meeting with Forrestal and the Joint Chiefs on May 13, Truman intended only to limit the FY 1950 defense budget to $15 billion, including $600 million of the stockpile of critical materials.[25] The obvious inference was that Truman had decided on a leveling-off of military measures to contain Soviet and communist expansion. Confirming his decision to freeze the defense budget, he told Forrestal on June 3 that it was "necessary to accelerate our national defense program at a steady rate rather than to attempt any immediate very large increase." And he added, "I am looking to your office to provide the necessary direction . . . to assure development of the military program in such a manner that the objectives and limitations set out . . . will be realized."[26] Forrestal, however, had somewhat different ideas. A month later, he suggested to Truman that the NSC staff should prepare a major study, one that would assess overall security needs and define whether the dangers were distant or immediate; from this estimate could be determined the nature of the most likely Soviet threat. Taken together, he informed Truman, these assessments would help the defense establishment "in determining the level and character of forces which it should maintain." All of this would be of assistance, Forrestal made clear, in drawing up new budget requests for FY 1950.[27]

From the start, Forrestal's call for an NSC input—an idea that had been percolating in his mind for months—met with doubts and skepticism from the White House. Truman wasted no time informing the secretary of defense that while he approved doing the study and would give its recommendations due consideration, preparations for FY 1950 should continue within the $15 billion ceiling. But he also left the door open to a change of policy should the situation change. "If the advice of the National Security Council or future developments warrant it," he told Forrestal,

> an adjustment can be made in the presently approved ceiling allowance for the National Military Establishment. Meanwhile, it is imperative that no time be lost in the formulation of the Establishment's 1950 program and budget within the stated allowance.[28]

This reaffirmation of his position, reflecting the continuing primacy in Truman's mind of fiscal and economic considerations, would form the crux of the famous fight over the FY 1950 budget. Ultimately, the outcomes of that fight would yield long-term consequences. By effectively ruling out the more costly conventional alternative, they would set the stage for policies and strategies more heavily dependent than ever on air-atomic retaliation against possible Soviet aggression.

NUCLEAR PLANNING ACCELERATED

Ironically, it was this very course—reliance on nuclear weapons—that Truman earnestly hoped to avoid. On May 6, 1948, reflecting on the previous day's JCS briefing on the current emergency war plan, codenamed HALFMOON, Truman expressed some misgivings. He questioned the plan's provision for an air offensive using nuclear weapons at the outset of hostilities. According to Admiral Leahy, the President wanted an alternate plan prepared that would "resist a Russian attack without using atomic bombs for the reason that we might not have them available either because they might at that time be outlawed or because the people of the United States might not at the time permit their use for aggressive purposes."[29]

No such plan ever materialized. In July, Forrestal, alluding to budgetary constraints, in effect told the Chiefs to forget the President's request.[30] But the prospect that such a plan might become a reality sent disturbing signals through the military. Secretary of the Army Kenneth C. Royall, who had been pressing for some time for clearer high-level guidance on military planning where the use of atomic weapons might be involved, was especially concerned. After learning of the President's interest in a nonnuclear plan, Royall circulated a memo on May 19 calling for a thorough review of America's atomic warfare policy.

Decisions about the use of the new weapon were, he asserted, urgently needed, since Army planners had hitherto assumed that such weapons would be available. Now, uncertainties abounded. If there were issues of morality, then these too should be addressed. Clearly, there were issues concerning target selection, the authority to use atomic weapons, the custody of the devices, and the organization best suited for directing their use, all of which, Royall said, should be studied without further delay.[31]

The next day (May 20), at an NSC meeting chaired by Secretary of State Marshall, Royall elaborated. He insisted that "if there are any qualifications on our use of atomic weapons," they should be known immediately. Secretary of the Air Force Stuart Symington thought Royall's proposed study was a "good idea," for "it would show how much we must rely on the bomb."[32] But in deciding what should be done, the council deferred action until its next meeting, when it authorized a two-pronged approach—an NSC study on US policy on "the initiation of atomic warfare in the event of war, including consideration of the time and circumstances of employment, and the type and character of targets against which it would be employed . . ."; and a separate study by the War Council, the Pentagon's most senior deliberative body, of the proper organization within the government "to insure optimum exploitation by the United States of its capabilities of waging atomic warfare."[33] Finally, nearly three years after TRINITY, and a year after the formation of the NSC, the question of strategic atomic warfare was on the agenda to be examined in broad and comprehensive terms. Yet resolving these problems amid the heightened tensions of that summer—the Berlin crisis especially—would, perforce, take the form of often imperfect and temporary solutions.

In sum, the first external jolts of 1948 had prompted American responses within carefully defined limits. Manpower needs had been addressed, new aircraft procurement voted within the framework of a 55-group Air Force, and other provisions for balanced forces accepted. But the response was not a stampede for new expenditures, nor was it an uncritical commitment to a series of expensive weapons systems. Neither the President nor the public was yet prepared to go faster on the military dimension of containment. The confidence engendered by unilateral possession of the bomb remained, for the time being, sufficient.

ONSET OF THE BERLIN BLOCKADE

The Berlin blockade, commencing on June 24, 1948, would prove one of the decisive events of the rapidly escalating East-West cold war. Not only was the blockade the culminating step in the Soviet-American failure to reach a common policy for Germany; it was also, in a very real sense, the turning point for American attitudes toward nuclear weapons. Combined with subsequent deliberations over the defense budget, the blockade became the final catalyst that thrust the United States into deepening and irreversible dependence on its nuclear arsenal. Beyond the confrontation itself, which several times (late June, mid-July, and mid-September) verged on open hostilities, tensions over Berlin prompted a series of spin-offs, each with its own consequences: a showdown between the AEC and the military over custody of nuclear weapons; urgent attention to the belated development of atomic energy policy; and, of course, a battle royal over the military budget.

For our purposes, the particulars of the Berlin crisis are less important than its strategic ramifications.[34] Early in the crisis, Truman, appearing to take a tough line, ordered support for Berlin through the airlift and assured his advisors that the United States was "going to stay, period." But as for how far he was prepared to go in backing up this statement, he failed to elaborate.[35] Then, on the morning of June 30, word reached Washington, via a wire service report, that the Soviets had sent up a barrage balloon obstructing British flight paths into Berlin and that the British were contemplating action to shoot down the balloon. This news (or rumor, as it turned out) prompted a major discussion later that same day among Forrestal and his senior advisors to assess the situation and to weigh the chances of war.

During the hastily convened meeting, a series of revealing pieces of information emerged.[36] First, Forrestal reported that he had been in touch by telephone with Under Secretary of State Robert Lovett, who had already consulted with Senator Arthur H. Vandenberg, chairman of the Foreign Relations Committee. According to Lovett, Forrestal said, Vandenberg opposed any Anglo-American action that breached the peace. Instead, the senator had counseled restraint and diplomatic protests, positions that Lovett had likewise endorsed. Second, and possibly more surprising, Adm. William D. Leahy, the President's chief of staff, revealed that Truman wanted US forces to stay in Berlin as long as possible, but not to the point of shooting down a barrage balloon and starting a war for which the United States did not have enough soldiers. The President, Leahy reported, "was quite positive on that." Royall, taking exception, argued that the barrage balloon might prove "a pretty good showdown issue." All tended to agree that if it came to that, the use of atomic weapons by the United States could not be avoided. Indeed, in Leahy's view, the United States should begin immediately to mobilize its nuclear assets. "We haven't very much," he noted, "but still we could make plans to use what we have. . . . I don't know what we could do but whatever we have we could use. It might be a very good idea to have them over there anyway." To this Royall responded that the dangers of war made completion of the NSC study on atomic warfare all the more urgent.

Royall's mention of the warfare study led to some illuminating exchanges. Gen. Hoyt S. Vandenberg, Air Force chief of staff, thought his people were studying potential targets, but he was not certain. Bradley thought a study involving target selection represented a civilian intrusion into the military domain. Forrestal, on the other hand, saw target selection as inherently political, since it could very well turn on such questions as "whether or not you gamble that a reduction of Moscow and Leningrad would be a powerful enough impact to stop a war." Reacting to similar comments from Adm. Sidney W. Souers, executive secretary of the NSC, Bradley asked whether an atomic weapon should ever be used on any political target. The question got no answer, however, since no one was eager to pursue such a sensitive issue; soon the discussion meandered. Nonetheless, all agreed on one item: the initial decision to use atomic weapons would be political, and that meant consulting the President.

The occasion for this meeting passed almost immediately, for, on July 1, word reached Washington that no balloon could be found. Even so, the possibility that the situation might take a further, sudden turn for the worse prompted the NSC to authorize a series of precautionary measures, including the deployment of the 301st Bombardment Group to western Germany on July 2 and a request shortly thereafter to move two additional bombardment groups—the 307th and 28th—to England. The British chiefs of staff, fearing that the tense situation in Berlin could go either way, proved eager to cooperate and promptly endorsed the proposed deployment, an action subsequently approved by the cabinet.[37] At the same time, the 509th Bombardment Group—containing the nation's only atomic-modified aircraft—went on 24-hour alert, although it remained in the United States.[38] Despite the absence of any firm agreement governing U.S. access to British bases other than the 1946 Spaatz-Tedder understanding, informal talks between Lt. Gen. Lauris Norstad, USAF, and Air Chief Marshal Tedder subsequently confirmed that the United States wanted to maintain "a permanent detachment in the U.K." consisting of one B-29 bombardment group and one fighter group "irrespective of whether an emergency in Western Europe existed or not." Tedder apparently offered no objection.[39] As Forrestal summarized it, these actions would show the seriousness of American intentions, give the Air Force some needed experience, and, most important of all, put the planes in place so they could become "an accepted fixture" before the British could have a change of heart.[40]

THE CUSTODY DISPUTE

With the decision to place the 509th on alert, prompt resolution of another issue became imperative. This concerned a dispute, simmering for some months, between the AEC and the military over whether the latter should have custody of atomic weapons, a change which under the law only the President could authorize. Though discussions had been underway since the fall of 1947, no progress whatsoever had resulted. The AEC concurred, as a matter of practicality, that the military needed access to nuclear weapons for training purposes, among other things; but it wanted to maintain a policy that kept the bombs under close control and supervision because of the military's lack of technical competence to handle and maintain them. Although the argument was not without merit, it was really somewhat disingenuous, used by Lilienthal and his colleagues on the Commission to stall for time. At issue was a basic principle they knew they could not defend indefinitely but refused to concede nevertheless. Indeed, they worried that ceding even the slightest degree of responsibility for custody to the military would be tantamount to overturning the letter and spirit of the Atomic Energy Act. The AEC would not, in short, make concessions that might surrender or dilute civilian control.[41]

With the onset of the Berlin crisis, Forrestal intensified his efforts to secure a solution to the custody dispute, only to find Lilienthal more resolutely opposed than ever to any change in procedures.[42] Finally, on July 15, after several inconclusive meetings with Lilienthal and his fellow commissioners, Forrestal warned Truman that the issue could no longer be ignored, since "there was a very serious question as to the wisdom of relying upon an agency other than the user of such a weapon, to assure the integrity and usability of such a weapon." Although Forrestal insisted that he was not asking for a decision on the weapon's use, Truman made it equally clear that he was not about to take any action that might result in putting the bomb in the hands of "some dashing lieutenant colonel." In that frame of mind, the President agreed to adjudicate the AEC and NME claims on the custody question.[43]

In the confrontation in the Oval Office on July 21, Lilienthal proved to be the more effective in-fighter. Donald F. Carpenter, chairman of the MLC, who argued the case for Forrestal, was simply unable to sway the President with his heavy, technical presentation. In an accompanying paper for Truman to review, the secretary of defense made several points more succinctly: a surprise attack might catch the services without any atomic weapons; the military needed to discover in peacetime how these weapons worked; and the growing number (now some 50 nuclear cores) meant that they could be dispersed to storage locations more convenient for military purposes.[44] Lilienthal deftly countered each and every point the military raised, keeping the custody and command issues sufficiently merged to awaken Truman's suspicions about what he might be surrendering.[45] His strategy worked. Two days later, on July 23, Truman notified Forrestal that he had decided in favor of the AEC, but expected the services and the commission to work out emergency transfer arrangements so as to prevent delays in a crisis. Though a rebuff for Forrestal, Truman's decision was to prove—as events would later dictate—but a temporary reprieve for the AEC.[46]

BERLIN AND THE RENEWED THREAT OF WAR

Despite the President's decision, problems connected with the custody question and possible use of the bomb persisted. Meanwhile, in early September came the breakdown of negotiations in Moscow aimed at finding a Berlin settlement. On September 13, Truman, faced with the renewed threat of hostilities, listened closely to an Air Force briefing on the problems of targets and bases and on the need for construction of huts at two British bases (Sculthorpe and Lakenheath) for the storage of nonnuclear assemblies. Having these facilities, he learned, might cut the time needed to implement a nuclear decision by ten days. Although the transfer/custody question did not come up, it was clear that construction of the huts implied it. This time, the services and Forrestal got more than partial satisfaction. While Truman "prayed" that use of the bomb could be avoided, he assured those present that "if it became necessary, no one need have a misgiving but what he would do so. . . ."[47] Truman's own note of the meeting poignantly confirms the seriousness of the moment: "Forrestal, Bradley, Vandenberg (the Air Force General, not the senator), Symington brief me on bases, bombs, Moscow, Leningrad, etc. I have a terrible feeling that we are very close to war."[48]

Three days later, on September 16, the President and his advisors confronted the atomic problem anew. Following a morning cabinet session, Marshall and Forrestal saw the President in private to press again for talks with the British on the construction of nuclear storage huts. This time Truman agreed, thereby opening the way for Lt. Gen. Lauris Norstad to head a secret mission to London. Marshall also suggested that the time might have come to reopen the custody question. But Truman, citing the political campaign, wanted matters in that regard left as they were.[49]

Later that same day, the NSC, with Truman absent, met to consider NSC 30, the long awaited report on atomic warfare. Drafted initially by the Air

Force in July, and revised slightly in early September, this document represented the NSC's response to Royall's earlier prodding about atomic war. Much to Royall's annoyance and disappointment, NSC 30 made no definite commitment to the use of nuclear weapons, though it did call for their inclusion in military plans. But its studied ambiguities, reaffirming that any final decision on use rested with the President, reflected the difficulties of trying to provide firm guidelines on such a sensitive subject. Two paragraphs summarized what was to become operative policy:

> 12. It is recognized that, in the event of hostilities, the National Military Establishment must be ready to utilize promptly and effectively all appropriate means available, including atomic weapons, in the interest of national security and must therefore plan accordingly.
>
> 13. The decision as to the employment of atomic weapons in the event of war is to be made by the Chief Executive when he considers such decision to be required.

Truman, without concurring or dissenting, took the paper's recommendations under advisement, and by so doing gave them quasi-official endorsement.[50]

Such considerations, vague though they may have been, reveal the essence of early nuclear strategy and deterrence theory. At first glace it would seem that Truman, by tacitly accepting NSC 30, remained fully in control of the how the nuclear arsenal would be used. But in reality he was giving up much more than he probably realized. By accepting the inclusion of nuclear weapons in military plans (something he had resisted just a few months earlier), Truman was saying in effect that it was also up to his military advisors to decide not only the nature of the targets to be attacked but also the probable circumstances in which those weapons would be used. Each new planning cycle had the paradoxical effect of curtailing the flexibility of the decision-maker and at the same time of providing him with more usable and increasingly dangerous options. However much the President may have preferred to keep the weapons-use question unsettled and open, his advisors—through the planning mechanisms of modern warfare—were in the process of limiting his choices. Truman and his successors would gradually discover that many fingers would be poised at, or near, the trigger mechanism.

In fact, by the end of September 1948, Truman was increasingly and uncomfortably aware that American preparations for a nuclear confrontation with the Soviets were well advanced. Contingency plans, hastily prepared, were still evolving with increasingly ominous overtones. Meeting with Forrestal on September 29, the Joint Chiefs laid out a status report. Check lists for each service, they confirmed, were ready; American commanders in Germany, Austria, and Trieste had their marching orders; the protection of AEC facilities was arranged; and the Air Force and the Armed Forces Special Weapons Project (AFSWP), the organization in charge of assembling and arming the bombs, were in the process of completing plans to accept the emergency transfer of custody of atomic weapons should the situation in Berlin worsen. Moreover, Norstad, now in England, had learned that Air Chief Marshal Tedder was in basic agreement with US thinking "about the immediate use of the A-Bomb." But as a precaution, should the British change their mind about having American aircraft stationed in their country, the Joint Chiefs continued to consider Spanish, Libyan, Italian, and Pakistani bases as alternative staging areas. Finally, and perhaps most foreboding of all, the Chiefs had also initiated studies to find an alternative command post "outside Washington in the event the Pentagon was destroyed."[51] In short, if a military confrontation could not be avoided, the United States would retaliate with the most devastating response it could devise. It was this sort of thinking that was steadily gaining ground, giving the bomb its claim to primacy in American strategy and policy.

THE BATTLE OVER THE BUDGET: FISCAL YEAR 1950

As critical as the Berlin crisis may have been in revealing American dependence on nuclear weapons, it was in the realm of fiscal matters that the American nuclear strategy took final shape. Truman's refusal to lift the $15 billion ceiling on the FY 1950 military budget effectively determined that nuclear weapons would be the mainstay of the country's defense posture. Although Truman repeatedly insisted that he wanted to reduce reliance on nuclear weapons and have them internationally controlled or banned, such sentiments became increasingly difficult to harmonize with his other objectives as 1948 progressed. This was especially true of his determination to hold down defense expenditures. As long as the American nuclear monopoly held, and as long as an overt Soviet nuclear threat to the United States appeared unlikely, advocates of increased US defense spending faced an uphill struggle.

Indeed, even as the Berlin crisis moved from one dangerous note to another, intelligence reports from US and allied sources sounded increasingly reassuring. Despite stepped-up tensions, British analysts deemed it unlikely that the Soviet Union would have a sufficient number of atomic bombs to offset the US preponderance anytime prior to the end of 1956.[52] In assessing the Soviet threat and risk of war, the analysts also found that:

> Russia almost certainly suffers from the grave disadvantage of not having any atomic bombs and this fact alone would make deliberate aggression a risky and unprofitable procedure for her. Her long range bomber force, being of comparatively recent growth, cannot yet have reached a high degree of efficiency whilst even her army, large as it is, is not yet wholly equipped and trained up to 1945 Western standards.[53]

The consensus within the American intelligence community was much the same—that the first point of real danger of a Soviet atomic attack would not occur before the mid-1950s. Until then, given the superiority the United States enjoyed in nuclear power, and barring a miscalculation on the Soviets' part, the West would remain relatively safe and secure.[54]

To some extent, then, as Truman was doubtless aware, nuclear weapons and the American monopoly dampened pressures which, in other circumstances, might conceivably have led to substantial increases in US military spending. The budget process thus went forward with Truman in a commanding position, although not always a comfortable one, given the pressures he was under from events abroad and the ongoing presidential campaign at home.

Meanwhile, during September and October, the NSC staff endeavored to satisfy Forrestal's request for a national security review. The work consisted in the main of assimilating a group of State Department and CIA studies under the serial heading of NSC 20, resulting in issuance of a final report (NSC 20/4) in November. At the same time, Forrestal found himself confronted again with dissension among the Joint Chiefs, not only over the overall size of the budget, but also over the allocation of resources among the services, with the Navy and the Air Force battling one another for larger shares. The resulting impasse among his military advisors convinced Forrestal that a budget limited to $15 billion was untenable and that an increase was the only realistic option in order to assure both national security and interservice harmony. Whether Truman would approve a raise, however, remained to be seen. His doing so was, as Forrestal fully realized, a long-shot possibility.[55]

Hoping to nudge Truman in his direction, Forrestal on October 31 wrote Secretary of State Marshall asking whether the international situation warranted a reduction in American forces or whether things had in fact grown worse, thus requiring a stronger military posture.[56] Marshall, acting on advice from Lovett and Kennan, hesitated to support Forrestal and risk becoming involved in the Pentagon's internecine quarrels. His response was appropriately and intentionally evasive. He felt, as he had the previous spring, that the United States should develop forces "within a balanced national economy, and that the country could not, and would not, support a budget based on preparation for war. This view still holds."[57]

Still, Forrestal continued to probe, personally touring Europe in early November to sound out leaders there on the situation.[58] When he returned, he submitted to the National Security Council a JCS paper (NSC 35) on US commitments abroad to help illustrate the dangers the country faced. The JCS addressed the threat question less from a bilateral Soviet-American perspective than from the general approach of what obligations the United States had incurred that might require the use of force. What is especially striking about the Chiefs' paper is the near absence of any mention of that threat. Its tone throughout was one of response to the overseas challenges and the execution of commitments abroad, with little mention of the possibility of an attack on the United States. Instead, the JCS opted for a more sustained, steady buildup.[59] When the Chiefs argued on that terrain, they naturally played the same game under a different set of rules in which both the President and the BoB were the more skilled practitioners.

If Forrestal still had hopes that NSC 20/4 would alter Truman's stance, he was soon to be disappointed. The completed report, adopted by the NSC on November 23, 1948, was not a document to turn the tide in a budget battle. Rather, its recommendations tended to be broadly worded and often imprecise—so much so that they were virtually useless in analyzing the relative merits of competing military programs, one of the functions for which Forrestal had requested the report in the first place. While acknowledging the grave danger posed by the Soviet Union to American security, the report sidestepped the issue of increased military preparedness by warning of the potential threat to the country's economic health caused by "excessive" armaments. Militarily, the Soviet Union possessed the capability to overrun Western Europe, the Middle East, and parts of Asia. But it would probably not be until the mid-1950s that the Soviets could mount "serious air attacks" against the United States with atomic weapons. Consequently, for the immediate future, the United States could afford to accept some degree of risk, while concentrating on isolating and containing Soviet influence through a variety of economic, military, and political tactics. A policy developed and applied on this basis, the report argued, would require "a level of military readiness which can be maintained as long as necessary as a deterrent to Soviet aggression"; it would also provide a foundation for rapid mobilization should the need arise. Although somewhat ambiguous as a statement of policy and vague as to the appropriate role of nuclear power, NSC 20/4 left no doubt that a military budget limited to $15 billion would not necessarily endanger national security.[60]

For its central purpose—helping to justify an increase in the size of the FY 1950 defense budget—NSC 20/4 was a failure. All the same, that did not stop Forrestal from continuing to press for a larger defense budget. On December 1, he submitted the first coordinated defense budget, or, more precisely, he submitted two budgets—one of $14.4 billion, which did not go above the presidential ceiling, and another of $16.9 billion, which Forrestal personally recommended as preferable in terms of addressing national security needs. (He dismissed as excessive a third set of estimates, submitted by the Joint Chiefs, for $23 billion.) After consultations with the State Department, Forrestal reported that General Marshall also favored the $16.9 billion budget as "better calculated . . . to instill the necessary confidence in democratic nations everywhere than would the reduced forces in a more limited budget."[61] But in Truman's view, the choice was easy. More ebullient and confident than ever after his recent come-from-behind election victory, he saw no need to make compromises with subordinates, especially one like Forrestal, whom he now knew he would soon replace. "I don't know why he sent two," Truman told Budget Director Webb. "The $14.4 billion budget is the one we will adopt."[62]

From Forrestal's standpoint, Truman's decision to adhere to the $15 billion ceiling now made increased reliance on strategic air power and nuclear weapons unavoidable. Forrestal, once the ardent advocate of "balanced forces," now dropped any pretense of believing them feasible, given the fiscal realities. As a fall-back position, he met with Truman on December 20 to argue for an additional $580 million for the Air Force to support six additional bombardment groups. His strategic rationale for the groups clearly embraced an atomic strategy. Air power, Forrestal contended, could be successfully used "against our most probable enemy." An air offensive, he argued, would not only prevent a US and allied defeat, but would buy time for the United States to mobilize and thus enable the war to be won with less expenditure of men and dollars. Because it could react immediately, Forrestal contended, air power provided the "most effective deterrent to Soviet aggression. It is the immediacy of the threat of retaliation that will stop Soviet aggression, if anything will."[63]

Forrestal's appeal brought no change, either in the allocation of funds or in Truman's budget priorities.[64] In fact, when Congress later added just such funds for more air groups in September 1949, the President refused to spend the money. Arguments based on strategic concepts were no more effective than threat assessments in breaking the ceiling. But other ramifications were equally important. First, the logic of the tight fiscal policy on overall strategic policy was emerging with greater clarity. Reliance on a strategic-atomic posture now formed an essential element of America's defense policy. The assumptions of the September discussions about atomic policy (NSC 30) were rapidly becoming part of the accepted strategic wisdom. Truman might talk of balanced forces, the budget might continue to be divided into triads for the Army, the Navy, and the Air Force, but the balance was more apparent than real. Indeed, even if Truman had changed his mind and agreed to the increases in the FY 1950 budget that Forrestal proposed, the results in terms of the US defense posture might not have been significantly different, given the ready acceptance and growing emphasis in JCS war plans on nuclear retaliation. As it happened, what had perhaps been implicit in the confusion of 1946 and 1947 became explicit: the atomic bomb was a part of both policy and operational planning for war with the Soviet Union. It would be the deterrent force, and if deterrence failed, it then would be utilized earlier rather than later against Soviet aggression. Face-to-face with the prospect of an explosive Soviet-American confrontation, and with inadequate US ground forces to match a Soviet push, the atomic advantage became crucial. Unfettered by any plan of international control, American planners could proceed. Slowly but surely, the faint outlines of what would latter be termed "massive retaliation" were beginning to emerge.

NOTES

1. "Annual Budget Message to Congress: Fiscal Year 1949," Jan. 12, 1948, *Public Papers of the Presidents of the United States: Harry S. Truman, 1948* (Washington, D.C.: G.P.O., 1964), 19-31. Also see Truman's press conference presentation on the budget, Jan. 10, 1948, *ibid.*, 11-19.

2. Rearden, *Formative Years,* 312-313.

3. Note by Felix Larkin, OSD, for Forrestal, Feb. 6, 1948, Henry Glass Papers, Misc. Material on Supplemental Approp. Mar.-May 1948 folder, Office of the OSD Historian (hereafter cited as Glass Papers). Also see Millis and Duffield, *Forrestal Diaries,* 377-378.

4. Ltr, Forrestal to Chan Gurney, Dec. 8, 1947, quoted in Millis and Duffield, *Forrestal Diaries,* 350-351.

5. Ltr, Spaatz to Kenney, Mar. 21, 1946, quoted in J.C. Hopkins and Sheldon A. Goldberg, *The Development of Strategic Air Command, 1946-1986* (Offutt AFB: Office of the Historian, HQ SAC, 1986), 2.

6. Memo, Gen. George C. Kenney to Gen. Carl Spaatz, Jan. 15, 1948, sub: SAC Strength and Capabilities, Spaatz Papers, box 257, Command-Strategic folder, L.C.

7. Little, *Foundations of an Atomic Air Force,* 221-222.

8. "Air Force Short Range Emergency Plan (HARROW)," [ca. Mar. 1948], Vandenberg Papers, Blitz Book, box 38, L.C.

9. Memo, Maj. Gen. W. E. Kepner, Chief, Special Weapons Gp, for DC/S, Materiel, Jan. 16, 1948, sub: Agenda for 2d Mtg USAF Aircraft and Weapons Bd, RG 341, 334 Committees and Rpts.

10. Little, *Foundations of an Atomic Air Force,* 155-156, 223, 227, 255.

11. Kenneth W. Condit, *The History of the Joint Chiefs of Staff: The Joint Chiefs of Staff and National Policy,* vol. II, *1947-1949* (Washington, D.C.: Historical Div., JCS, 1976), 285-293. For the Air Force's view on these disputes, see John T. Greenwood, "The Emergence of the Postwar Strategic Air Force, 1945-1953," in Alfred F. Hurley and Robert C. Ehrhart (eds.), *Air Power and Warfare* (Washington, D.C.: Office of Air Force History and U.S. Air Force Academy, 1979), 224-236. For the Navy view, see David Alan Rosenberg, "American Postwar Air Doctrine and Organization: The Navy Experience," *ibid.,* 245-271. The best overall view of service planning during this period is Steven T. Ross, *American War Plans, 1945-1950* (New York: Garland, 1988).

12. Testimony by Wedemeyer before House Armed Services Committee, Jan. 12, 1948, Glass Papers, Budget NME 1950 folder, OSD Historical Office.

13. Millis and Duffield, *Forrestal Diaries,* 374-377.

14. Bradley memo, Mar. 11, 1948, *FRUS 1948,* I, 539-540.

15. See Rearden, *Formative Years,* 154-155, 172-173, 185; NSC 5/3 (Greece), *FRUS 1948,* IV, 93-95; NSC 1/3 (Italy), Mar. 12, 1948, *ibid.,* III, 765-769; and memo, Leahy (for JCS) to Forrestal, Apr. 3, 1948, sub: Palestine, RG 330, CD 6-2-47.

16. "Report to the President from the Secretary of Defense," Feb. 28, 1948, CF, box 4, Defense Dept. Rpt. folder, Truman Papers, HSTL.

17. Millis and Duffield, *Forrestal Diaries,* 392-394.

18. Diary entry, Mar. 16, 1948, in Robert H. Ferrell (ed.), *Truman in the White House: The Diary of Eben A. Ayers* (Columbia: University of Missouri Press, 1991), 247.

19. Yergin, *Shattered Peace,* 353; "Special Message to the Congress on the Threat to the Freedom of Europe," Mar. 17, 1948, *Truman Public Papers, 1948,* 182-186; Millis and Duffield, *Forrestal Diaries,* 397.

20. Memo, Marshall to Forrestal, Mar. 23, 1948, *FRUS 1948,* I, 541-542. Also see Robert Cutler, *No Time for Rest* (Boston: Little, Brown, 1965), 248-253.

21. U.S. Congress, Senate, Committee on Armed Services, *Hearings: Universal Military Training,* 80:2 (Washington, D.C.: G.P.O, 1948), 325-332.

22. For a detailed account of congressional action on the FY 1949 supplemental, see Edward A. Kolodziej, *The Uncommon Defense and Congress: 1945-1963* (Columbus: Ohio State University Press, 1966), 74-81.

23. Mins. of Mtg, Forrestal, Webb, Leahy, Spaatz, Denfeld, Bradley, McNeil, Gruenther, Mar. 20, 1948, Glass Papers, Key West Conference Mar. 1948 folder, OSD Historical Collection, Pentagon; Mins. of Mtg, May 6, 1948, Forrestal Diaries, vol. XI, 2231-2233, Forrestal Papers; Forrestal to Truman, May 13, 1948, Glass Papers, Finletter Rpt and Material file; and McNeil memo, May 8, 1948, sub: Supplemental Budget, *ibid.*

24. Diary entry, Apr. 21, 1948, in Ferrell (ed.), *Ayers Diary*, 253.

25. Statement by the President to SecDef, Service Secretaries, and Chiefs of Staff, May 13, 1948, Truman Papers, PSF, Subject file; Millis and Duffield, *Forrestal Diaries*, 435-438.

26. Ltr, Truman to Forrestal, June 3, 1948, RG 330, CD 9-2-4.

27. Ltr, Forrestal to Truman, July 10, 1948, *FRUS 1948*, I, 592-593.

28. Ltr, Truman to Forrestal, July 15, 1948, PSF/Subject file, Truman Papers.

29. Leahy Diary, May 6, 1948, L.C.

30. Millis and Duffield, *Forrestal Diaries*, 458.

31. Memo, Royall to NSC, May 19, 1948, sub: Atomic Weapons, *FRUS 1948*, I, 572-573.

32. Memo to the President, May 21, 1948, [sub: 11th Mtg NSC, May 20, 1948], PSF/NSC file, Truman Papers, quoted in Rearden, *Formative Years*, 435.

33. Mins., 12th Mtg NSC, June 3, 1948, PSF/NSC file, box 203, NSC Mtg No. 12 folder, Truman Papers, HSTL.

34. Among the extensive accounts of the Berlin blockade crisis, see especially W. Phillip Davison, *The Berlin Blockade: A Study in Cold War Politics* (Princeton, N.J.: Princeton University Press, 1958); Avi Shlaim, *The United States and the Berlin Blockade, 1948-1949* (Berkeley, Calif.: University of California Press, 1983); and Daniel F. Harrington, "American Policy in the Berlin Crisis, 1948-1949," (Ph.D. diss., Indiana University, 1979).

35. Millis and Duffield, *Forrestal Diaries*, 452-455; Truman, *Years of Trial and Hope*, 123.

36. The source materials on this meeting are: "Conference of the Secretary of Defense with Joint Chiefs of Staff, held in the office of the Secretary of Defense, 30 June 1948, 11 A.M.," (verbatim transcript), RG 330, CD 9-3-13; and memo by John H. Ohly, June 30, 1948, sub: Mtg with JCS, Forrestal Papers, box 2, Suitland. A brief summary also appears in Leahy Diary, June 30, 1948, L.C.

37. DEFE 4/14, Mins., C.O.S. (48), 96th Mtg Chiefs of Staff Committee, July 9, 1948; and 99th Mtg, July 14, 1948, Public Record Office, London (Kew). Also see Avi Shlaim, "Britain, the Berlin Blockade and the Cold War," *International Affairs* (London) 60 (Winter 1983/4): 8-9.

38. Little, *Foundations of an Atomic Air Force*, 234.

39. CAS memo, Sep. 24, 1948, quoted in Ian Clark and Nicholas J. Wheeler, *The British Origins of Nuclear Strategy, 1945-1955* (Oxford: Clarendon Press, 1989), 129.

40. Millis and Duffield, *Forrestal Diaries*, 457.

41. *Lilienthal Journals*, 362 and *passim;* Hewlett and Duncan, *Atomic Shield*, 154-184.

42. See Rearden, *Formative Years,* 428-430.

43. Millis and Duffield, *Forrestal Diaries,* 458.

44. Ltr, Forrestal to Truman, July 21, 1948, RG 330, CD 12-1-30. Stockpile numbers estimated from Rosenberg, "U.S. Nuclear Stockpile," 26.

45. Memo, Lilienthal to Truman, July 21, 1948, PSF, Truman Papers; *Lilienthal Journals,* 388-392.

46. Ltr, Truman to Forrestal, Aug 6, 1948, RG 330, CD 12-1-30; Millis and Duffield, *Forrestal Diaries,* 461

47. Forrestal Diary, Sep. 13, 1948, vol. XII, 2494, Forrestal Papers, Princeton. An abridged version of this entry appears in Millis and Duffield, *Forrestal Diaries,* 487.

48. Robert H. Ferrell (ed.), *Off the Record: The Private Papers of Harry S. Truman* (New York: Harper and Row, 1980), 148-149.

49. Forrestal Diary, Sep. 16 and 17, 1948, vol. XII, 2501-2502, Forrestal Papers, Princeton.

50. Mins., 21st Mtg NSC, Sept. 16, 1948, PSF/NSC file, Truman Papers; NSC 30, Sept. 10, 1948, "United States Policy on Atomic Warfare," *FRUS 1948,* I, 625-628.

51. Memo, Col. Robert J. Wood to SecDef, Sep. 29, 1948, Forrestal Papers, box 2, Suitland.

52. DEFE 4/16, J.P. (48) 70 (Final), Rpt by the Joint Planning Staff, Chiefs of Staff Committee, sub: World Strategic Review, Sep. 11, 1948, enclosure to C.O.S. (48) 128th Mtg Chiefs of Staff Committee, Sept. 14, 1948, P.R.O.

53. DEFE 4/14, J.P. (48) 63 (Revised Final), June 26, 1948, Rpt by the Joint Planning Staff, Chiefs of Staff Committee, sub: Western Union Defense Policy, enclo. to Mins. C.O.S. (48) 90th Mtg, June 30, 1948, P.R.O.

54. Memo, Hillenkoetter to Truman, July 6, 1948, PSF/Intelligence file, Truman Papers.

55. For the internal debates over the budget, see Rearden, *Formative Years,* 343-347; K. Condit, *JCS and National Policy, 1947-1949,* 232-250; and Warner R. Schilling, "The Politics of National Defense: Fiscal 1950," in Warner F. Schilling, Paul Y. Hammond, and Glenn H. Snyder, *Strategy, Politics, and Defense Budgets* (New York: Columbia University Press, 1962), 135-213.

56. Ltr, Forrestal to Marshall, Oct. 31, 1948, *FRUS 1948,* I, 644-646.

57. Cable, Marshall to Lovett, Nov. 8, 1948, *ibid.,* 654-655; cable, Marshall to Forrestal, Nov. 8, 1948, *ibid.,* 655.

58. Millis and Duffield, *Forrestal Diaries,* 521-526.

59. NSC 35, "Rpt to the NSC by the SecDef.," Nov. 17, 1948, enclosing memo, Leahy (for JCS) to SecDef, Nov. 2, 1948, sub: Existing International Commitments Involving the Possible Use of Armed Forces, *FRUS 1948,* I, 656-662.

60. NSC 20/4, "U.S. Objectives With Respect to the USSR To Counter Soviet Threats to U.S. Security," Nov. 23, 1948, *ibid.,* I, 662-669.

61. Ltr, Forrestal to Truman, Dec. 1, 1948, *FRUS 1948,* I, 669-672.

62. Memo, Truman to Webb, Dec. 2, 1948, PSF, Truman Papers. For an excellent account of the 1948 election campaign and the confidence that winning fostered in Truman's outlook, see David McCullough, *Truman* (New York: Simon and Schuster, 1992), 653-719.

63. Untitled Memo, ca. Dec. 16 or 20, 1948, prepared in the Office of the Chief of Staff, USAF, Forrestal Papers, Suitland, Exhibit C: Supplement.

64. As presented to Congress in January 1949, the administration's FY 1950 defense budget called for a roughly equal three-way split of funds: $4.5 billion for the Army; $4.3 billion for the Navy; and $4.6 billion for the Air Force. See Rearden, *Formative Years, 352.*

V

Move and Counter-move: The Development of a Nuclear Arsenal

By the beginning of 1949, an American defense strategy that relied increasingly on the retaliatory power of nuclear weapons had acquired clear and distinct outlines. What was also emerging was a closer, more dynamic competition with the Soviet Union that would, with time, sharply escalate tensions and give nuclear weapons an even more prominent role in East-West relations. The unexpected Soviet explosion of a nuclear device in late August 1949 dramatically altered the framework of the Soviet-American relationship. Not only did it end the American monopoly months, if not years, ahead of most predictions, giving the competition a new sense of urgency and reality; it also accelerated the US decision to develop a thermonuclear device, thereby further solidifying the American commitment to a nuclear strategy. Moreover, the Soviet surprise set in motion the bureaucratic process that would lead to the most thorough postwar examination of US objectives and policy—NSC 68—yet undertaken.

As important and formative as the Soviet detonation may have been, it was not the only consideration bearing on the size and nature of the US nuclear effort. First, the Soviet explosion, for all of its dramatic impact, did not produce any immediate alteration in the size of US military expenditures. On the contrary, the budget submitted to Congress in January 1950 for Fiscal Year 1951 (July 1, 1950, to June 30, 1951) was outwardly oblivious (save for comparatively modest increases for the Atomic Energy Commission) of the Russian achievement. In fact, the budget projected outlays for defense that were $2 billion less than the year before. Economy was still the Truman administration's watchword, and would remain so until the Korean War prompted an abrupt but unavoidable reversal.

Second, the Soviet detonation caught the American atomic program in a state of pregnant expectation, already poised to move to a new plateau. The shape of the subsequent atomic and thermonuclear program did not, therefore, entirely owe its inception to the sobering news of early September. And third, the Air Force was finally beginning to acquire a significant delivery capability built around an expanding and re-energized Strategic Air Command. Once the political environment shifted in favor of a nuclear-oriented strategy, the process of acquiring and refining the capabilities could go forward with greater assurance as well. The net effect—even before the Soviet explosion took place—was increased emphasis on, and readiness for, air-atomic warfare.

EXPANDING NUCLEAR CAPABILITIES

As we have already seen, Truman's decision to hold the US defense budget to $15 billion in FY 1950 gave considerable impetus to a nuclear-oriented defense strategy. Concurrent with these developments was the spread of a new way of thinking, one that by 1949 increasingly regarded the atomic bomb—as supposedly demonstrated by the events of the Berlin crisis—as the proven first line of defense and principal deterrent against Soviet aggression. In contrast to doubts he had expressed only a year or so earlier, Truman in February 1949 privately declared "that the atomic bomb was the mainstay and . . . that the Russians would have probably taken over Europe a long time ago if it had not been for that."[1] With this as his frame of reference, Truman also began to exhibit a stronger-than-ever willingness to contemplate the bomb's use. On April 6, 1949, he publicly defended the magnanimous nature of the Baruch Plan, justified his decision to drop the bomb on Japan, and said that if "the democracies of the world are at stake, I wouldn't hesitate to make it again."[2] This public pronouncement simply mirrored discussions within the government. At a War Council meeting on February 8, 1949, all present (including Forrestal, Bradley, Souers, Eisenhower, and Vannevar Bush) agreed that the decision of the previous September on NSC 30 "regarding the use of the atomic bomb was definite and that the public believed we would use the bomb."[3]

At the same time, though, Truman was obviously uneasy over the direction in which events seemed to be headed, especially in view of stepped-up pressure from the Air Force to expand its air-atomic capabilities. By the beginning of 1949, Air Force plans and preparations were in fact showing marked improvement, with 120 nuclear-modified B-29s and B-50s now available (compared with only 30 the previous spring) and with six bomb assembly teams trained and organized. In addition, SAC had recently acquired its first B-36 intercontinental bombers and had activated its first squadron of tankers (modified B-29s), making it possible to extend the range of some of its planes through inflight refueling.[4] Still, those in charge believed that much remained to be done. The leader of the effort was Lt. Gen. Curtis E. LeMay, who had coordinated the Berlin airlift in Germany until returning to Washington in October 1948 to succeed Gen. George C. Kenney as SAC's commander. Tough, dedicated, and exacting, LeMay set out, as he later put it, to turn SAC into "a real strong and efficient outfit."[5]

LeMay's first priority was to maximize SAC's capabilities, a task he interpreted as developing a more effective capacity to wage air-atomic warfare. "When I first came back from Germany," he recalled, "there wasn't any doubt in my mind that if we had to go to a full scale war, we would use nuclear weapons. That was the capability we worked on, to go to nuclear weapons."[6] At the time he took over at SAC, however, Air Force plans still envisioned a combination of nuclear and conventional bombing due to the scarcity of atomic weapons in the stockpile and of planes equipped to deliver them.[7] To help overcome these problems, the Air Force assembled a panel of senior officers who in February accepted LeMay's recommendations for major changes in air procurement policy.[8] These included cancellation of the B-54, a medium-range follow-on to the B-29, and several lighter aircraft programs, in order to transfer the funds thereby available into the procurement of 75 more intercontinental B-36s. Instead of two B-36 bombardment groups, as provided for in the FY 1950 budget, LeMay wanted four, plus a fifth for reconnaissance, a force sufficient to deliver the entire US nuclear stockpile, then around 130 weapons.[9]

In late March 1949, Director of the Bureau of the Budget Frank Pace alerted the White House to the proposed change in Air Force procurement, which needed Truman's approval before it could go into effect. "If the revised program increases the strategic emphasis on the use of atomic weapons," Pace warned the President, "it may create a situation which would not permit the President any alternative as to their use in time of emergency."[10] Truman then queried his Air Force aide, Brig. Gen. R. B. Landry, on whether the United States might be putting "all its eggs in one basket" by giving priority to strategic air power. In his reply, Landry (speaking for the Air Force) assured Truman that American strategy was a balanced one, with the Air Force merely having the task of responding immediately "as distinguished from forces to become available later through mobilization build-up."[11]

Subsequently, Gen. Hoyt S. Vandenberg, the Air Force chief of staff, briefed Truman on Air Force plans in an apparently less than convincing presentation. At the urging of his naval aide, Rear Adm. Robert Dennison, Truman on April 21 requested the new secretary of defense, Louis Johnson, to look into the "chances of successful delivery of bombs as contemplated by this plan, together with a joint evaluation of the results to be expected by such bombing."[12] Earlier, in the fall of 1948, Forrestal had posed similar questions to the Joint Chiefs, with the result that by the time Truman became interested in these matters, formal studies were either already underway or in the process of being organized. The Joint Chiefs had assigned one study, on weapons effects, to an ad hoc JCS committee headed by Lt. Gen. Hubert R. Harmon, USAF; another study, still not yet fully organized, on delivery capabilities, they had given to the Weapons Systems Evaluation Committee (WSEG), a newly created JCS technical advisory body.[13] But it would be quite some time, possibly as much as a year, Johnson advised, before the full results were known.[14] On May 4, Truman, seeing no grounds for further delay, approved the transfer of funds so that procurement of the 75 additional B-36s could proceed as proposed.[15]

Had he waited a little longer, however, Truman might have reconsidered. For a week later, on May 12, the Harmon committee submitted its report to the Joint Chiefs. Initially resisted and resented by the stubborn LeMay, who had to be reminded by Vandenberg to cooperate,[16] the committee's inquiry turned up findings that awkwardly straddled two stools. On the one hand, the report doubted that strategic bombing would produce the results that the Air Force envisioned. Although the planned air offensive, if successful (an assumption that the WSEG study had yet to test), would produce substantial damage and casualties in the millions, it probably would not "bring about capitulation, destroy the roots of Communism or critically weaken the power of the Soviet leadership." But at the same time, the committee saw no realistic alternative to the use of nuclear weapons and regarded them as "the only means of rapidly inflicting shock and serious damage to vital elements of the Soviet war-making capacity."[17]

Truman never saw the Harmon report. How it would have affected his thinking cannot, therefore, be gauged. Clearly, though, the report raised serious questions about the effectiveness of the current air-atomic strategy and the wisdom of depending on a nuclear arsenal. Such concerns were, of course, commonplace throughout the Navy, which saw the Harmon report as partial confirmation of its repeated warnings against placing too much faith in strategic bombing and as a strong argument for reviving the more versatile supercarrier program, abruptly canceled by Secretary of Defense

Johnson for money-saving reasons just a month earlier. But because of the report's highly sensitive nature, controversial findings, and high classification, its distribution within the government was limited. Although the Joint Chiefs forwarded several copies to Johnson's office on July 28, he apparently did not see or read the report until October. At that time he notified Truman of the report's existence but, acting on the advice of a subordinate, declined to provide him with a copy until completion of the WSEG feasibility study.[18] The net effect, as David Alan Rosenberg has pointed out, was that "the president was never fully exposed to the military arguments against an atomic air offensive that it [the Harmon report] contained."[19]

FISCAL RESTRAINT: THE BUDGET FOR 1951

Still, even if Truman had seen the Harmon report, it might well have made no difference. For the worries and concerns that animated Truman's thinking were never so much military as they were political and economic. And by the time the Harmon report was finished, two other issues had come to claim Truman's attention: the apparent need for even closer fiscal restraint, necessitating a new round of budget cuts; and a pending decision on whether to step up production of fissionable material. Taken together, the resolution of these issues would effectively pre-empt any further serious debate within the administration over whether a nuclear-oriented strategy was in the country's best interest.

Once again, the fiscal situation took priority, this time with an outcome that would make military options even more limited. Earlier, Truman had tentatively assured the services that they could count on a defense budget for FY 1951 of $15 billion, the same as the previous fiscal year. But it became increasingly apparent as 1949 progressed that he would have difficulty keeping his promise. On April 5, Budget Director Pace briefed the President on the budget/receipt forecasts for the coming fiscal year. Even under the most optimistic assumptions and with a defense budget of $13.5 billion, the anticipated federal deficit, because of a downturn in the economy, would be $5.4 billion. In fact, congressional experts thought the deficit could reach $6 to $7.5 billion. And Pace said, "it appears reasonable to conclude that the deficit for each of the next four years may range from $4 to $8 billion, without the initiation of any major new expenditure programs." While he had hopes for a surplus in FY 1953, such a goal could only be achieved through reductions in the security field. With this memorandum, the BoB had (as Webb had done the year before) established de facto the FY 1951 budget ceiling for military programs. In essence, what followed thereafter in 1949 was the forging of a defense budget within the framework of $13.5 billion.[20]

Louis Johnson and the Joint Chiefs did not, of course, yet realize the nature of these fiscal restraints. Nor did Gen. Dwight D. Eisenhower, who had agreed to act as unofficial chairman of the Joint Chiefs to adjudicate competing service claims, an interim assignment until Congress authorized a legal chairman that summer. But there were hints, some of which Eisenhower noted in his diary. "One of our greatest troubles is inability to plan for a given amount of money," he complained to himself. "We work like the devil on an agreement on a certain sized budget, and then are told to reduce it. . . . Of course the results will not show up until we get into serious trouble. We are repeating our own history of decades, we just don't believe we ever will get into a real jam."[21]

Meanwhile, the Bureau of the Budget went about preparing its case for presentation to the Pentagon. On April 25, for instance, Pace wrote Johnson about the joint intelligence estimates, urging him to be particularly critical in reviewing the basic assumptions on which "these estimates are made and evaluate the deficiencies which will undoubtedly result because of fiscal limitations in augmenting the 1951 program. You will need to have the alternatives evaluated and some relative measure of the calculated risk involved." In this review he urged the secretary to make full use of CIA and NSC viewpoints.[22]

A week later, on May 2, Pace invited Johnson to discuss the overall budget situation for FY 1951. In their session on May 12, Johnson argued the case for the maintenance of the current force levels at a total cost of $16.5 billion, receiving strong support from the Joint Chiefs, who regarded $15 billion as the absolute minimum for national defense. Johnson took care to remind Pace that the JCS believed "that such gains as may have been made in the cold war are attributable in great measure to military strength." Any diminution of forces would have an "adverse effect." Amid these pleas, only one note of realism seems to have appeared: the observation by Wilfred McNeil, Johnson's special assistant for budgetary matters, that the projected deficit might put the military budget figure at $13 billion. And McNeil added, "being practical about it, probably the only way the President could justify such a situation [i.e., a higher defense budget] would be for a deterioration of the international situation."[23]

McNeil's guess proved correct. While Eisenhower and the JCS struggled during June to work out budget allocations under a $15 billion ceiling, Pace and Truman were busily preparing the groundwork for an overall review of basic national security programs within the framework of a $13 billion defense budget. On July 1, Truman hosted a special meeting with his national security advisors to deliver the news that defense and international programs (excluding the Marshall Plan) would have to be curtailed, with $2 billion slated to be cut from the defense budget.[24] At a time when recent inflation rates of 7 to 8 percent had progressively eaten into the diminished postwar budgets, some existing programs would have to be curtailed. Something had to give, and when it did, it tended to be conventional rather than strategic forces. In assessing the impact of the President's recent action, Eisenhower drew the logical conclusion: that further reliance on strategic air was now unavoidable, indeed inevitable. "Since we have always stressed the value of military preparation as a deterrent to war," he advised Johnson, "it seems to me obvious . . . that we cannot and must not fail to provide a respectable long range strategic bombing force. . . . I am quite certain that if we are erring in any direction it is in failure to allocate a sufficiently high percentage of our reduced appropriations to the certainty that we can launch and sustain a vigorous bombing offensive on a moment's notice."[25] However unsettling the Harmon report's findings may have been, they tended to lose much of their impact amid the brutal realities of the budget process.

Subsequently, in late September, the NSC at Truman's request tendered its views on the implications and effects of the proposed cutbacks. Prepared in late August and early September, before the Soviet detonation became generally known, the report made no mention of the Soviet test or its possible ramifications. Rather, it concentrated on reaffirming the need for security within the context of sound fiscal and budgetary policies, emphasizing the need for spending restraints in order "to avoid permanently impairing our economy and the fundamental values and institutions in our way of life." For the Defense Department, which would have to begin making reductions immediately, the $13 billion ceiling would allow the maintenance of "the same degree of military strength, readiness, and posture during FY 1951 which it will maintain in FY 1950."[26] Whatever the rhetoric of the cold war and its ideological impetus, whatever blasé assumptions the new Soviet capability might have shaken, the defense budget for FY 1951, as presented to Congress a few months later, would be the lowest in three years.[27]

FROM SCARCITY TO PLENTY:
MORE FISSIONABLE MATERIAL

The other area of activity at this time—a study of whether to increase the production of fissionable materials—reflected concerns of another sort and yet would ratify the nuclear strategy even further. Beyond the immediate issue of stockpile needs and the AEC's capacity to meet them, there was the larger question of whether the commission and the military could establish a working partnership. Exactly how closely SAC and the AEC were in fact coordinating their efforts by 1949 is still unclear. Custody of weapons, as Truman had decreed the previous summer, remained firmly with the AEC, and would stay there until the summer of 1950, when events in Korea would compel him to alter his policy. Even before then, however, there were several exercises in late 1948 and early 1949 to test emergency transfer procedures, along with stepped-up efforts to train military crews in the handling and assembly of nuclear weapons.[28] But the central problem—a continuing paucity of weapons—was on the verge of being solved.

The breakthrough had come with the SANDSTONE tests held in the spring of 1948, the results of which amazed and astounded those connected with the nuclear program. Most importantly, the tests demonstrated two new technological improvements in bomb design: the levitated core, which made for greater efficiency, increasing yield by up to 75 percent; and the composite plutonium-uranium core, which allowed cheaper and more available U-235 to be used in combination with plutonium to produce a nuclear explosion. The implications of these discoveries were enormous. Not only would weapons soon be more plentiful, using smaller amounts of fissionable material than the bombs currently being stockpiled, but they could also be of increasingly diverse design, from lightweight "tactical" nuclear weapons for battlefield use to larger bombs approaching 50 kilotons for strategic purposes.[29] Initially, because of continuing production and ore-supply problems, the AEC doubted whether it would be able to keep pace with the JCS schedule set in December 1947, which called for a stockpile of 400 Nagasaki-type (MARK III) implosion bombs by the beginning of 1953. But after reassessing the SANDSTONE data, the commission withdrew its earlier opinion and confidently estimated that it could meet the Joint Chiefs' requirements by January 1, 1951, two years ahead of the original timetable.[30]

Once this became known, the Joint Chiefs, at the urging of the Military Liaison Committee, began to formulate a shopping list that could only be accommodated through expanded production facilities. On December 9, 1948, they notified Forrestal of their desire to reopen the question of military needs, including the possibility of stepping up ore procurement in order to assure "the continued production of fissionable material on a long-term basis."[31] On March 12, 1949, Maj. Gen. K. D. Nichols, Chief of the Armed Forces Special Weapons Project, the group in charge of bomb assembly and training, briefed Eisenhower on the numerous possibilities.

"I recommended," Nichols recalled, "that we should be thinking in terms of thousands of weapons rather than hundreds."[32]

Despite their differences over strategy and weapons systems, the Joint Chiefs were firmly united in their support of a larger nuclear stockpile, for with more bombs available there would be less reason for competing claims. Accordingly, on June 14, 1949, the Joint Chiefs approved a new list of weapons requirements through 1955, though the number (still classified) fell "far too low" to exploit the amount of fissionable material (plutonium and U-235) that only two weeks earlier the MLC had unofficially told the AEC would be needed. Rather than blunt its case for further expansion, and not anxious to make their superiors appear somewhat foolish and ignorant on atomic energy matters, the MLC simply ignored this contradiction and let stand the new statement of production requirements to the AEC, omitting any mention of bomb numbers.[33]

Thus, while Truman was reassessing his budget options for FY 1951, the stage was being set for a confrontation over the scale of the atomic energy program. Of crucial importance to the outcome, of course, was Truman's attitude on the issue of atomic energy, markedly changed from only a year before. What had once been one of his top goals—to obtain international control of atomic energy—was now a fading memory. As he told a group of congressional leaders in July: "I am of the opinion we'll never obtain international control. Since we can't obtain international control we must be strongest in atomic weapons."[34]

Not surprisingly, then, Truman was inclined from the beginning to approve the increase. Not only would it give the country a larger nuclear stockpile, it would at the same time, he may have assumed, offset the effect of some of the recently mandated cutbacks elsewhere in the defense effort. The net result, as some would later call it, would be "a bigger bang for the buck." Even so, Truman hesitated to rush into any program that would necessitate large and perhaps unanticipated expenditures. Consequently, he ignored a suggestion from Senator Brien McMahon, chairman of the Joint Committee on Atomic Energy (JCAE), to approve the proposed production increase without further delay.[35] Instead, on July 26, he opted to establish a special NSC committee on atomic energy, composed of the secretaries of state and defense and the chairman of the AEC, to consider the need for new production facilities in light of the military's revised requirements. Apprised that initial expansion costs could run to $300 million, he wanted the group to concentrate on the following questions: (1) Would the present program be adequate to January 1956? (2) Could additional security be obtained from an increase over current efforts, including development of improved atomic bombs and applications in the field of guided missiles? (3) What impact would the timing have on budgetary stringency, research advances, and probable international reaction? And (4) could reductions be made elsewhere in defense spending to permit atomic acceleration without any budget increases? To these specific questions he added two admonitions: he did not want a technical report, and the entire study must involve a minimum number of persons.[36]

At Truman's suggestion, the special committee named a working group of experts to explore the problem in detail and to provide preliminary recommendations. While the AEC and State Department wanted an examination of the impact of expanded production upon the entire strategic situation, Pentagon representatives, with Johnson's firm support, held out for restricting the effort to assessing the technical feasibility of the problem and its international impact. In the end their persistence paid off.[37]

Thus the special committee's final report, presented to Truman on October 10, was simply a composite of the three agency perspectives. On the whole it was largely uninfluenced in either content or tone by the Russian success of the previous August. The preponderant arguments for increased production came, naturally enough, from the JCS. Familiar points—the SANDSTONE breakthroughs, the failure of international control efforts, and the possibility of more efficient utilization of raw materials—were adduced to justify an expanded program. More novel were their other reasons: that recent military assistance talks had revealed a Europe even more defenseless than had been previously imagined; that atomic devices allowed more economy and more efficiency in war planning; and that an adequate weapons stockpile was required, since production plants might be knocked out in a war. With 1956 set as the target date for the new production goals, the JCS believed overwhelming American superiority would—despite the recent Soviet achievement—"continue to act as a deterrent to war." David Lilienthal, the chairman of the AEC, personally doubted that the proposed increase was necessary. But the commission, in its contribution to the report, acknowledged that the expansion was technically feasible, that material not used for military purposes could later be shifted to peaceful uses, and that the financial ramifications ($319 million in capital and $54 million in annual operating costs) could be handled through the AEC budget.

The State Department remained ambivalent about the proposed expansion. State believed that, "on balance," the expansion would not be "untimely" from the international point of view. It would indicate the continuing American determination to lead the field, bolster European morale, and help in forthcoming conversations with the United Kingdom and Canada regarding ore allocations.

"Other nations," the department observed, "in all probability, already assume we are producing atomic weapons to the full extent of our capabilities." The report concluded with two separate, noteworthy observations. First, the accelerated production should be "understood to be a projection of previous plans based upon our own capabilities, rather than as counter-development to the Soviet explosion." And second, the new costs "should not be at the expense of other areas of the national defense program," meaning not from the Defense Department or the military assistance program.[38]

Truman accepted the committee's report and approved its recommendations without hesitation. But because he sought to avoid any appearance of responding to the Soviet success, he decided to defer a supplemental request to Congress for the additional financing until January. Until then, the AEC was authorized to spend $20 million from other funds on the preliminary work needed for the production increases.[39] On this issue, therefore, the element of continuity and past practice appeared to dominate. A stubborn Truman seemed unwilling to make any move that might betray panic. Nonetheless, a crucial decision enabling the acceleration of production and the guarantee of plentiful weapons had been taken. The atomic strategy had, de facto, been further endorsed; it was economical, efficient, intimidating, and—above all—more available than ever.

THE H-BOMB DECISION

Discussions about expanding nuclear production were, in their later stages, overshadowed by the government's growing preoccupation with the ramifications of JOE I, the Soviet atomic test of August, 29, 1949. Many shared Senator McMahon's view, expressed in a Joint Committee on Atomic Energy report on October 13, that "Russia's ownership of the bomb, years ahead of the anticipated date, is a monumental challenge to American boldness, initiative, and effort."[40] How would the United States respond? Not, as we have seen, with a dramatic upsurge of defense spending. Nor, since Truman's assent on expanded production remained largely internal (and, by his own desire, muted), by waving the threat of multiple new atomic weapons. Rather, the answer would be the decision to develop a thermonuclear device. That this was indeed the response owes much to the intrusion into the political process of two participants seen only marginally in the analysis until now: Congress and the scientific community.

Congressional-AEC relations were never in the early years exactly smooth, getting off to a particularly poor start with the controversy over the appointment of David Lilienthal as AEC chairman. After 18 months of relative calm, 1949 had seen a Congressional investigation of alleged "incredible mismanagement" of the AEC facilities. These accusations, which Senator Hickenlooper exploited, all but destroyed the tenuous cohesiveness among the disparate commissioners. Commissioner Lewis L. Strauss broke away and became the principal in-house agitator. Simultaneously, Brien McMahon, thanks to the 1948 election that restored a Democratic majority in Congress, resumed the chairmanship of the JCAE. Not only did he have a keen interest in the atomic issue, he also had an aggressive, inquisitive young staffer—William L. Borden—anxious to push him along. The upshot, as Truman noted in September 1949, was two senators (Hickenlooper and McMahon) up for re-election in 1950, each using the JCAE to further their political ambitions. Of the two, McMahon's role was the more crucial.[41]

Over the months from September 1949 to January 1950, the Connecticut senator's efforts on behalf of the Super bomb took a variety of forms. Direct appeals to the President were one avenue. Not only did he press Truman again in late September to approve a supplemental budget increase for stepped-up nuclear production, but he repeatedly made known his fears that a decision against the Super "would almost guarantee disaster for if Russia got the H-Bomb, the catastrophe becomes all but certain—whereas if we get it first, there exists a chance of saving ourselves. . . ."[42]

McMahon also worked to elicit strong, unhesitating support and cooperation from the military establishment. Indeed, as 1949 progressed, McMahon and the committee drew the services more into their confidence than ever before. Time and again, since its creation two years earlier, the JCAE had queried the military about the adequacy of the atomic program, only to receive vague or noncommittal replies. Finally, on March 16, 1949, the committee got the MLC to state unequivocally that the military did not have "enough bombs nor are we getting them fast enough."[43] From this point on, protests from the military about the atomic energy program's shortcomings became almost routine. On October 7, for example, Secretary of the Air Force Stuart Symington and General Vandenberg, under intense questioning from committee members, admitted dissatisfaction with the stockpile of bombs, while adding that it was up to others to set those figures. General LeMay, on the other hand, took a more cautious view. He told the committee that "he has not recently looked at atomic stockpile figures and preferred not to." But with SAC increasingly dependent on the nuclear arsenal, it was only a matter of time before he, too, would be clamoring for more and bigger weapons.[44]

The issue of the fusion bomb, coupled with the adequacy question, thus offered McMahon a further opportunity to forge a working alliance between Capitol Hill and the Pentagon. In this he was, of course, helped by the views of senior figures within the defense establishment, including Robert LeBaron, who became chairman of the MLC in October 1949. LeBaron was a research chemist whose background in nuclear physics dated from the 1920s, when he had studied with Madame Marie Curie in Paris. He was fully cognizant that development of the Super would mean less material for regular fission bombs and that the device might not work. Nonetheless, he advocated taking the risk. America, he told Deputy Secretary of Defense Stephen T. Early in November, could not play "ostrich." "The crux of our military concept of peace through power lies on the belief that the atomic weapon gives us the necessary force in a tight package with simple logistic support. If Russia can make a super and we forego the task, what happens to our military thesis?"[45] The JCS were even more emphatic. On November 23, they wrote Louis Johnson that: "Possession of a thermonuclear weapon by the USSR without such possession by the United States would be intolerable," while possession by the United States alone might "act as a possible deterrent to war." Brushing aside moral and psychological objections to its development, the JCS asserted emphatically that America's failure to act would not "prevent the development of such a weapon elsewhere."[46]

During several appearances before the JCAE, Gen. Omar Bradley, chairman of the Joint Chiefs since August, reiterated these sentiments. On October 14, 1949, he told the committee that the military definitely favored both the Super and more atomic weapons.[47] During a later appearance on January 20, 1950, he elaborated further. Cautious and restrained, he nevertheless left no doubt that the military strongly favored the development of the hydrogen bomb. But the General's backing was tempered with resignation. He observed that while there were differences of opinion, if war came, "we would eventually win it, and what kind of shape we would be in after having spent our resources and the destruction and so, is something else again. . . . [C]ertainly you wouldn't have Europe left as we know it."[48] If the emotional McMahon was more enthusiastic about the Super than Bradley, he had effectively secured the latter's strong support. This backing was a kind of trump card, useful to hold in reserve if Truman faltered in his decision, and conveniently intimidating in the meantime. Moreover, in forging the military-JCAE link, both parties gained. The military had an ally against the AEC on future issues, such as weapons custody, while the committee had a potential ally for a more extensive and active atomic energy program.

The third area of McMahon's activity concerned the AEC. Throughout the fall of 1949, McMahon and the committee peppered Lilienthal and the AEC with demands for action. His prodding about production facilities, especially the needed plant expansion, allowed the AEC no respite. The net effect was substantial. By early 1950, the commission was clearly on the defensive. A weary Lilienthal quit at the end of his term in mid-February, leaving behind at least three commissioners more attuned to the committee's priorities and wishes. What McMahon had succeeded in doing, along with Hickenlooper's earlier attacks on Lilienthal, was to erode the AEC's cohesiveness, independence, and willingness to resist.[49]

The fourth area of McMahon's activity was in expanding the activities and inquisitiveness of the JCAE itself, in particular using the committee's hearings as a vehicle to gather information. On October 17, 1949, for example, Rear Adm. Roscoe H. Hillenkoetter, director of Central Intelligence, discussed American intelligence forecasts and the Soviet atomic success. The admiral confronted a committee alarmed at the presumed American intelligence failure, worried about the possible military implications of the Soviet advance, and bewildered by the triumph of Soviet technology. In the exchanges, Hillenkoetter steadfastly insisted that the United States had not been "taken by surprise" by the explosion. Rather, it was clear that the five-year estimate for the Soviet timetable was correct; the error had come in dating initial Soviet work on the project in 1945 instead of 1943. In any case, the Soviets now had two piles in operation, would soon add a third, and would probably have ten bombs by the end of the year, with production capacity for 25 bombs a year thereafter.[50]

Regardless of the number of weapons, however, Hillenkoetter did not foresee any Soviet military action "in the immediate future." "At any time that they [the Soviets] get into a military adventure," he explained, "you don't know how that thing is going to go, and they are not going to take a chance. Every dictatorship that has been in power has never lost by its own people overthrowing it; it is always the result of an outside military movement that gets them." Offsetting this evaluation, however, from the committee's standpoint, was the fact that the Soviets had surprised the United States in the technological field. Not only did they now have the bomb, but they had also successfully copied the B-29, had built a jet fighter (the MiG-15) possibly superior to any American counterpart, and were on the verge of reaping the fruits of a communist triumph in China. In these circumstances, could the United States take a chance on not developing the thermonuclear weapon? Or, as McMahon put it, "frankly, if they [the Russians] should get it and we should not have it . . . it might well mean the difference between our existence as a nation and not existing."[51] Should war come and the US atomic effort be found inadequate, McMahon wanted to have a "clear conscience" in declaring before a "board of inquiry" that he had done his best.[52]

Besides Congress, the thermonuclear issue also drew a strong and active response from the scientific community. Since 1943, senior figures in the Manhattan Project and later in the GAC had intermittently considered the feasibility of a fusion reaction. Each time, however, they had concluded that the uncertain theoretical possibilities, probable costs, and detrimental effects on the atomic program did not warrant an effort in that direction. The Soviet explosion prompted a reconsideration of the fusion question. The labyrinthine details of the scientific lobbying for the Super need not concern us. Edward Teller, Ernest O. Lawrence, and their allies ultimately managed to overturn the institutional position of the GAC. In the process, their efforts would not only divide the senior members of the scientific establishment and prompt creation of a second major weapons laboratory, but also open the way for insidious personal feuds and congressional opprobrium toward members of the GAC.[53]

Little of this could have been anticipated by the AEC or the GAC when the latter assembled in October to consider the feasibility question anew. The prestige of victories past, a record of support for expanding the fission program, and the legacy of wisdom would seem to have ensured that the GAC would continue to occupy the dominant position. This status, in turn, made the GAC's unanimously negative report a crucial move in the decision process and effectively delayed Truman's final action on the matter from early November to late January 1950, causing him in the meantime to reconvene the NSC special committee. In doing so, he not only delayed his own decision but allowed the other forces to have their say. The net loser, in the long run, would be the GAC.

The GAC's opposition to the H-bomb, first declared in October 1949 and reaffirmed early the following December, testified eloquently to the problems of mingling the pros and cons of security with those of ethics and morality. The arguments advanced by the GAC against the Super took the following form: that its feasibility could only be determined by a test, that its costs were unknown, that it could only be used for "exterminating civilian populations," and that American development of it would precipitate similar actions by other nations. Some, including Lee DuBridge, James Conant, and J. Robert Oppenheimer, thought the H-bomb should never be developed at all, while others—Enrico Fermi and Isidor I. Rabi, most notably—reserved final judgment, pending a clearer picture of what the Soviets might do. All agreed, however, that smaller atomic weapons were adequate, that the Super was a "weapon of genocide" and necessarily an evil thing in any light, and that the H-bomb would be intrinsically different from anything else in the atomic effort. With this in mind, the committee urged a policy of self-restraint as a way to convince the world of America's good intentions. If it were too late to cap the atomic volcano, perhaps there was still time to avert a quantum jump to an entirely new plateau of destruction.[54]

A majority of the AEC commissioners—Lilienthal, Sumner T. Pike, and Henry Smyth—found this reasoning acceptable and convincing. Their own report to the President on November 9 incorporated many of the same points.[55] The other two commissioners—Lewis Strauss and Gordon Dean—adopted a different position.[56] Taking the lead, Strauss wrote President Truman on November 25, advising that there was a 50-50 chance the Super would work and that there was the added danger that the Soviets might already have launched a Super bomb project of their own.[57] Further, wrote Strauss, it was "the historic policy of the United States not to have its forces less well armed than those of any other country (viz., the 5:5:3 naval ratio, etc. etc.)." Nor did Strauss fail to note that the military wanted the weapon for both offensive and defensive reasons. And finally, he stressed the inconsistency of those favoring atomic weapons on the one hand and opposing thermonuclear ones on the other. The new weapon would be horrible, but, he said, echoing the military, "all war is horrible." He thus hoped that the President would not accept the AEC report and would instead direct the commission "to proceed with all possible expedition to develop the thermonuclear weapon."[58]

The force of these arguments was impressive. Already vulnerable in their technical stance against the H-bomb, the GAC (and the three AEC commissioners who were against the H-bomb as well) had centered their opposition upon the terrible nature of the new weapon and its moral implications. Those arguments, while certainly not invalid, were less compelling than those stressing Russia's possession of a Super. No argument could weigh more heavily with the President than the possibility that the Soviet Union might achieve an additional scientific triumph. Strauss had, in effect, masterfully outflanked those who wanted to foreswear the Super.

Whether a bitterly divided commission could ever have convinced the President to accept the GAC report was at best problematical. With each passing week, Lilienthal found his strength—politically and personally—ebbing. With his resignation from the AEC pending, he did not bring the same tenacity as earlier into his fights with Strauss, the military, or McMahon. The President continued to treat him respectfully, almost as if they were both confronting forces too great for either to deflect. Yet there was no White House intervention or signal that might have reversed the trend against Lilienthal's conception of the AEC. The central arena, in which he still participated, though with increasing ineffectiveness, had now become the NSC special committee, revived by Truman on November 19.[59]

By the time the reconstituted special committee—Johnson, Secretary of State Dean Acheson, and Lilienthal—began to function, the State Department had already devoted hours of attention to the various ramifications of the Soviet explosion. Within the Policy Planning Staff there was clear recognition, albeit limited enthusiasm, for the growing atomic nature of American strategy. George Kennan, who had been uncomfortable with the presence of nuclear weapons all along, now disliked reliance on them more than ever. He believed they would make it "difficult if not impossible to do any thing else when the time [came] to make a decision." All that would happen, he thought, should the United States launch an atomic attack, would be to "stiffen the courage and the will to resist of the Russian people."[60] But in drawing such sweeping conclusions, Kennan clearly spoke more from visceral conviction than from any solid information about the capabilities of the US nuclear program. In fact, he never knew—and never asked to know—how many atomic bombs the United States actually had on hand at any one time or, for that matter, how powerful they were.[61]

Still, Kennan was not alone in the State Department in believing that the Soviet atomic test had possibly rendered US nuclear strategy suspect. As Paul H. Nitze, Kennan's deputy and soon to be his successor as PPS director, told the staff on October 11: "Conventional armaments and their possession by the Western European nations, as well as by ourselves, [become] all the more important." To help redress the imbalance, Nitze thought that Europe would have to devote more of its resources in this direction, and even accept some decrease in its standard of living.[62] Acheson, though he regarded the prospect of European sacrifice somewhat skeptically, did not contest the Kennan-Nitze critique of the atomic strategy.[63]

On another familiar topic—international control—there were renewed discussions within the State Department during October and November. Expert testimony was, on the whole, profoundly ambiguous both about the chances for an accord with the Soviet Union and about any benefits to the United States from the process of trying. But there was support for keeping the Baruch Plan before the UN, despite the President's pessimism over its prospects. To withdraw it might hurt American prestige and contribute to a sense of panic. Still, State Department officials tended to concur that the hopeful days of 1945-46 had long passed and might never return.[64]

Acheson did not like the long-term prospects. Unless, he commented on November 3, there was some "kind of mechanism of control or prohibition of such weapons, when you do have a war it will eventually (between one and one-half and two and one-half years after its inception) be an atomic war." To avert this, he suggested a different tack—a renewed effort for step-by-step political, strategic, and economic negotiations with Moscow, linked perhaps to a moratorium on the development of the Super. While conceding past difficulties with the Soviets on these points, the secretary nevertheless saw this multifaceted approach as a possibility.[65] But this approach reflected the thinking of a calmer, more orderly time, when progressive negotiations might have been politically possible, before the loss of China, the Soviet explosion, the Alger Hiss trial, and signs of McCarthyism looming on the horizon.

Nor did resurrection of the special committee promise a more orderly resolution of the problem, in view of the strained relations among its members. The Johnson-Acheson feud, already being well reported in the press, showed no signs of abating, while the Johnson-Lilienthal relationship was tenuous at best. In fact, relations among the committee's members were so discordant that the committee held only two formal meetings, a stormy one on December 22, and a strained one on January 31, 1950, after which it submitted its report to the President. This state of affairs meant that the regular members' deputies, functioning in effect as the committee's staff, had an even bigger share of the responsibility than usual. The outcome was a set of recommendations which, while more integrated than the October report on fissionable material, fell short of constituting a major review of the country's atomic energy policy.

Yet if the cooperation and level of analysis left something to be desired, the NSC study did force the military to disclose some thoughts and assumptions about the strategic uses of a fusion weapon. Possibly the most revealing disclosures came in a December memorandum prepared by the JCS, outlining the military implications of thermonuclear weapons. In addition to making several predictable points about a fusion weapon bestowing flexibility and acting as a possible deterrent, the memorandum also noted the "blackmail potential" of such a weapon in Soviet hands. Such a potential, the military held, would have a "profoundly demoralizing effect on the American people" and might tempt Moscow to some act of aggression. "The inevitable jeopardy to our position as a world power and to our democratic way of life would be intolerable," the paper concluded.[66]

The JCS also argued that it was imperative to make the developmental effort if only to see whether such a weapon was possible. Otherwise, planners would be placed in an untenable dilemma: to risk wasting resources in anticipation of an attack that might never come, or to risk no resources and face an attack that might very well someday materialize. In this predicament, the Chiefs maintained that "the cost involved in a determination of the feasibility of a thermonuclear explosion is insignificant when compared with the urgency to determine firmly the ceiling of atomic development." Thus, they concluded, the United States ought to make the effort, ought to develop an ordnance and carrier program simultaneously, and ought to wait on production until feasibility was determined.[67] These conclusions would, as it turned out, form the crux of the special committee's final report.

The development of the special committee's recommendations proceeded piecemeal. On December 20, Acheson dictated a long, thoughtful (if somewhat meandering) memorandum in which he attempted to sort out the key issues. At the outset, he postulated that American security had become dependent on an atomic strategy "more subtly than through any articulate major premise," and that, with the new European commitments, the United States did "not have any other military program which seems to offer over the short run promise of military effectiveness." Given these realities, it was time to clarify American policy and spell out guidance for defense planning. Without such guidance, the drift would continue; American policy would remain contradictory and unclear and the nature of the crisis responses unpredictable. Acheson was particularly troubled by the contradiction of advocating the international control of atomic energy on the one hand, while relying on an atomic strategy on the other. But he could not avoid concluding that a stated policy of retaliation with atomic weapons would probably do much to reduce the chances of an attack on the United States.[68]

On December 22, the special committee assembled to assess where it stood. Earlier, Nitze and Lilienthal had discussed the possibility of a compromise. Lilienthal had expressed deep reservations about developing the bomb until there was some idea of the effect it might have on the overall international situation and Soviet-American relations in particular. He deemed the bomb morally objectionable and, like Kennan, saw it as another step toward ever greater reliance on nuclear weapons. Nitze concurred that there were legitimate grounds, including moral ones, for concern, but he disagreed with Lilienthal's suggestion that development of the bomb should be postponed until its international ramifications could be studied. Having talked at length with Teller, Lawrence, Oppenheimer, and others, he could not rule out the possibility that the Soviets had already initiated an H-bomb development program of their own. In such circumstances, he thought it prudent, and so advised Acheson, to press ahead with H-bomb research, concurrently with a review of US basic national security policy. "The upshot of this," he found, "was to satisfy Lilienthal's basic argument."[69]

As it happened, the meeting on December 22 produced no agreement whatsoever and turned into a quarrelsome confrontation between Johnson and Lilienthal. Johnson wanted the issue decided as the fission production problem had been addressed a few months earlier, on the narrow technical question of whether the bomb was feasible to build. Lilienthal, on the other hand, thought a broader discussion was in order, one that would address such fundamental issues as "the purpose and course of mankind." Acheson, realizing that his was the "swing" vote, was thoroughly frustrated and disgusted with the lack of progress. He blamed the deadlock on what he later termed "the acerbity of Louis Johnson's nature." The committee adjourned and did not meet again until January 31, when it issued its final recommendations.[70]

Within the State Department, meanwhile, the control issue received one last flicker of attention. On the eve of stepping down as director of policy planning, Kennan drafted a long memorandum in which he expressed hope that the quest for international control would not be abandoned. He urged in the meantime, as an alternative, the adoption by the United States of a unilateral "no-first-use" policy toward nuclear weapons.[71] Among those to respond was Nitze, Kennan's successor as head of the Policy Planning Staff. Perceptive, coherent, and increasingly influential with Acheson, Nitze placed the control problem in the larger context of the Super decision. Aligning himself solidly in the development camp on the H-bomb, he argued that "the military and political advantages which would accrue to the U.S.S.R. if it possessed even a temporary monopoly of this weapon are so great as to make time of the essence." But he also agreed with Kennan that Soviet possession of an atomic device, and later a thermonuclear one, made a no-first-use strategy worth exploring. Such a stance need not, asserted Nitze, undermine the deterrent effect of the bomb, for the Soviets could never be "quite certain that we would in fact stick to such a policy if the nature of their aggression too deeply upset the moral sense and vital interests of the people of the United States and the world in general." The other side of the issue—what to substitute for atomic superiority—was far more complex. On the prospects for control generally, Nitze expressed reservations. He wanted, most importantly, to be sure that no control schemes put the United States in a worse strategic position than the absence of control. He hoped the forthcoming policy review would confront this problem as well.[72]

If Acheson's principal subordinates could not make the case for addressing the Super issue through international control, neither could the secretary. As January progressed, his remaining inclinations in the direction of international control and of questioning the need for the H-bomb gradually dissipated. He recognized that the military case for development was strong, that Congressional interest was becoming keener, that public discussion was now starting, and that Truman could not wait much longer for a decision. On January 24, Acheson approved a draft report prepared at his request by R. Gordon Arneson, special assistant for atomic energy matters, on the development of the fusion bomb, circulating it to Johnson and Lilienthal the same day.[73]

Arneson's draft would (with but a few changes) become the special committee's final report to the President. Although its recommendations were familiar, the report's argumentation and analysis stamp it as a key document in the history of the US nuclear stockpile. Arneson began by observing that the development of a Super need not involve a crash program at the expense of the fission bomb effort. During the projected three years that it would take to explore the feasibility of a fusion reaction, work on other weapons and their delivery would continue unimpeded. Chances of success were put at even; the other requirements for ordnance and delivery vehicles were judged to be "within the capabilities of the United States from the point of view of money, materials, and industrial efforts." Should the device work, then the question of production, stockpiles, and possible utilization would arise. At that point a thorough review of American policy would have to be considered, including the possibility of an international control agreement.

Ruling out unilateral restraint by either side on the development issue, Arneson insisted that the United States could not take the chance that the Soviets might gain sole possession of the new bomb. Rather, the question became: would an American decision accelerate a Soviet program in the same direction? The answer, put simply, was "probably." But, the report continued, it did not appear that US policy would "have a decisive effect" on Soviet military developments or be the cause of an arms race. "The Soviet decision," Arneson observed, "to reequip its armies and devote major energies to developing war potential, after the end of the war and at a time when we were disbanding our armies, was based on considerations more profound than our possession of the atomic weapon." And since these same forces would possibly work for the Soviet Super, there was little reason to think any effort for international control or mutual self-restraint would be either practical or safe.

From this analysis, the recommendations, essentially the same as those Nitze had discussed with Lilienthal earlier, flowed easily: (1) that the

President direct the AEC to determine the feasibility of an H-bomb, with the "scale and rate of effort" determined jointly by the AEC and Defense Department; (2) that no decision about production of the Super be taken at this time; (3) that the President direct a re-examination of US policy in view of the Soviets' new and potential capabilities; and (4) that the President say all this publicly and then make no further pronouncement.[74]

Attached to Arneson's draft, in the final report, were three appendices— a history of the thermonuclear issue, an AEC report on the technical problems, and a Defense Department study of the Super. The last contained much of the JCS mid-December memorandum on the military implications of the fusion weapon, but it refined several old arguments, stressing that the military wanted no "crash" or "all-out" program but, on the contrary, "an orderly and economical solution to the problem." The report estimated that for a price, roughly $100 to $200 million, the United States might acquire a fusion bomb with a blast area 50 times greater than a fission bomb. Not only would the new weapon reduce the number of fission bombs required, it would increase the assurance of success against certain strategic and tactical targets of the highest importance. The problem of delivery was conceded but with a new twist. Instead of a manned bomber, the H-bomb would probably be most effective if mated to a "supersonic unmanned vehicle," for the more powerful the warhead, the "less demanding for refinements in the guidance system of the final delivery missile." These points, which forecast much of the strategic weapons activity of the 1950s, gave added impetus to the case that Johnson, LeBaron, and the Joint Chiefs had constructed.[75]

On January 31, 1950, the principals and their advisors met in the Old Executive Office Building to review Arneson's draft and recommendations, making only minor changes in the proposed press release and deleting, at Johnson's suggestion, any reference to the question of production. All agreed that production per se was not at issue, though this would soon change. In an impassioned valedictory, Lilienthal reiterated his concerns about overreliance on nuclear weapons and the need to examine the fundamental assumptions of military strategy. With this, the special committee proceeded to complete its task. The members had only to report to the President, which they did, without delay, at noon. They found Truman eager to accept their report, endorse their recommendations, and announce the decision publicly. His mood was perhaps best caught in an aside to Lilienthal, who confided in his diary that Truman "recalled another meeting that he had had with the National Security Council concerning Greece a long time ago; that at that time everybody predicted the end of the world if we went ahead, but we did go ahead and the world didn't come to an end. He felt this would be the same case here."[76]

Truman's role in the H-bomb decision deserves further comment. From the moment the Soviet blast was detected, the President strove to avoid any public display of alarm. Nor, as we have already seen, did he allow it to disturb his earlier decisions about the size of the defense budget. Publicly, his demeanor remained cocky, confident. Privately, his actions suggest more than token concern. Not only did he renew his inquiries about the status of the strategic attack plans,[77] but also he thoroughly agreed with the recommendations to expand the production of fissionable materials. More important, he appears to have been receptive to the early October arguments of Lewis Strauss about the potential value of a Super bomb. He encouraged Strauss to have the GAC consider the matter and then, upon their negative report, decided to appoint an NSC group to reconsider the fusion question. Although there was no guarantee that the special committee would come up with recommendations that accorded with Truman's preferences, it seems clear nonetheless that this was what Truman wanted.

Amid these developments, the President faced a new element—indirect pressure from the military chiefs. For most of 1949, the service chiefs had presented Truman and the nation with the continuing spectacle of discord. The feud over the flush-deck supercarrier and the B-36, the hearings before the House Armed Services Committee, the firing of Adm. Louis Denfeld, and the continuing internecine conflict over the military budget were all too familiar. But on the H-bomb question, as on the fission bomb question earlier, the Joint Chiefs closed ranks, presenting Truman, the AEC, and the State Department with a coordinated front. Some credit for this obviously belongs to Bradley's unifying presence as JCS chairman. Some belongs to the nature of the problem—whether or not to develop the H-bomb was much easier to decide than which service would actually deliver the device. But whatever its origins and however formed, the JCS position—because of the newfound harmony—acted as one more reason for Truman doing what he already preferred to do.

The JCS arguments reached Truman in mid-January in the form of a commentary upon the military views of the scientists on the GAC. The most salient points, beyond a ringing endorsement of the thermonuclear proposal, were to express opposition to a no-first-use posture, to say that the bombs were not intended "to destroy large cities," and to warn that if the Soviets got the Super, the American public might demand defensive efforts on such a scale that the United States would be hard pressed "to generate sufficient offensive power to gain victory" in the event of war. The study also reminded the President that the American public expected the government to do "everything possible to prevent a war while at the same time being prepared to win a war should it come." Finally, on the moral issue, the JCS held that the arguments of national security outweighed "moral objections," for "it is difficult to escape the conviction that in war it is folly to argue whether one weapon is more immoral than another. For, in a larger sense, it is war itself which is immoral, and the stigma of such immorality must rest upon the nation which initiates hostilities."[78]

Upon reading the JCS paper, Truman could have had few illusions about the military reaction if he accepted the GAC conception of national security. Moreover, as he also learned shortly, the H-bomb might be the only weapon in the arsenal that would give credence to the atomic strategy. On January 23, he finally received the briefing he had requested months earlier on the feasibility of the Air Force's strategic bombing plans. While the President listened, Lt. Gen. John E. Hull, director of the Weapons Systems Evaluation Group, sketched the gloomy findings—the bombing campaign as planned would entail enormous sacrifice and effort, with limited results. Although 70 to 85 percent of the bombers would reach their targets, only 50 to 70 percent would return; and while the destruction would be considerable, permanently crippling damage would be confined to one-half to two-thirds of the Soviet industrial facilities in the targeted areas.[79] A year or so earlier, such findings would almost certainly have triggered a wholesale reassessment of strategy and defense policy. But by the beginning of 1950, too many commitments had been made for Truman to back out. Although the WSEG report made no mention of the H-bomb, the implication was clear that without the added force of these weapons, the atomic strategy would continue to be open to question.

Truman may not have needed the subtle nudge of the WSEG report, but it was there anyway. The growing pressures incumbent in deciding about a major weapon system, pressures which Truman's successors would encounter with more frequency, were at work. Both the JCS paper and WSEG-1 tended to reinforce the President's opinions, while reducing his options. Thus, when Acheson, Johnson, and Lilienthal arrived at the Oval Office at noon on January 31, they found a more than receptive President. They found one eager to end the confusion and anxious to curtail further public discussion about the thermonuclear matter. Hence the abruptness of their session (less than ten minutes) and the promptness of the subsequent public announcement that same day.

In a very real sense, then, Harry Truman ratified the decision to develop the H-bomb; he did not make the decision. Like the use of the bomb against Japan in 1945, he acceded to a preprogrammed course of action. Of the major national security decisions of his Presidency up to this time—Hiroshima, the Truman Doctrine, Berlin—the hydrogen bomb required less thought than any, and more an acceptance of international and domestic political realities. His assent was crucial to the bomb's development, but his ability to withhold that approval was virtually nonexistent. The financial costs for development were almost incidental, the production and deployment decision still months if not years away, and the atomic arsenal adequate in a way it had not been before 1949. Indeed, had the Soviet success come in 1948, the choice of whether to divert precious fissionable materials for the H-bomb would have been more crucial, given the relatively modest stockpile of weapons at that time. The Super thus offered an economical and convenient response. To have seen Truman decide against its development would be to have seen him align himself with a small group of dissident scientists, a narrow majority of the AEC, and a relatively small segment of American opinion, ranged against the Defense and State Departments, the JCAE, most of Congress, and probably the majority of the public. In these circumstances, and with these odds, Presidents seldom decide; they acquiesce.

In going ahead, Truman had not, of course, made any other decision about the bomb. Production of thermonuclear weapons to be stockpiled remained an open issue. This would almost certainly have continued to be the case for months, had it not been for the arrest in England on February 3, 1950, of Klaus Fuchs on charges of espionage for the Soviets. A major review of what might have been betrayed now assumed urgent proportions. Most accounts, in assessing the impact of Fuchs's treachery, focus on his participation in the Manhattan Project, his presence at a 1946 H-bomb conference at Los Alamos, and the possibility that he had relayed a preliminary H-bomb design to Moscow.[80] But the most disturbing aspect of Fuchs's treason was the likelihood that he had compromised classified data about the radar fusing mechanism of the Nagasaki-type fission bomb, thus rendering suspect the ability of the bombs to detonate on target. Until a new back-up fusing device could be perfected and installed, the effectiveness of the entire atomic arsenal would be in question.[81] In these circumstances, development of the Super appeared more urgent than ever, as did production of at least some Supers for insurance purposes.

Louis Johnson wrote the President on February 24 that the implications of Fuchs's affair were "literally limitless." The JCS, he told the President, had considered the matter and believed the United States had "to proceed forthwith on an all-out program of hydrogen bomb development if we are not to be placed in a potentially disastrous position with respect to the comparative potentialities of our most probable enemies and ourselves."[82] Once again, Truman responded by convening the NSC special committee to consider the matter, with Sumner T. Pike representing the AEC.

This time the deliberations were quick and generally smooth. On March 9, the President got a further report on the thermonuclear program recommending that the AEC and Defense Department plan not only to develop the fusion weapon but also to produce and deploy it at an estimated additional cost of $95 million. Assuming the President's acceptance of these recommendations, the special committee expected a fusion test in 1952 and a prototype weapon available a year later. And should the fusion principle work, these steps would ensure only a limited hiatus between experimentation and military availability. In this way, the damage, both actual and potential, of Fuchs' defection might be offset. Without giving the matter a second thought, Truman concurred.[83]

In retrospect, there can be no doubt that Truman's decision in early 1950 to develop and stockpile the H-bomb marked the close of one era and the beginning of another. What had begun in 1945 at TRINITY with the test of an experimental device had gradually evolved, five years later, into a wholly new defense posture that placed nuclear weapons in the forefront of American security. With the initiation of the H-bomb program, acceptance of the atomic strategy had come full circle and would not be challenged again during Truman's presidency. Among defense planners and policymakers alike, the atomic strategy was fast becoming, in effect, part of the American ethos.

NOTES

1. *Lilienthal Journals*, 464.
2. "Remarks to a Group of New Democratic Senators and Representatives," Apr. 6, 1949, *Public Papers: HST, 1949*, 200.
3. War Council Mins, Feb. 8, 1949, Ohly Collection, OSD Historian.
4. Rosenberg, "Hydrogen Bomb Decision," 71; Hopkins and Goldberg, *The Development of Strategic Air Command, 1946-1986*, 13.
5. Quoted from a 1971 interview with LeMay in Thomas M. Coffey, *Iron Eagle: The Turbulent Life of General Curtis LeMay* (New York: Crown, 1986), 280.
6. Quoted in Richard H. Kohn and Joseph P. Harahan (eds.), *Strategic Air Warfare* (Washington, D.C.: Office of Air Force History, 1988), 95.

7. USAF Briefing Paper for the President, Dec. 16 and 20, 1948, box 2, Forrestal Papers, Suitland; JCS 1952/1, Dec. 21, 1948, in Thomas H. Etzold and John Lewis Gaddis (eds.), *Containment: Documents on American Policy and Strategy, 1945-1950* (New York: Columbia University Press, 1978), 357-360.

8. See Robert Frank Futrell, *Ideas, Concepts, Doctrine: Basic Thinking in the United States Air Force, 1907-1984* (2 vols.; Maxwell AFB: Air University, 1989), I, 242-245.

9. Memo, Symington to Forrestal, Feb. 25, 1949, Eisenhower Pre-Presidential Papers, Dwight D. Eisenhower Library, Abilene, Kansas; "History of B-36 Procurement Presented to House Armed Services Committee by Maj. Gen. F.H. Smith, Jr., " (Mimeo; ca. 1949), sec. 1, Center of Air Force History collection, Bolling AFB, Washington, D.C.; Harry R. Borowski, *A Hollow Threat: Strategic Air Power and Containment Before Korea* (Westport, Conn: Greenwood, 1982), 151. Stockpile numbers are unofficial. See John Lewis Gaddis, *The Long Peace* (New York: Oxford University Press, 1987), 111.

10. Memo, Pace to Truman, Mar. 28, 1949, RG 51, BoB Series 47.3.

11. Memo, Landry to Truman, Apr. 16, 1949, RG 330, CD 12-1-8.

12. Memo, Truman to Johnson, Apr. 21, 1949, RG 330, CD 23-1-19.

13. Memo, Forrestal to JCS, Oct. 23, 1948; memo, Forrestal to JCS Oct. 25, 1948; and memo, Lalor for Harmon, et al., Jan. 12, 1949, all in RG 330, CD 23-1-19. Also see John Ponturo, *Analytical Support for the Joint Chiefs of Staff: The WSEG Experience, 1948-1976* (Arlington, Va.: Institute for Defense Analyses, 1979), 51-54.

14. Ltr, Johnson to Truman, Apr. 27, 1949, RG 330, CD 23-1-19.

15. Smith, "History of B-36 Procurement," sec. 26; Futrell, *Ideas, Concepts, Doctrine,* I, 245.

16. Ltr, Vandenberg to LeMay, Feb. 15, 1949, Vandenberg Papers, Command-Strategic (4) folder, box 45, L.C..

17. "Evaluation of Effect on Soviet War Effort Resulting from the Strategic Air Offensive," May 11, 1949, portions in Etzold and Gaddis (eds.), *Containment: Documents on American Policy and Strategy, 1945-1950,* 360-364.

18. Memo, Denfeld (for JCS) to Johnson, July 28, 1949, RG 330, CD 23-1-19; ltr, Johnson to Truman, [Oct. 18, 1949], *ibid.*; also see memo, Ohly to Johnson, Oct. 12, 1949, *ibid.*

19. Rosenberg, "Hydrogen Bomb Decision," 77-78.

20. BoB memo to the President, Apr. 5, 1949, RG 51, BoB Series 47.3; undated memo to the President, sub: Budget Alternatives for 1951, *ibid.*

21. See Robert H. Ferrell, *The Eisenhower Diaries* (New York: Norton, 1981), 159.

22. Memo, Pace to Johnson, Apr. 25, 1949, Glass Papers, OSD Historian.

23. Memo, Pace to Johnson, May 2, 1949, *ibid.*; memo, McNeil to Johnson, May 11, 1949, *ibid.*

24. NSC 52, "Governmental Programs in National Security and International Affairs for FY 1951," July 5, 1949, *FRUS 1949,* I, 349; ltr, Truman to Souers,

July 1, 1949, *ibid.*, 350-352; NSC 52/1, July 8, 1949, *ibid.*, 352-353. For a summary of the July 1 meeting, see Rearden, *Formative Years*, 371-372.

25. Memo, Eisenhower to Johnson, July 14, 1949, Eisenhower Pre-Presidential papers, Abilene, Kansas; also in RG 330, CD 16-1-17.

26. NSC 52/3, "Governmental Programs in National Security and International Affairs for Fiscal Year 1951," Sep. 29, 1949, *FRUS 1949*, I, 385-393.

27. For details, see "Annual Budget Message to the Congress: Fiscal Year 1951," Jan. 9, 1950, *Truman Public Papers, 1950*, 44-106.

28. Little, *Foundations of an Atomic Air Force*, 107-108.

29. Hewlett and Duncan, *Atomic Shield*, 164-165; Robert S. Norris, Thomas B. Cochran, and William M. Arkin, "History of the Nuclear Stockpile," *Bulletin of the Atomic Scientists* (Aug. 1985): 106-109.

30. Rosenberg, "Hydrogen Bomb Decision," 71; Hewlett and Duncan, *Atomic Shield*, 178.

31. Memo, Leahy (for JCS) to SecDef, Dec. 9, 1948, RG 330, CD 25-1-38.

32. Nichols, *Road to Trinity*, 269.

33. JCS 1823/14, June 14, 1949, RG 218, CCS 471.6 (8-15-45), sec. 15; U.S. Congress, Joint Committee on Atomic Energy, "The Scale and Scope of Atomic Production: A Chronology of Leading Events," Jan. 30, 1952 (galley proofs), RG 330, 471.6 (A-Bomb). Hereafter cited as "JCAE Chronology."

34. Statement by President Truman at a Meeting at Blair House, July 14, 1949, *FRUS 1949*, I, 481.

35. Ltr, McMahon to Truman, July 14, 1949, *ibid.*, 482-484.

36. Ltr, Truman to Souers, July 26, 1949, *ibid.*, 501-503.

37. Memo, William Webster (CMLC) to Johnson, Sep. 2, 1949, enclosed with draft rpt.; and memo, John H. Ohly to Johnson, Sep. 30, 1949, both in RG 330, CD 19-2-17.

38. Ltr, Souers to SecState, SecDef, and Chm AEC, Oct. 10, 1949, w/enclosures, RG 330, CD 19-2-17; portions printed in *FRUS 1949*, I, 559-564. For Lilienthal's skepticism, see *Lilienthal Journals*, II, 501-502, 508-511, 527-528.

39. Ltr, Truman to Lilienthal, Oct. 19, 1949, CF, Truman Papers; Hewlett and Duncan, *Atomic Shield*, 380.

40. Extract, Oct. 13, 1949, "JCAE Chronology."

41. Hewlett and Duncan, *Atomic Shield*, chs. 11 and 14, covers the issue of AEC-Congressional relations especially well. Also see the "JCAE Chronology," and Harold P. Green and Alan Rosenthal, *Government of the Atom: the Integration of Powers* (N.Y.: Atherton Press, 1963), 233-252. Truman's remark about elections is in *Lilienthal Journals*, II, 564.

42. Ltr, McMahon to Truman, Sep. 28, 1949, *FRUS 1949*, I, 543-544; extract for Nov. 1, 1949, "JCAE Chronology." Also see ltr, McMahon to Truman, Nov. 21, 1949, *FRUS 1949*, I, 588-595.

43. Extract for Mar. 16, 1949, "JCAE Chronology."

44. Extract for Oct. 7, 1949, *ibid.*

45. Memo, LeBaron to Early, [ca. Nov. 10, 1949], RG 330, CD 16-1-17.

46. Memo, Bradley (for JCS) to Johnson, Nov. 23, 1949, *ibid.*

47. Extract for Oct. 14, 1949, "JCAE Chronology."

48. "Stenographic Transcript of Hearings before the Joint Committee on Atomic Energy, Congress of the United States," Jan. 20, 1950, vol. I: "Projected Development of Super Weapons," RG 330, CD 471.6 (A-Bomb).

49. Hewlett and Duncan, *Atomic Shield,* ch. 12; Lewis L. Strauss, *Men and Decisions* (Garden City, N.Y.: Doubleday, 1962), 215-230; *Lilienthal Journals,* II, 564-636.

50. Hearings before the Joint Committee on Atomic Energy, Oct. 17, 1949, Department of Energy files.

51. *Ibid.*

52. "Stenographic Transcript," vol. I, Jan. 20, 1950, RG 330, CD 471.6 (A-Bomb).

53. For a concise and informative account of the infighting among members of the scientific community, see Herbert York, *The Advisors: Oppenheimer, Teller, and the Superbomb* (San Francisco: W.H. Freeman, 1976).

54. Hewlett and Duncan, *Atomic Shield,* 381-385; ltr, Oppenheimer to Lilienthal, Oct. 30, 1949, with attachments, RG 330, CD 16-1-17, portions printed in *FRUS 1949,* I, 569-573.

55. Ltr, Lilienthal to Truman, Nov. 9, 1949, with enclosures, *FRUS 1949,* I, 576-585.

56. For Dean's views, see Roger M. Anders (ed.), *Forging the Atomic Shield: Excerpts from the Office Diary of Gordon E. Dean* (Chapel Hill: University of North Carolina Press, 1987), 48-50, 57-64.

57. This prediction proved correct. In fact, the Soviets had been pursuing theoretical studies at least since 1947, and on or about November 1, 1949, Stalin approved a high-priority development program that resulted in the test of a boosted fission bomb with thermonuclear characteristics in August 1953 and demonstration of a weaponized model in 1955. See David Holloway, "Soviet Thermonuclear Development," *International Security* 4 (Winter 1979-80): 192-197.

58. Ltr, Strauss to Truman, Nov. 25, 1949, *FRUS 1949,* I, 596-599. Also see Strauss, *Men and Decisions,* 219-222.

59. *Lilienthal Journals,* II, 597-598.

60. Mins., 148th Mtg of the Policy Planning Staff, Oct. 11, 1949, *FRUS 1949,* I, 399-403.

61. Bundy, *Danger and Survival,* 201.

62. Minutes of the 148th Mtg PPS, Oct. 11, 1949, *FRUS 1949,* I, 402.

63. Paul H. Nitze, "The Relationship of Strategic and Theater Nuclear Forces," *International Security* 2 (Fall 1977): 124-125.

64. Mins. of 8th Mtg of the Policy Planning Staff on the International Control of Atomic Energy, Oct. 28, 1949, *FRUS 1949,* I, 204-205.

65. Mins., Mtg of the Policy Planning Staff, Nov. 3, 1949, *ibid.,* I, 573-576.

66. "Memo Circulated by the Defense Members of the Working Group of the Special Committee of the National Security Council," ca. Dec. 16, 1949, *ibid.,* I, 604-610.

67. *Ibid.*
68. Memo by Acheson, Dec. 20, 1949, *ibid.,* I, 612-617.
69. Memo by Nitze, Dec. 19, 1949, *ibid.,* I, 610-611; Paul H. Nitze, *From Hiroshima to Glasnost: At the Center of Decision—A Memoir* (New York: Grove, Weidenfeld, 1989), 87-92; Interview No. 3 with Nitze by Richard D. McKinzie, Aug. 4, 1975, Northeast Harbor, Maine, Oral History Collection, Truman Library, p. 8.
70. Dean Acheson, *Present at the Creation* (New York: Norton, 1969), 348; *Lilienthal Journals,* II, 613-614.
71. Memo by Kennan, Jan. 20, 1950, *FRUS 1950,* I, 22-24. Also see Kennan, *Memoirs, 1925-1950,* 471-476.
72. Memo by Nitze, Jan. 17, 1950, *FRUS 1950,* I, 13-17.
73. Memo of Telcon by Acheson, Jan. 19, 1950, *ibid.,* I, 511; Hewlett and Duncan, *Atomic Shield,* 399-409; G. Gordon Arneson, "The H-Bomb Decision," *Foreign Service Journal* (May 1969), 27, and (June 1969), 25.
74. "Report by the Special Committee of the National Security Council to President Truman," Jan. 31, 1950, RG 330, CD 16-1-17.
75. *Ibid.*
76. *Lilienthal Journals,* II, 623-633. Also see Arneson, "The H-Bomb Decision," pt. 1, 27-28; and Acheson, *Present at the Creation,* 348-349.
77. Memo, Truman to Johnson, Nov. 17, 1949, RG 330, CD 23-1-19.
78. Memo, Exec Sec NSC to SecState, Jan. 19, 1950, w/enclosure, Memo, Bradley (for JCS) to Johnson, Jan. 13, 1950, *FRUS 1950,* I, 503-511.
79. JCS 1952/11, WSEG Rpt No. 1, Feb. 10, 1950, RG 218, CCS 373 (10-23-48) sec. 6, Bulky Package. Ponturo, *WSEG Experience,* 73-75; and Philip M. Morse, *In at the Beginning: A Physicist's Life* (Cambridge, Mass: MIT Press, 1977), 258-259, summarize the briefing.
80. See for example Robert Chadwell Williams, *Klaus Fuchs, Atom Spy* (Cambridge, Mass.: Harvard University Press, 1987); and Gregg Herken, *The Winning Weapon: The Atomic Bomb in the Cold War, 1945-1950* (New York: Knopf, 1980), 322-323.
81. Alice Cole, et al., *History of Strategic Arms Competition, 1945-1972, Chronology—U.S.* (2 vols; Washington, D.C.: Historical Office, Office of the Secretary of Defense, 1974), I, 101.
82. Ltr, Johnson to Truman, Feb. 24, 1950, RG 330, CD 16-1-17.
83. "Report to the President by the Special Committee of the National Security Council on Development of Thermonuclear Weapons," Mar. 9, 1950, *ibid.*

VI

Re-arming for the Cold War

As averse as Truman was to nuclear weapons in principle, his decision to develop the H-bomb clearly reflected the mindset of a pragmatist. Critics at the time were correctly concerned about where the decision would ultimately lead. But Truman had never doubted that maintaining a strong, up-to-date nuclear arsenal came first. What good it would do over the long term, or what its effective uses might be, were secondary considerations if they mattered at all. For Truman, the key issue was American nuclear superiority and its continuance for as long as possible.

Even so, Truman recognized that the development of a thermonuclear weapon, if indeed possible, could only come in several years. What happened in the meantime was the matter deserving more urgent attention. Thus, the more immediate result of the H-bomb decision was to set in motion the first thorough review since 1948 of basic US national security policy. This effort would lead to the completion in April 1950 of NSC 68, considered by some the "blueprint" of American cold war strategy. While approving development of the H-bomb, Truman also signed a letter (based on the compromise reached between Acheson and Lilienthal) directing the secretaries of state and defense "to undertake a re-examination of our objectives in peace and war and of the effect of these objectives on our strategic plans, in light of the probable fission bomb capability and possible thermonuclear bomb capability of the Soviet Union."[1] The resulting report, doubtless much broader and more probing than Truman expected, would break new ground.

LOOKING TO THE FUTURE: NSC 68

Much has been said and written about NSC 68, but its precise impact is still open to question.[2] Clearly, though, as far as Acheson was concerned, the study sought to stem the increasingly one-dimensional defense policy emerging from the President's thrifty defense budgets and growing reliance on nuclear weapons. Even though he had recommended development of the H-bomb, Acheson had done so reluctantly. He now sought to minimize the impact of that decision on the future posture of America's armed forces. Unlike Truman, Acheson remained skeptical of America's ability to maintain nuclear superiority indefinitely. The H-bomb, he calculated, simply bought a little more time. In staff discussions, Acheson left no doubt that he saw atomic weapons offering a diminishing return in light of the Soviet Union's capacity to demonstrate a similar capability. According to Nitze:

> Acheson made the point that, over time, the Soviets were bound to narrow America's technological lead in the nuclear field. The margin of American nuclear superiority would tend to become less and less significant as the years went by. Therefore, the United States and its allies should address themselves to restoring the conventional military balance.[3]

Acheson's assessment was, of course, by no means new or unique. Others, including Kennan and many in the Navy who opposed strategic bombing and were dubious of the military utility and morality of nuclear weapons, had tried to make similar points almost from the inception of the nuclear age. But these views, coming as they did from the administration's senior cabinet member—and increasingly Truman's closest advisor—represented a most formidable challenge to the then-current trend in American defense planning.

Acheson's concerns were first and foremost of a practical nature. Since becoming secretary in January 1949, and especially after the conclusion of the North Atlantic Treaty that April, Acheson had regarded European security as his number-one foreign policy concern. But by the beginning of 1950, he lacked confidence that existing American capabilities, conventional as well as strategic, provided adequate protection, for what would later be known as "extended deterrence." As time went on, he reasoned, a defense posture resting on nuclear retaliation would steadily lose credibility as the Soviets acquired more nuclear weapons of their own. The result, he feared, would be "a trend against us which, if allowed to continue, would lead to a considerable deterioration in our position."[4] This did not mean that Acheson regarded war with the Soviet Union as imminent or even inevitable. But with unavoidable US defense obligations to NATO and implied obligations elsewhere as in the Far East, he became convinced that such a possibility had to be addressed more seriously than it had been in the past.

A clear indication of Acheson's thinking came in his decision to replace Kennan as director of the Policy Planning Staff with Paul H. Nitze. A career foreign service officer with an intellectual bent, Kennan enjoyed the reputation both inside and outside the government, as well as abroad, as America's foremost authority on Soviet affairs. But with Acheson's advent, Kennan's influence waned. Kennan was no pacifist, but he put more trust in diplomacy than in the exercise of power—especially military power—to resolve the kinds of differences that had arisen between Washington and Moscow since World War II. He was especially dubious of the Pentagon's emphasis on nuclear weapons and allegedly stated that two well drilled divisions of Marines could effectively restrain Soviet and communist expansion.[5] Although Acheson was also skeptical of relying on nuclear weapons, he considered Kennan's faith in diplomacy and his aversion to military power, including even nuclear power, naive and inappropriate. From Acheson's perspective, a vigorous, forceful policy made more sense and, in the long run, stood a better chance of success. "The only way to deal with the Soviet Union," he believed, "is to create situations of strength."[6]

In choosing Nitze as Kennan's successor, Acheson purposefully sought out someone with views closer to his own. In later years, Acheson would remark that he found Nitze "a very able person and one with whom I find myself in agreement about 99 per cent of the time."[7] In contrast to his view of Kennan as the sensitive, introspective scholar, Acheson saw Nitze as "a Wall Street operator," a pragmatist who knew how to get things done.[8] After a successful career as an investment banker in New York in the 1930s, Nitze had come to Washington in 1940. There, he served in a variety of capacities during World War II, mainly dealing with economic mobilization and overseas procurement. As the war drew to a close, he joined the US Strategic Bombing Survey, serving as one of its directors in Europe and as acting vice-chairman during the Pacific phase of the survey's investigation. It was in the latter capacity, while trying to assess the significance of the atomic attacks on Hiroshima and Nagasaki, that Nitze began to refine his thoughts, many of which would appear in NSC 68, on the future imperatives of American security. "In preparing contingency policies," he later wrote of his experience in the bombing survey, "we thought that, while much had changed from the pre-nuclear era, the basic principles of military strategy were not entirely laid to waste. They had been deeply modified, but they still should play a major role in the development of military strategy in the nuclear era."[9]

The first task that Acheson assigned to Nitze was to establish closer liaison with strategic planners in the Defense Department, an assignment that

Nitze found continually frustrating with Secretary of Defense Louis Johnson at the Pentagon. While Acheson wanted to broaden State-Defense contacts, Johnson wanted to narrow them. In fact, he required subordinates to conduct any business they might have with State through his immediate office.[10] Many of Johnson's prohibitions were impossible to enforce, and some were simply ignored as a matter of expediency. But the overall effect was to create an atmosphere of severely strained relations that fueled press speculation of an Acheson-Johnson feud. Acheson eventually concluded that Johnson must have been "mentally ill." "His conduct," Acheson recalled, "became too outrageous to be explained by mere cussedness. It did not surprise me when some years later he underwent a brain operation."[11]

In fairness to Johnson, the situation in the Pentagon verged on anarchy. His ironfisted methods reflected a desperate effort to maintain control. Many of his troubles, to be sure, were the product of his coarse, abrasive, and dictatorial manner. But others—intense interservice rivalry for funds, quarrels over competing weapons systems, and brooding anxieties, especially in the Navy, over the ultimate effects of the 1947 unification law—were inherited from his predecessor, James Forrestal. Nor did Truman's desire to hold down military expenditures help Johnson win friends and influence within the services. Having placed a ceiling of $13 billion on the military budget for Fiscal Year 1951, Truman wanted further reductions the following year. Accordingly, on March 1, 1950, Johnson circulated a "tentative planning budget ceiling" for FY 1952 that limited new military spending to $12.1 billion.[12] By all accounts politically ambitious and eager for a run at the presidency, Johnson worked hard to meet Truman's goals, apparently hoping to build a reputation for himself as a tough-minded administrator. Any loss of strength from cutbacks, he implied repeatedly in public statements, would be more than made up by increased reliance on strategic air power.[13]

Unlike Acheson, Johnson had no enthusiasm for the policy review ordered in connection with the H-bomb decision. Perhaps afraid of what it would uncover, he had argued against the need for such a study. When forced to accept it nonetheless, he gave it low priority, almost to the point of ignoring it. Consequently, even though the review was supposed to have been a collaborative effort, Johnson by default let the initiative pass to Acheson and his people. The resulting paper was written mainly by members of State's Policy Planning Staff, with Nitze, Robert Tufts, and Robert Hooker spearheading the effort. Contributions from the Defense Department came largely from the JCS representative, Maj. Gen. Truman H. Landon, USAF. Landon initially presented modest proposals to correct minor deficiencies in the existing force structure, but he soon became persuaded, in Nitze's estimation, that the purpose of the project was a fundamental review of policy and not "a mere horse-trading budget exercise." The rapidity of the change in Landon's outlook convinced Nitze that there was a revolt brewing in the Pentagon against Johnson's policies, especially his emphasis on economy over preparedness.[14]

After nearly six weeks of work and several drafts, Nitze deemed it time for Acheson and Johnson to meet to examine the review group's progress. This meeting, held on March 22, 1950, at the State Department, nearly killed the project. Nitze had kept Acheson advised with daily briefings, but Johnson apparently knew little about the process apart from occasional memos drafted by his personal representative on the study group, Maj. Gen. James H. Burns, his coordinator for politico-military affairs. When Johnson arrived, he cut short Nitze's oral summary of the review group's work, denounced the State Department for numerous past discourtesies, and declared that he would take no position until he had read the study group's papers in detail. Acheson took Johnson aside, but their inability to hold a civil conversation led to the collapse of the meeting. Johnson stalked out while Acheson relayed word of the impasse to the White House. "Within the hour," he recalled, "the president telephoned me, expressing his outrage and telling me to carry on exactly as we were doing."[15]

Almost immediately, Johnson's influence within the administration declined as his differences with Acheson became more pronounced. A week later, while Johnson was at The Hague for a meeting of the NATO defense ministers, the review group circulated its report and slipped a copy to Truman. Acheson, the Joint Chiefs, and the three service secretaries all endorsed its recommendations. Faced with the choice of concurring or of offering an embarrassing lone dissent, Johnson likewise endorsed the report and urged Truman to put it before the NSC for further study.[16] Finding that he could not suppress the report, Johnson decided to accept it, though he remained skeptical whether it would lead to any significant change in policy. In April 1950 the report entered the council's serial number file as NSC 68.[17]

A substantial document of over 60 pages, NSC 68 offered the first truly integrated assessment of basic national security requirements in the postwar era. In this regard, three points stand out. First is the report's ready acceptance of Acheson's view of the Soviet threat (and, by implication, his remedies for dealing with it), centering on his contention that "the Soviet Union has one purpose and that is world domination."[18] Going a step further, NSC 68 found that "the Soviet Union, unlike previous aspirants to hegemony, is animated by a new fanatic faith, antithetical to our own, and seeks to impose its absolute authority over the rest of the world." As evidence of this "Kremlin design," NSC 68 cited Moscow's continuing pressure on noncommunist countries in Europe and Asia; its inordinately large investment of resources (estimated at 40 percent of the Soviet Union's gross national product) in war-supporting industries; and its amassing of military capabilities "far in excess of those necessary to defend its national territory." In other words, all evidence indicated that the Soviet Union was "developing the military capacity to support its design for world domination."[19]

Whether NSC 68 purposefully overstated the Soviet military threat remains a matter of some conjecture. Nitze, in defense of the report's findings, subsequently cited the limited range of information available to the review group and the unavoidable use of existing agreed intelligence estimates. "Later," he conceded, "the intelligence people would state that of their estimated 175 Soviet divisions, one third were at full strength, one third were at partial strength, and the final third were cadres."[20] But Acheson, hinting at another reason for the overestimate, recalled in his memoirs that: "The purpose of NSC-68 was to so bludgeon the mass mind of 'top government' that not only could the President make a decision but that the decision could be carried out."[21] This suggests that, insofar as Acheson was concerned, the content and accuracy of the report were less important than the results it produced. According to historian Paul Y. Hammond: "Acheson was more interested in the polemic value of NSC-68 than in its precise rationality. Evidently he saw it as a device for challenging established policies and premises which he thought needed reexamination."[22] What Acheson wanted, it seems, was a hard-hitting study that would draw attention to world problems as he saw them, and, at the same time, steer policy in his direction.

The second point followed logically from the first and built upon the Achesonian doctrine of "situations of strength." As outlined in the report, the first priority should be "a rapid and sustained buildup of the political, economic, and military strength of the free world," culminating no later than 1954—the year of "maximum danger"—when the Soviet Union was expected to have sufficient nuclear capabilities to threaten serious damage to the United States.[23] The aim, as NSC 68 made clear, was to present the Soviet Union with such a formidable adversary that Moscow would not dare risk war. "The frustration of the Kremlin design," the report argued,

> requires the free world to develop a successfully functioning political and economic system and a vigorous political offensive against the Soviet Union. These, in turn, require an adequate military shield under which they can develop.[24]

In indicating what should be done, however, NSC 68 gave off mixed signals. The buildup, it said, should be phased and balanced, a recommendation probably intended as much as anything to avoid interservice wrangling over the allocation of resources. Although NSC 68 accorded priority to the strengthening of conventional forces, it also grudgingly acknowledged the West's continuing dependence on, and need for, strong nuclear capabilities. Indeed, it ruled out a US pledge of no-first-use of atomic weapons. The ideal solution would be "assurance that atomic weapons had been effectively eliminated from national peacetime armaments."[25] But since this seemed highly unlikely, as experience dating from the ill-fated Baruch Plan indicated, the United States and its allies had to accept the grim reality that an arms competition with the Soviet Union was now well underway. At the same time, the report conceded that, until the West achieved significantly more effective conventional capabilities, nuclear weapons would have to remain the West's premier military asset, preferably as a retaliatory option but with pre-emption not excluded either. Although this was hardly the reorientation of defense policy that Acheson had hoped to see, it represented a shift in direction and was expected by the drafters to require a change of priorities over time.[26]

Finally, Acheson used NSC 68 to argue his case that fiscal conservatism in defense matters must be abandoned if American foreign policy were to continue to function effectively. While NSC 68 contained no specific cost estimates (a purposeful omission, according to Acheson), Nitze and others on the review group privately estimated the need for increased expenditures anywhere in the range of $35 to $50 billion annually.[27] Though it is undocumented whether Acheson ever communicated these figures to Truman, Nitze seems to think he did, at least in some general way that would avoid later surprises.[28] In any case, Acheson wanted to present as cogent a brief as possible for raising the country's overall level of preparedness. The implications, he felt, spoke for themselves.

Contrary to the assertion in Acheson's memoirs, Truman did not approve NSC 68 as soon as he officially received it in April 1950. In fact, his initial reaction was one of typical caution. Reluctant to commit himself to any new or enlarged programs without knowing what they might cost, he directed the creation of an ad hoc interagency committee on NSC 68, with heavy representation from his economic advisors, to assess the report's potential budgetary impact.[29] At the same time, Secretary of Defense Johnson ordered the Joint Chiefs to prepare an itemized listing of force-level deficiencies.[30] These studies were still in progress when the Korean War erupted on June 25, 1950. Confronted with the sudden outbreak of war and fearing an escalation of communist aggression elsewhere, Truman sent US combat troops into Korea and notified Congress that he would need supplemental appropriations for defense and military assistance. Finally, in late September, he got around to signing a memorandum (NSC 68/1) approving NSC 68 "as a statement of policy to be followed over the next four or five years."[31]

Whether Truman would have approved NSC 68 had the Korean War not intervened cannot be known. NSC 68 represented a major departure of policy, toward a peacetime re-armament program that radically altered the distribution of resources at home and drastically expanded the scale and scope of American commitments abroad. Instead of acting immediately on its recommendations, Truman in customary fashion turned the report over to his budget advisors and let them whittle away at it while he pondered his next move. As it happened, he took more than five months to make up his mind and then acted only after events seemed to dictate the course he should take.

Still, even without Korea, the available evidence suggests that Truman would have approved the report and acted on its recommendations, though perhaps not so fully as its authors hoped. This, at least, appears to have been his inclination when he met with his director of the Bureau of the Budget, Frederick J. Lawton, on May 23, 1950. According to Lawton's notes of their meeting: "The President indicated that we [the Bureau of the Budget] were to continue to raise any questions that we had on this program and that it definitely was not as large in scope as some of the people seem to think."[32] Events, beginning with the North Korean attack, soon caused Truman to revise his thinking considerably.

THE IMPACT OF KOREA

By championing an all-around military buildup, NSC 68 offered something for everyone—more divisions for the Army, more ships and carriers for the Navy, and, of course, more planes, including long-range strategic bombers, for the Air Force. Although the report stressed the need for augmented and improved conventional forces, its failure to go beyond generalizations or to stipulate requirements made it a poor guide for planning purposes. When the Korean emergency erupted, each of the services was thus more or less on a par in making claims on resources. The result was a significant expansion in the size and capabilities of the armed forces but no real reordering of priorities. On the contrary, the longer the emergency lasted and the more costly the NSC 68-inspired buildup proved to be, the more tempting it became to rely ever more heavily on nuclear capabilities.

The immediate concern was, of course, the emergency in Korea, a problem that Congress and the administration readily agreed required significant augmentation of US forces. Accordingly, on July 18, the Joint Chiefs gave Secretary of Defense Johnson a complete set of new requirements that envisioned a substantially enlarged force structure, with greatly strengthened conventional capabilities, resulting by the end of the fiscal year in an Army of 11 divisions, all at or near full strength; a Navy with 282 major combat ships and 12 carrier air groups; a two-division Marine Corps; and an Air Force expanded from 48 to 58 wings. To support these force-level increases, Truman asked Congress for $10.5 billion in supplement appropriations, the first of several such requests that would eventually send the FY 1951 defense budget soaring from $13 to $48 billion.[33]

In tentatively approving the new force-level goals, Truman acknowledged that the ongoing buildup was not transient but rather a course of action for "the next four or five years." At an NSC meeting on July 27, he also mentioned that "despite our preoccupation with the developments in Korea," he worried that the Soviets might be tempted to make moves elsewhere, possibly in the Persian Gulf or Black Sea Straits in order to secure and protect access to adequate oil reserves for a war against the West.[34] Senior advisors, including Acheson, Johnson, and the Joint Chiefs of Staff, shared this view. None doubted that developments in Korea marked a serious turn for the worse, that they represented an unprecedented Soviet boldness, or that they should not be treated as an isolated phenomena. Indeed, in assessing the prospects, one NSC paper pointedly warned that events in Korea might well be "the first phase of a general Soviet plan for global war."[35]

In spite of plans and preparations for a military buildup heavily weighted toward conventional forces, Truman and his advisors realized that it would take time to see significant results. As Marc Trachtenberg has found, senior policymakers and intelligence analysts alike seriously worried that the West would face a "window of vulnerability" that could last into 1952 or later.[36] Though unappealing to Truman, his only readily available countermeasure remained the nuclear arsenal, which was under the custody and control of the AEC. Although preparations had been under way for some time to train military personnel to take over these functions, the Korean emergency accelerated the timetable and prompted the Joint Chiefs in July 1950 to request again that the President transfer custody of some nuclear weapons to the military. In contrast to his sharp resistance to such a request in 1948, Truman this time readily agreed, though he limited the transfers to nonnuclear components. Some went to a storage site on Guam where they would be readily available for use in Korea if needed; but most, having been earmarked for a war against the Soviet Union, were loaded and stored aboard aircraft carriers steaming in Atlantic or Mediterranean waters. Later, as facilities became available, nonnuclear components were also deployed to Newfoundland and Great Britain. Not until January 1953, however, just before leaving office, did Truman approve the transfer of completed weapons assemblies as well.[37]

Despite these preparations for a possibly larger emergency, Truman remained cautious about the bomb, even in the face of growing pressure to adopt stronger measures that would inevitably have involved the use of nuclear weapons. Meeting on August 10 with Secretary of State Acheson, several prominent members of Congress left no doubt that they considered a preventive war against the Soviet Union an increasingly realistic possibility. One—Senator Estes Kefauver of Tennessee—warned that "sentiment throughout the country was building up" to support such action and that "bold ideas were required" to head off further movement in that direction.[38] Two weeks later, Secretary of the Navy Francis P. Matthews, in an apparently unauthorized speech in Boston, advocated "instituting a war to compel cooperation for peace," a thinly veiled threat that caused a considerable stir in the press.[39] While Matthews quickly acknowledged that he had spoken out of turn, he clearly echoed a growing segment of public opinion. Barely had the furor over Matthews's speech died down when Maj. General Orvil A. Anderson, commandant of the Air War College and a strident advocate of strategic bombing, urged a pre-emptive strike against the Soviet Union's atomic energy facilities. "Give me the order to do it," he reportedly said, "and I can break up Russia's five A-bomb nests in a week."[40] But unlike Matthews, who got off with a wrist slap, Anderson was immediately suspended from duty and forced into early retirement.

Truman and his immediate advisors found these calls for preventive war unsettling. Not only did they exacerbate an already tense and delicate situation, but also, if taken seriously, they would have revealed the truly weakened posture of the country's armed forces, largely a product of the administration's frugal defense-spending policies since the end of World War II. Shortages of personnel and equipment, just to meet the needs of the emergency in Korea, were apparent from the onset of the crisis and continued to plague military planners for months to come.[41] More importantly, as the Hull report (WSEG-1) had revealed earlier, not even the planned strategic air offensive could be counted on to deal the Soviet Union's warmaking effort a decisive blow. In other words, as those with inside information (such as Matthews and Anderson) doubtless must have known or suspected, a preventive war did not represent a realistic option in 1950 even if the United

States had known for sure that the Soviet Union was about to launch attacks elsewhere. Initiating a preventive war would have been risky enough; sustaining it would, in all probability, have been impossible.

In fact, Truman's main objective was to limit, not widen, the conflict, if for no other reason than to curb the growing demands of the military buildup. As he told his budget director, Lawton, early in the war, he had no desire to put "any more money than necessary . . . in the hands of the Military."[42] At the time, plans under discussion in the Pentagon looked ahead to a buildup that would peak in 1954—the "year of maximum danger" cited in NSC 68—in a 12-division army, a navy of 324 major combat vessels, and a 69-wing air force.[43] But when the fighting in Korea intensified over the summer, so too did urgings from the Defense Department to step up the size and pace of the re-armament effort. Having reassessed the situation, the Joint Chiefs on September 1 dramatically escalated their military requirements. They now indicated that they would need an 18-division army, a 395-ship navy, and a 95-wing air force in order to meet NSC 68 goals by the agreed target date. Of the 95 wings recommended for the Air Force, 37—or nearly 40 percent—were to be assigned to the Strategic Air Command.[44] Budget estimates developed separately by the President's ad hoc committee on NSC 68 projected total annual costs of around $40 billion, thus consuming around 15 percent of the US gross national product—more than three times the size of pre-Korean War military spending. Moreover, in arriving at its figures, the committee had used somewhat smaller force levels than the Pentagon's and candidly conceded that its calculations might be "too conservative."[45]

When the Chiefs' estimates reached Truman's desk in late September, events in Korea, starting with Gen. Douglas MacArthur's daring Inchon invasion on the 15th, appeared to signal the impending collapse of the North Korean aggression. Ironically, just before the tide turned, Truman fired the hapless Louis Johnson and made him the scapegoat for the early reverses in Korea. Cautiously optimistic that the worst might be over, Truman began to rethink his position on the buildup, telling one senior White House aide that he preferred to delay any commitment to the re-armament programs that the JCS had laid before him.[46] At a meeting of the NSC on September 29, Truman, while approving NSC 68 "as a statement of policy to be followed over the next four or five years," also delayed any decision on implementation until mid-November, noting that "the programs and estimated costs were not final." Gen. George C. Marshall, Johnson's successor as secretary of defense and former secretary of state, agreed that it would be beneficial "to have more time to study the programs and cost . . . particularly from the Congressional and public aspect." Only Acheson, who sensed the drift of the

President's thinking, expressed concern. "The only thing that is more dangerous than undertaking this program," he said, was "not undertaking it." Despite Acheson's lame protest, Truman was obviously having second thoughts about what to do.[47]

Truman had come too far, setting in motion too much machinery and making too many promises and commitments, to back off entirely from a policy of re-arming. Even so, with the situation in Korea seeming to improve by the early fall of 1950, the President's enthusiasm for an expensive military buildup was clearly wavering. Publicly, to be sure, he usually sounded as committed as ever since the outbreak of the war to strengthening the country's defenses, telling an audience in San Francisco in mid-October: "We must devote more of our resources to military purposes, and less to civilian consumption. . . . We are going ahead in dead earnest to build up our defenses. There will be no letdown because of the successes achieved in Korea."[48] A week later, while addressing the UN General Assembly, he reiterated his determination "to build up strength for peace as long as it is necessary." But at the same time, he also sounded a cautionary note, hinting that his commitment to an arms buildup was not unalterable and resurrecting themes he had not used publicly since the collapse of the Baruch Plan. "We must continue to strive, through the United Nations," he insisted, "to achieve international control of atomic energy and the reduction of armaments and armed forces. . . . Disarmament is the course which the United States would prefer to follow."[49]

The clearest indication of a reassessment came at the Pentagon, where, from mid-October through early November, budget analysts in the Office of the Secretary of Defense queried and then trimmed the JCS requests. Here, the concern was over the practical consequences of the proposed buildup— how Congress would react, and whether the economy could withstand the drain on manpower and raw materials, the diversion of production facilities for new equipment, and possible adverse side-effects such as inflation. There were also obvious policy implications, which Deputy Secretary of Defense Robert Lovett described as the need to achieve balance between "priorities of danger and priorities of need," a process that in the current circumstances would doubtless necessitate "adjustments downward."[50] Reluctantly, the Joint Chiefs scaled back their estimated requirements, in effect pushing back the date for completion of the buildup from 1954 to 1956.[51]

At a meeting of the NSC in late November, Truman reiterated his commitment to a general strengthening of the armed forces and said he would support an additional supplemental to the FY 1951 budget. Still, he worried "about the economic situation in this country," especially the maintenance of "domestic production in order to obtain the necessary tax income to meet the costs of the military program." He wanted, he hinted, to see where the recent intervention of Chinese communist troops in Korea would lead. But if, as Truman put it, "the Chinese Communist threat evaporates," he seriously doubted whether "an almost hostile Congress" could be persuaded to vote military appropriations exceeding $45 billion annually over the next several years.[52] In other words, barring some unpredictable emergency, Truman anticipated an unavoidable leveling-off of the buildup as declining congressional support reacted to a diminished threat.[53]

Whether Truman would have followed through with his apparent intention to restore ceilings on military spending, effectively attenuating the buildup, will, of course, never be known for sure. Certainly, though, there was nothing in his previous behavior to indicate his willingness to endorse a defense program such as the Joint Chiefs had proposed. But by early December 1950, instead of "evaporating," as Truman hoped they might, the Chinese communists launched a massive counteroffensive, catching MacArthur and his command totally off-guard and forcing UN troops into an ignominious retreat back down the Korean peninsula. Reeling from this unexpected setback, MacArthur urgently warned his superiors: "We face an entirely new war."[54]

In the wake of these ominous developments in Korea, a virtual state-of-siege mentality gripped Washington. "I've worked for peace for five years and six months," Truman confided to his diary, "and it looks like World War III is here."[55] At a news conference on November 30, the President, in answer to a reporter's question, revealed that the use of nuclear weapons in Korea was and had been for some time under "active consideration," though he declined to be more specific.[56] Distressed by the President's remarks, British Prime Minister Clement Attlee urgently requested consultations and flew to Washington to urge the United States to exercise restraint. As Attlee told a visiting French delegation on the eve of his departure, he thought that atomic weapons could not "be regarded as on a level with other weapons," and that their "use would bring about a new era in warfare with consequences which no one could appreciate." Attlee considered it urgent and imperative, therefore, that the whole question of when and whether to use the bomb "be decided at the highest political level and not by one Power alone."[57]

By the time he arrived in early December, however, British fears of precipitate American action had largely dissipated.[58] In fact, using nuclear weapons in Korea had been a subject of high-level discussion within the US government off and on since the beginning of the war and would continue to be until the 1953 armistice. But the lack of suitable targets and "obvious considerations of possible adverse psychological reaction" made the Strategic Air Command reluctant to recommend such action unless undertaken "as part of an overall atomic campaign against Red China."[59] For the time being, in any case, the matter was closed.

Meanwhile, reacting to warnings from intelligence sources, defense planners and senior policymakers again considered the possibility that the Soviet Union might be preparing for a wider conflict.[60] From the ensuing review by the NSC emerged a proposal not only to approve the Joint Chiefs' September force-level goals but to accelerate the buildup by two years and make mid-1952, not mid-1954, the target date for completion.[61] Although Truman continued to express concern over the "economic picture," events in Korea and the rising tide of alarm in Washington virtually compelled him to support and endorse the buildup and to look ahead to the possibility of additional increases as well.[62] How long until Truman changed his mind, though, remained to be seen.

REASSESSING THE DANGER: THE BUDGET FOR FY 1953

By the beginning of 1951, the military services were well on their way to a formidable, across-the-board expansion of what were, for all intents and purposes, "peacetime" capabilities. Despite the emergency in Korea, most of the increases were for forces slated for duty in other theaters, including a sizable deployment to Europe.[63] Not only would the resulting force structure be considerably larger; it would also be equipped with the latest tanks, ships, and aircraft, including (starting in 1951) the medium-range B-47, the first of a whole new generation of jet bombers designed exclusively for air-atomic warfare.[64] But by and large, the buildup remained consistent with the earlier practice of allotting money within a tripartite framework. As finally sorted out after the various supplementals, the FY 1951 defense budget made available in new obligational authority $19.4 billion for the Army, $15.9 billion for the Air Force, and $12.5 billion for the Navy. In addition, the Air Force and the Navy received contract authority for procurement of ships, planes, and other sophisticated equipment, items with long leadtimes for which payment would not come due for several years. That the Army's share of the budget was somewhat larger than the other services' reflected not so much the administration's determination, as NSC 68 had urged, to achieve a more balanced force posture, as it did the immediate demands of the war in Asia.[65]

This ordering of priorities, with generous allowance for conventional re-armament, held firm only so long as the emergency in Korea fed fears in

Washington of a possibly wider conflict. When the situation seemed to stabilize, around a battlefield stalemate in the summer of 1951, assumptions changed accordingly, reverting to a more business-as-usual pattern of thinking regarding military expenditures. Until then, however, the operating assumption in Washington and in other western capitals was that the West's weakness had invited the Soviet-directed aggression in Korea. The corollary belief was that Moscow would continue to exploit its relative strength at each and every opportunity, whether in Asia, Europe, or the Middle East. Re-armament, in short, continued to be the order of the day and would have to remain so, in the opinion of the Joint Chiefs of Staff, for at least the next two to three years. "If war comes during this period," they warned, "though we would probably not lose it, we would have a difficult time winning it."[66]

Throughout the tensions, nuclear weapons and strategic bombing still played a leading role in US defense strategy and would continue to do so, military planners assumed, until the conventional buildup made possible a viable alternative strategy. Even though the fighting was confined to Asia, a persistent worry in Washington was that Korea might be a diversion; the real danger lay in a possible surprise Soviet invasion of Western Europe. Consequently, one top priority continued to be strategic forces, which might (1) deter a Soviet attack by threatening nuclear retaliation, or (2) retard advancing Soviet armies or strike directly at the Soviet Union's warmaking capacity in the event of a war. Even with the exceedingly heavy demands for tactical air in Korea, Air Force programming was such that SAC's needs for air-atomic operations generally came first. This applied also to SAC assets earmarked for duty in Korea. Indeed, throughout the war, SAC forces sent to Asia were exceedingly modest, limited to about 100 aging B-29s flown by recalled reservists and equipped with World War II-vintage electronics.[67]

Further increases, not just to reinforce strategic bombing capabilities but to bolster the entire defense establishment, were just ahead. On April 30, 1951, Truman sent Congress his defense budget for FY 1952, which reflected his decision of the previous December to accelerate the buildup by two years. Although the military services had originally thought that $82.3 billion would be needed, arm-twisting and judicious paring had brought the figure down to $56.2 billion. Four months late in arriving, the budget produced scattered rumblings of discontent among legislators who felt they were not being allowed enough time to give it a proper screening. But in the end, they generally went along with the administration's recommendations, voting $55.5 billion.[68]

Paradoxically, the defense budget for FY 1952 would be the high-water mark of the Korean re-armament effort.[69] For by the time Congress finished work on the appropriations bill in October 1951, a substantially improved international situation cast doubt on the need for more arms. Not only had the long-awaited Soviet invasion of Western Europe failed to materialize, but there were indications that the conflict in Korea might be nearing resolution. Truman's decision in April to fire MacArthur for insubordinate remarks (MacArthur had claimed that his superiors were holding him back from ending the communist aggression) clearly indicated that the administration had no desire to extend the war beyond the Korean peninsula.[70] And, gesturing their own interest in containing the conflict, the Chinese communists that summer agreed to armistice talks. Not even the announcement in October of the second and third Soviet atomic tests provoked much public alarm.[71] In these circumstances, the congressional consensus that had previously supported and sustained the re-armament effort through four supplementals to the FY 1951 defense budget showed signs of breaking down. "It may or may not be necessary to spend this money," said Republican Senator Robert Taft, as Congress was wrapping up action on the 1952 budget, "but we ought not to spend it without realizing that if we are going to continue such a scale of expenditures, we will plunge the country into economic difficulty."[72]

Although Truman had anticipated this turn of events, the congressional shift came at a time when the Joint Chiefs, supported by the State Department, were pressing anew for further military expansion. Having achieved on paper, at least, most of their immediate goals with respect to NSC 68, the services now sought to get whatever more they could before the momentum generated by Korea ran out. Each wanted sizable increases. But it was the Air Force that had the biggest appetite, seeking to expand from 95 to 143 wings, including 57 wings assigned to SAC.[73] To realize their aims, the services seized on a set of NSC studies (the NSC 114 series) encompassing a review by the State and Defense Departments of accomplishments under NSC 68, and a parallel assessment, ordered by Truman in the summer of 1951, of the assumptions that should underlay the FY 1953 budget (scheduled for presentation to Congress in January 1952).[74] The first report (NSC 114) in the series, submitted to the President in August 1951, agreed that while the United States and its allies still faced "a period of acute danger," the level of US military production and preparedness could not meet readiness targets approved the previous winter. At the same time, a lag in the flow of military assistance to allied countries worried the State Department. Part of the problem, to be sure, came from a shortage of materials due to competing civilian demands and earlier-than-expected delivery dates that stemmed from the acceleration of the buildup. But there was a political dimension to the problem as well, one that divided the President's advisors and cast serious doubt on the entire future of the buildup.[75]

The dispute centered on the question of objectives—whether to continue the process of re-arming at breakneck speed, or to consolidate the gains already achieved around a force posture stressing mobilization potential (rather than forces in-being) that could be maintained for an indefinite period of time. The Joint Chiefs and the State Department favored the first course, while Marshall, Lovett, and their chief budget advisor in the Office of the Secretary of Defense, Wilfred J. McNeil, leaned toward the latter. In critiquing the schism for Acheson, Nitze drew attention to sharply different experiences that had produced sharply different outlooks. "Secretary Marshall," he said,

> and many others who lived through the bleak days of minuscule military budgets during the 20's and 30's are very dubious whether the U.S. people and the Congress will support military budgets at a level even of $20 billion a year over an extended period. They therefore tend to view the present program . . . as a one shot authorization which may well be followed only by normal pay, maintenance, and replacement budgets.

Though Nitze did not challenge this argument directly, he disagreed that "in an atomic age" the United States and its allies could afford to rely on mobilization capabilities as the basis for security while the Soviet Union steadily enhanced its nuclear capabilities. On the contrary, although the United States currently held an edge in nuclear weapons, thus "restraining the USSR from taking actions which in their estimation would bring on general war," there was no assurance that America's nuclear superiority would not—like the monopoly it had once had—cease to be. "It appears to us essential," Nitze concluded, "to achieve preparedness prior to the substantial reduction of our atomic superiority."[76]

Truman's stance in this debate is not entirely clear. At one point, he appeared to feel that, with the increases already incorporated into the FYs 1951 and 1952 budgets, "the programs were adequate."[77] Later, though, after reading NSC 114, he judged it to have "great merit," a remark suggesting that he may have been inclined to side with the State Department and JCS position.[78] Nevertheless, as a former chairman of the Senate Special Committee to Investigate the National Defense Program in World War II, he may only have been referring to the report's advice for overcoming mobilization problems, a subject of increasing concern both in the press and on Capitol

Hill, where rumors of fraud and corruption in the procurement process were rife.[79]

Truman, in any event, did not have to be explicit about his preferences, since they always tended in the direction of fiscal prudence. And with armistice talks underway in Korea, he noticed that the "sense of urgency" that had previously driven both Congress and the American people was now "seriously lacking." In these circumstances, he believed, a way had to be found for maintaining security that would be generally acceptable and effective against a Soviet that threat was likely to remain formidable for some time to come.[80] The solution, in Marshall's opinion, should there be a cease-fire or some other settlement in Korea, was readily apparent. "In order to avert any let-down," he advised, ". . . we might then take the occasion to build up our air forces, sort of as a psychological move, and advertise it widely."[81] But it fell to Lovett, who succeeded Marshall in September 1951 as secretary of defense, to work out the details in the FY 1953 budget. Faced with the usual array of service disagreements over their respective needs, Lovett broke the impasse by opting for nominal increases for the Army and the Navy and an Air Force filled out to 126 wings, with emphasis on strategic air capabilities and air defense.[82] In developing the budget for FY 1953, he urged the Chiefs to bear in mind "the necessity for continually reviewing our military expenditures with a view to obtaining the greatest return."[83] Even though Lovett's allocation of resources in the 1953 budget gave the Air Force less than it had originally requested, it still marked a distinct turning point in the buildup. The concept of the balanced forces approach of NSC 68 gave way again to reliance on ready forces stressing air power and, by extension, the atomic bomb. All in all, it was a relatively cheap, safe, and, in view of the precedents, wholly predictable outcome.

Truman, however, having finally made up his mind, wanted to go even further in curbing the buildup. Although he approved the force structure Lovett had proposed, he told a meeting of his national security advisors in late December 1951 that he remained deeply troubled by the impact that the continuation of large defense budgets would have on the economy. Earlier, the Bureau of the Budget, Truman's trusted ally in such matters, had warned that even under the "minimum" Defense Department estimates proposed by Lovett, the federal deficit in FY 1953 could reach $10 billion and climb to $12 billion the following year. "In view of this," the bureau advised, "the economic risks involved in larger security programs must be weighed against the security risks involved in limiting further expansion of those programs."[84] Truman took the hint. As a first step toward avoiding larger deficits, he ordered "a stretch-out of the period in which readiness is to be developed." In practical terms, this meant a ceiling of $52 billion on the defense budget (the services had asked for $71 billion) and a delay in completion of the buildup and modernization of forces until 1956 at the earliest, if even then. All the services were affected by the stretch-out, but the Army and the Navy felt it the hardest, finding their shares of the defense budget reduced to around 28 percent apiece, as opposed to 44 percent for the Air Force.[85]

Thus, as the pace of the Korean War buildup slackened, the allure of air power, built around the awesome power of the nuclear arsenal, reasserted itself. Though perhaps not fully aware of it at the time, Truman was sealing his country's commitment—and that of its allies, by their willingness to defer to American leadership—to a defense posture dependent in the first instance on strategic air and nuclear weapons. Not only did the FY 1953 budget set the pattern of defense spending for years to come, it also assured that the Air Force would operate in the forefront of military planning for the next generation or more. The newest service would provide the bulk of the forces for strategic deterrence or for general war should the occasion arise. What the years of the Truman presidency had initiated, the "new look" defense policies of the ensuring Eisenhower administration would confirm and institutionalize.

REFINING ATOMIC ENERGY POLICY

Truman's decision to attenuate the Korean War conventional buildup in preference to reliance on strategic air power was only one of a series of crucial policy actions at roughly this same time that helped solidify a nuclear-oriented US defense posture. The more committed the military establishment became to a nuclear strategy, the more it needed assurance of a sufficient stockpile of usable weapons and, equally important, guidance from above on how they were to be employed. As in the past, controversy surrounded these issues. But with dependence on nuclear weapons now becoming more apparent than ever, building a consensus was somewhat easier.

The most difficult questions involved weapons-use policy. Although the NSC had endorsed a general statement of principles (NSC 30) in 1948, its practical applications were never fully clear. Final decision on use of the atomic bomb rested with the President as commander in chief, while for planning purposes the military services were left on their own. About the only restraints were the size of the nuclear stockpile, the number of available delivery vehicles, and the President's own proclivity to vacillate when queried on the subject. As the gist of his public statements over the years indicated, he seemed prepared, as one State Department study cautiously put it, "to make a decision as to the use of atomic weapons when circumstances so require."[86]

If Truman's overt commitment to the use of the bomb may have appeared somewhat hazy, it was no less explicit than that of America's closest allies, the British. Although British defense planners put great stock in the bomb as a deterrent to Soviet aggression in Europe, they had little appreciation of the actual circumstances in which nuclear weapons might be used, probably because Britain had yet to acquire an atomic capability. Anglo-American planning talks on the conduct of a future war had been held on an intermittent basis since 1948, but the most important subject of all—the strategic employment of atomic weapons—was barred by the Americans from discussion on the grounds that it involved too many sensitive and speculative considerations.[87] With the outbreak of hostilities in Korea, senior British officials became apprehensive that the United States would escalate the conflict through the use of nuclear weapons against North Korea and Communist China.[88] As mentioned, Truman's casual observation during a press conference in late November 1950, following the Chinese intervention, that retaliation with nuclear weapons could not be ruled out, set off a minor furor in London, and brought Prime Minister Attlee scurrying to Washington in hopes of eliciting an American promise not to use the bomb without prior consultations. According to the American record of the proceedings, Truman, while agreeing to keep the British informed, gave no assurances that they would be brought into the decision-making process. Not only were there the provisions of the McMahon Act to consider, but also, as Secretary of State Acheson pointed out, the President had a constitutional duty as commander in chief "to authorize use of the atomic weapon if he believed it necessary in the defense of the country."[89]

The British record of the discussions was somewhat different. It said that the President had indeed affirmed that he would take no action without prior consultation, even though he could offer no written agreement and was unable to include in the conference communiqué any reference to this understanding.[90] The communiqué said simply that it was the President's hope that world conditions would never call for the use of nuclear weapons, but that it was his desire in any case to keep the Prime Minister fully informed of developments should a change in the situation occur.[91] But despite the apparent breakdown of communications and the resulting misunderstanding, both sides seemed reasonably satisfied that the conference had solved the immediate problem.

Further consideration of the weapons-use issue soon became entangled with another matter—whether to increase yet again the production of fissionable materials. Even though Truman had already approved two such increases—one in 1949 and another shortly after the outbreak of the Korean War—he faced mounting pressure to authorize a third. Truman himself may have inadvertently contributed to this situation when, in early September 1951, while in San Francisco for the Japanese peace conference, he told a group of Democratic party loyalists that the United States was constructing "new weapons" with "fantastic" capabilities.[92] He probably meant recent technical breakthroughs from the RANGER and GREENHOUSE tests, which suggested new designs for tactical nuclear weapons as well as a workable design for the H-bomb. But by highlighting the possibilities, he was at the same time encouraging those who wanted even greater reliance on nuclear weapons.

Once again, it was the ambitious and indomitable senator from Connecticut, Brien McMahon, chairman of the Joint Committee on Atomic Energy, who seized the initiative. Convinced that nuclear weapons were the key to future national security, McMahon had hounded both the Defense Department and the AEC since the outbreak of the Korean War to put more effort into developing a nuclear-armed military establishment.[93] On September 18, 1951, in a major speech to the Senate, he elaborated on what he thought should be done, beginning with a reordering of priorities that would end, as he saw it, wasteful spending on costly and less effective conventional arms. "At the rate we are moving," he contended, citing the record defense budgets that Congress was being asked to pass, "I can see ahead only two ultimate destinations: military safety at the price of economic disaster or economic safety at the price of military disaster." The way out of this dilemma, McMahon believed, was to step up the production of fissionable materials—plutonium and U-235—by some 200 percent, not only to bolster strategic forces, but to arm and equip battlefield troops as well—to have, in other words, "an atomic army, an atomic navy and an atomic air force." "If we mass-produce this weapon, as we can," he argued, "I solemnly say . . . that the cost of a single atomic bomb will become less than the cost of a single tank."[94]

McMahon's speech, as it developed, set the stage for another Defense-AEC confrontation. Seizing on the opportunity McMahon had presented, the Joint Chiefs in October 1951 gave the AEC a wholly new set of increased production requirements to be met from 1956 on—a 50 percent increase in plutonium production and a 150 percent increase in U-235. Though less than the 200 percent expansion that McMahon had thought necessary, the Chiefs hedged their position by describing these as "interim" requirements, a hint that requests for still further increases might be in the offing.[95] With this, the Pentagon and the AEC steeled themselves for what seemed another impending battle royal. But with the commission now chaired by Gordon Dean, one of the original advocates of the H-bomb, rather than David Lilienthal, the atmosphere in which deliberations took place was decidedly more collegial.

As he had done in the past with such matters, Truman turned the problem over to the Special Committee of the National Security Council on Atomic Energy, which consisted of the secretaries of state and defense and the chairman of the AEC. Opinions quickly divided along familiar lines. Realizing that the conventional buildup he had so strongly supported had peaked, Secretary of State Acheson accepted that there was no choice but to fall back on nuclear weapons. Thus he endorsed the expansion as a means of assuring the United States continued nuclear superiority at a time of growing Soviet atomic capabilities. Dean and his AEC colleagues likewise concurred in the expansion, but still wanted to know more about the military basis for stepping up the output of fissionable materials.[96] To this Secretary of Defense Lovett objected. Instead of a simple ruling on production quotas, Lovett sought a once-and-for-all resolution of the many other divisive issues that had complicated atomic energy policy for years. "The time has come," he told the Joint Chiefs, seeking their advice and, coincidentally, suggesting how they ought to respond, "to delineate clearly the responsibilities between the Department of Defense, which has primary interest in atomic weapons requirements, and the Atomic Energy Commission, which has primary responsibility for scientific development."[97] The Chiefs' reply, subsequently forwarded to the President, was unequivocal. "It must be recognized," they said, ". . . that the atomic weapon has become such an integral part of our plans and preparations for the conduct of a major war that it constitutes a vital element in the attainment of full military preparedness on the part of the United States." It followed, then, that while the Chiefs were open to any suggestions the AEC or any other agency might choose to offer, "it is the ultimate responsibility of the Department of Defense to determine how many and what types of atomic weapons are needed for the defense and security of the United States." The same, they added, held true should the question arise of where and when to use atomic weapons.[98]

Lovett got some, but not all, of what he wanted. On January 16, 1952, Truman, while meeting with the Special Committee at the White House, approved the proposed expansion plan but took no action on other related issues. As he had done in the past, Truman expressed regrets at having to make the decision, comparing the investment in nuclear weapons with the manufacture of poison gases in World War II "even though we devoutly hoped that they would not have to be used, which turned out to be the case." Indeed, even his military advisors were by now coming to look upon nuclear weapons as a wasting asset, whose value would steadily erode as time went on. According to Gen. Hoyt S. Vandenberg, the Air Force chief of staff: "... the time will come when both the United States and the Soviet Union will have sufficient stocks of atomic bombs to deal one another the gravest kind of blow. . . . After that point has been reached . . . all bombs would in a sense be surplus and the crucial advantage would lie with the power which was in a position to make the best tactical use of atomic weapons." In other words, more nuclear weapons did not necessarily promise more security, a rather odd admission at a rather odd time, to say the least.[99]

Even so, Truman's decision opened the way for the most dramatic increases yet in the size of the US nuclear arsenal, which would balloon from slightly less than 1,000 weapons by the time he left office to 18,000 by the end of the decade. This increase, in turn, reflected not only the enormous growth in production capacity initiated under Truman, but also the erection of an extensive industrial system for weapons research and development. By the end of Truman's presidency, the AEC had added a second atomic research laboratory at Livermore, California, and had established new plants for manufacturing and assembling weapons at Rocky Flats, Colorado, Kansas City, Missouri, Burlington, Iowa, and Amarillo, Texas. As a growth industry, atomic energy was hard to rival.[100]

Still, even if he had wanted to, Truman was in no position to oppose the increase. His personal preferences notwithstanding, he found himself too committed politically to a nuclear-oriented defense posture to change course at this point. True, a further increase was expensive and burdensome on the economy, not to mention potentially hazardous environmentally, a lurking danger as yet barely perceived. But it was bound to be supported in Congress—more so, to be sure, than additional expenditures on conventional weapons. And with each and every increase in the production of fissionable materials, there was always that attractive prospect of heading off growth in future defense budgets, with nuclear weapons taking up the slack. All in all, by approving the increase, Truman had much to gain and little to lose.

Lovett, meanwhile, continued to press for a broad statement of policy that would confirm the military's paramount role in atomic energy affairs. He wanted the Defense Department to be able to decide not only weapons-use and requirements policy but also such other questions as the future custody and control of weapons, the sharing of information with other countries, and even weapons storage and security arrangements. His efforts, however, met with mixed success. Although Truman agreed that solutions to these issues were needed, he seemed to be growing tired of the whole nuclear problem and deferred again to action through the Special Committee. Consequently, Acheson and Dean, intent on preserving their own agencies' influence, effectively blocked the military from usurping control of policy.[101] The net result was a watery statement of "Agreed Concepts Regarding Atomic Weapons," approved by Truman in September 1952 but still awaiting implementation when he left office the following January.[102] As far as Truman was concerned, it appears, he had wrestled with these problems long enough; now it was up to his successors.

All the same, Truman left a distinct and lasting legacy. Not only had he ordered the use of the atomic bomb in World War II, thereby demonstrating its awesome power; he had also presided over the creation of a defense establishment whose mainstay was nuclear weapons at a time, indeed, when nuclear weapons were becoming the country's first line of defense. Even though Truman often voiced regret over his decisions leading to this situation, it is hard to see how it could have been otherwise. The nuclear past was part of the future.

NOTES

1. Ltr, Truman to Acheson, Jan. 31, 1950, *FRUS 1950*, I, 141-142.
2. The bibliography on NSC 68 is large and growing. See in particular Samuel F. Wells, Jr., "Sounding the Tocsin: NSC 68 and the Soviet Threat," *International Security* 4 (Fall 1979): 116-158; Joseph M. Siracusa, *Rearming for the Cold War* (Los Angeles: Center for the Study of Armament and Disarmament, 1983); Sam Postbrief, "Departure from Incrementalism," *Naval War College Review* 33 (March-April 1980): 34-57; Paul Y. Hammond, "NSC-68: Prologue to Rearmament," in Warner R. Schilling, Paul Y. Hammond, and Glenn H. Snyder, *Strategy, Politics, and Defense Budgets* (New York: Columbia University Press, 1962); and John C. Donovan, *The Cold Warriors: A Policy-Making Elite* (Lexington, Mass.: D.C. Heath, 1974), ch. 4.
3. Paul H. Nitze, "The Relationship of Strategic and Theater Nuclear Forces," *International Security* 2 (Fall 1977): 124-125.
4. Acheson memcon, Mar. 24, 1950, *FRUS 1950*, I, 207.
5. Huntington, *Common Defense*, 41; Hammond, "NSC-68: Prologue to Rearmament," 287. The most thorough analysis of Kennan's thinking is David Mayers, *George F. Kennan and the Dilemmas of U.S. Foreign Policy* (New York: Oxford University Press, 1988).
6. Dean Acheson, "'Total Diplomacy' to Strengthen U.S. Leadership for Human Freedom," *Department of State Bulletin*, XXII (Mar. 20, 1950): 427.

7. Ltr, Acheson to Edward B. Burling, Sept. 20, 1961, in David S. McLellan and David C. Acheson (eds.), *Among Friends: Personal Letters of Dean Acheson* (New York: Dodd, Mead, 1980), 212.
8. Nitze, *From Hiroshima to Glasnost*, 50.
9. Paul H. Nitze, "Military Power: A Strategic View," *The Fletcher Forum* 5 (Winter 1981): 154.
10. Memo, Johnson to SecArmy, et al., Aug. 31, 1949, OASD (ISP) collection, OSD Historian.
11. Acheson, *Present at the Creation*, 374.
12. Walter S. Poole, *The History of the Joint Chiefs of Staff: The Joint Chiefs of Staff and National Policy*, vol. IV, 1950-1952 (Washington, D.C.: Historical Div., Joint Secretariat, JCS, 1976), 28.
13. Carl W. Borklund, *Men of the Pentagon: From Forrestal to McNamara* (New York: Frederick A. Praeger, 1966), 86. Also see "Johnson Relies on Our Air Force for Resisting Any Atomic Attack," *New York Times*, Mar. 4, 1950.
14. Nitze, *From Hiroshima to Glasnost*, 94. Also see the Oral History Interview with Nitze by Richard D. McKinzie, Aug. 4, 1975, Northeast Harbor, Maine, No. 4, Oral History Collection, HSTL.
15. Acheson, *Present at the Creation*, 373; Memcon, Mar. 22, 1950, *FRUS 1950*, I, 203-206.
16. Memo, Johnson to Truman, Apr. 11, 1950, RG 330, CD 16-1-17.
17. For Johnson's skepticism, see Rearden, *Formative Years*, 533-534.
18. Acheson memcon, Mar. 24, 1950, *FRUS 1950*, I, 207.
19. "NSC-68: A Report to the National Security Council by the Executive Secretary on United States Objectives and Programs for National Security," Apr. 14, 1950, *Naval War College Review* 27 (May-June 1975): 53, 64. Hereafter cited as "NSC-68".
20. Paul H. Nitze, "The Development of NSC 68," *International Security* 4 (Spring 1980): 173.
21. Acheson, *Present at the Creation*, 374.
22. Hammond, "NSC-68: Prologue to Rearmament," 372.
23. "NSC 68," 108.
24. *Ibid.*, 98.
25. *Ibid.*, 84-85.
26. Ltr, Robert W. Tufts to Steven L. Rearden, Apr. 14, 1989, copy in Nitze papers, L.C.
27. Hammond, "NSC-68: Prologue to Rearmament," 321.
28. This is based on the authors' conversations with Nitze.
29. Ltr, Truman to Exec. Sec. NSC, Apr. 12, 1950, *FRUS 1950*, I, 234-235; Mins., 55th Mtg. NSC, Apr. 20, 1950, PSF, NSC Series, box 207, Mtg. No. 54 folder, Truman Papers.
30. Mtg, Armed Forces Policy Council, Apr. 25, 1950, Ohly Collection, OSD Historian; memo, Johnson to Service Secretaries, et al., May 25, 1950, RG 330, CD 16-1-17.

31. Mins, 68th Mtg NSC, Sep. 29, 1950, PSF, NSC Series, box 209, Mtg. No. 68 folder, Truman Papers.

32. Memo for the Record, May 23, 1950, sub: Mtg with the President, box 6, Mtgs with the President folder, Frederick J. Lawton Papers, HSTL.

33. Doris Condit, *History of the Office of the Secretary of Defense: The Test of War, 1950-1953* (Washington, D.C.: Historical Office, Office of the Secretary of Defense, 1988), 224-227, 241.

34. Memo to the President, July 27, 1950, sub: Discussion at 62nd Meeting NSC, July 27, 1950, RG 273, Records of the NSC, NARA.

35. NSC 73/4, *FRUS 1950*, I, 378.

36. See Marc Trachtenberg, "A 'Wasting Asset': American Strategy and the Shifting Nuclear Balance, 1949-1954," *International Security* 13 (Winter 1988/89): 11-17.

37. D. Condit, *Test of War*, 463-464; Hewlett and Duncan, *Atomic Shield*, 524-525; Norman Friedman, *U.S. Aircraft Carriers: An Illustrated Design History* (Annapolis, Md.: Naval Institute Press, 1983), 248.

38. *FRUS 1950*, III, 197-204.

39. *New York Times*, Aug. 26, 1950: 1,6.

40. Quoted in Futrell, *Ideas, Concepts, Doctrine, 1907-1960*, 295.

41. D. Condit, *Test of War*, 58-62; James F. Schnabel, *United States Army in the Korean War: Policy and Direction—The First Year* (Washington, D.C.: Office of the Chief of Military History, 1972), 86-99; Acheson memcon, Oct. 10, 1950, *FRUS 1950*, I, 401.

42. Memo for the Record, July 22, 1950, sub: Mtg with the President, box 6, Mtgs with the President folder, Lawton Papers.

43. Rearden, *Formative Years*, 534.

44. Futrell, *Ideas, Concepts, Doctrine, 1907-1960*, 318.

45. Poole, *JCS and National Policy, 1950-1952*, 53-56; memo to NSC Staff, Aug. 23, 1950, sub: Mtg. Ad Hoc Committee on NSC 68, Aug. 22, 1950, *FRUS 1950*, I, 373-374.

46. Memo, James S. Lay, Jr., to Truman, Sep. 28, 1950, [sub: Instructions on Handling of NSC 68], PSF, NSC Series, box 209, Mtg. No. 68 folder, HSTL.

47. Memo to the President, Oct. 2, 1950, [sub: Summary of Discussion at 68th Mtg NSC, Sep. 29, 1950], PSF, NSC file, box 220, NSC Mtgs 1950 folder.

48. "Address in San Francisco at the War Memorial Opera House," Oct. 17, 1950, *Truman Public Papers, 1950*, 676-677.

49. "Address in New York City Before U.N. General Assembly," Oct. 24, 1950, *ibid.*, 685-686.

50. Lovett quoted at Mtg, Armed Forces Policy Council, Oct. 17, 1950, in D. Condit, *Test of War*, 232.

51. Memo, JCS to SecDef, Nov. 19, 1950, sub: US Objectives and Programs for National Security (NSC 68), summarized in Poole, *JCS and National Policy, 1950-1952*, 64-65.

52. Truman's reference to a "hostile Congress" probably reflected his irritation over the outcome of the 1950 congressional elections which reduced the

Democratic majority in the Senate from 12 to 2 and cut it by two-thirds in the House of Representatives.

53. Memo to the President, Nov. 24, 1950, sub: Discussion at the 72d Mtg NSC (Nov. 22, 1950), PSF, NSC file, box 220, NSC Mtgs 1950 folder, HSTL.

54. Cable, MacArthur to JCS, Nov. 28, 1950, *FRUS 1950*, VII, 1237.

55. Quoted in Ferrell (ed.), *Off the Record*, 204.

56. *Truman Public Papers, 1950*, 727.

57. Record of mtg, Dec. 2, 1950, in H. J. Yasamee and K. A. Hamilton (eds.), *Documents on British Policy Overseas*, series II, vol. IV, *Korea, June 1950-April 1951* (London: HMSO, 1991), 235.

58. M. L. Dockrill, "The Foreign Office, Anglo-American relations and the Korean War, June 1950-June 1951," *International Affairs* (London) 62 (Summer 1986): 465.

59. Cable, LeMay to Vandenberg, Dec. 2, 1950, LeMay Papers, box B-196, B-8552 folder, L.C. Also see Roger Dingman, "Atomic Diplomacy During the Korean War," *International Security* 13 (Winter 1988/89): 50-91.

60. See NIE-3, Nov. 15, 1950, sub: Soviet Capabilities and Intentions, *FRUS 1950*, I, 414-416.

61. NSC 68/4, Dec. 14, 1950, *ibid.*, 467-474.

62. Memo to the President, Dec. 15, 1950, sub: Discussion at 75th Mtg NSC, Dec. 14, 1950, PSF, NSC file, box 220, NSC Mtgs 1950 folder, HSTL.

63. Most of the additional forces were scheduled to become part of the strategic reserve in the United States, with a substantial allocation of forces—4 army divisions and 35 air wings—earmarked for deployment to Europe. See Ernest R. May, "The American Commitment to Germany, 1949-55," *Diplomatic History* 13 (Fall 1989): 440-444; and Poole, *JCS and National Policy, 1950-52*, 57.

64. Marcelle Size Knaack, *Encyclopedia of U.S. Air Force Aircraft and Missile Systems*, vol. II, *Post-World War II Bombers, 1945-1973* (Washington, D.C.: Office of Air Force History, 1988), 99-157.

65. D. Condit, *Test of War*, 223-242.

66. Memo, Record of State-JCS Mtg, Jan. 24, 1951, *FRUS 1951*, I, 35. Also see NIE-15, Dec. 11, 1950, sub: Probable Soviet Moves to Exploit the Present Situation, *ibid.*, 4-7.

67. Memo, Col. David A. Burchinal to Asst. for Programming, DCS/O, et al., Nov. 23, 1951, sub: Air Force FY 1953 Program, Twining Papers, box 117, AF Council 1951-52 folder, L.C.; Daniel T. Kuehl, "Refighting the Last War: Electronic Warfare and U.S. Air Force B-29 Operations in the Korean War, 1950-53," *Journal of Military History* 56 (Jan. 1992): 87-111.

68. D. Condit, *Test of War*, 250-260.

69. In fact, the FY 1952 defense budget set a record that not even the Reagan buildup of the 1980s broke. Measured in constant (FY 1988) dollars, the budget for FY 1952 came to $349.8 billion, compared with the largest defense budget request of the Reagan years (FY 1989) which came to $323.3 billion. See U.S. Department of Defense, *National Defense Budget Estimates for FY 1988/1989*

(Washington, D.C.: Office of the Assistant Secretary of Defense [Comptroller], May 1987), 98-100.

70. John W. Spanier, *The Truman-MacArthur Controversy and the Korean War* (Cambridge, Mass: Harvard University Press, 1959).

71. Hewlett and Duncan, *Atomic Shield*, 558-559.

72. U.S. *Congressional Record*, Sep. 11, 1951, vol. 97, Pt. 8, 11134-11135. Also see Kolodziej, *The Uncommon Defense and Congress, 1945-1963*, 150f.

73. Futrell, *Ideas, Concepts, Doctrine, 1907-1960*, 323-325; D. Condit, *Test of War*, 261-262.

74. Memo, Lay to NSC, July 12, 1951, sub: US Objectives and Programs for National Security, *FRUS 1951*, I, 101-103.

75. NSC 114/1, Aug. 8, 1951, sub: Status and Timing of Current US Programs for National Security, *ibid.*, 127-148.

76. Memo, Nitze to Acheson, July 31, 1951, sub: The Issues in NSC 114, *ibid.*, 110-112.

77. Memo to the President, June 28, 1951, sub: Summary of Discussion at 95th Mtg NSC, RG 273, NARA.

78. Memo to the President, Aug. 2, 1951, sub: Summary of Discussion at 98th Mtg NSC, Aug. 1, 1951, PSF, NSC file, box 220, NSC Mtgs 1951 folder, HSTL.

79. See Kolodziej, *The Uncommon Defense and Congress, 1945-1963*, 151.

80. Memo to the President, Oct. 18, 1951, sub: Summary of Discussion at 105th Mtg NSC, Oct. 17, 1951, PSF, NSC file, box 220, NSC Mtgs 1951 folder, HSTL.

81. Memo to the President, June 28, 1951, sub: Summary of Discussion at 95th Mtg, NSC, RG 273, NARA.

82. Futrell, *Ideas, Concepts, Doctrine, 1907-1960*, 325.

83. Memo, SecDef to JCS, Nov. 9, 1951, quoted in Poole, *JCS and National Policy, 1950-1952*, 116.

84. BoB memo, Oct. 16, 1951, sub: Budgetary Implications of Major National Security Programs, Harriman Papers, box 323, Budget Bureau folder, L.C.

85. U.S. Congress, Committee on Appropriations, *Hearings: Department of Defense Appropriations for 1953*, 82:2 (Washington, D.C.: G.P.O., 1852), 89; D. Condit, *Test of War*, 276-283.

86. Draft Memo by Arneson, Apr. 24, 1951, *FRUS 1951*, I, 823.

87. Gowing, *Independence and Deterrence*, I, 310.

88. N. J. Wheeler, "British Nuclear Weapons and Anglo-American Relations, 1945-54," *International Affairs* (London) 62 (Winter 1985/86): 73-75.

89. Acheson, *Present at the Creation*, 484. For the US record of these talks, see *FRUS 1950*, II, 1698-1788.

90. See Makins to Bevin, Jan. 10, 1951, in *Documents on British Policy Overseas: Korea, June 1950-April 1951*, 310-312.

91. Gowing, *Independence and Deterrence*, I, 314.

92. *New York Times*, Sep. 5, 1951: 36.

93. See D. Condit, *Test of War*, 467-471; and Hewlett and Duncan, *Atomic Shield*, 522-525, 547-549.

94. U.S. *Congressional Record,* Sep. 18, 1951, vol. 97, Pt. 9, 82:1: 11496-11499.

95. D. Condit, *Test of War,* 471.

96. Hewlett and Duncan, *Atomic Shield,* 576. Also see Dean's diary entries in Anders (ed.), *Forging the Atomic Shield,* ch. 4.

97. Memo, Lovett to JCS, Nov. 3, 1951, quoted in Poole, *JCS and National Policy, 1950-52,* 152.

98. "Statement of the Views of the Joint Chiefs of Staff on Dept. of Defense Interest in the Use of Atomic Weapons," enclosure to memo, Lovett to Lay, Feb. 6, 1952, *FRUS 1952-54,* II, 863-868.

99. Memo to the President, Jan. 17, 1952, [sub: Discussion on Jan. 16, 1952, of Special Committee of the NSC on Atomic Energy], *FRUS 1952-54,* II, 861-858.

100. Roger M. Anders, *Institutional Origins of the Department of Energy: The Office of Military Application* (Washington, D.C.: U.S. Dept. of Energy, 1980), 4-5. Stockpile figures are unofficial estimates, from Thomas B. Cochran, William M. Arkin, and Milton M. Hoenig, *Nuclear Weapons Databook,* vol. I, *U.S. Nuclear Forces and Capabilities* (Cambridge, Mass.: Ballinger, 1984), 15.

101. Poole, *JCS and National Policy, 1950-52,* 154, 159; *FRUS 1952-54,* II, 947-953, 969-973, 973-979, 984-988.

102. *FRUS 1952-54,* II, 1011-1013.

VII

SAC and the Anglo-American Connection

The Korean re-armament was a multibillion-dollar effort, the first of its kind in the "peacetime" history of the United States. Not only did it more than treble the size of the American defense budget, but also it earmarked substantial additional funds for foreign military assistance, anti-Soviet propaganda on an unprecedented scale, and stepped-up covert operations. NSC 68 had posited that a major objective of the defense buildup was less American dependence on nuclear weapons. But, as we have already seen, the costs and other consequences of such a policy appeared, or so it seemed, both prohibitive and beyond the willingness of American decision-makers to risk. Thus, by 1952, a curtailment of the re-armament program gradually began, with conventional forces the most immediately affected. Once more, strategic air power and nuclear weapons became the bulwark of American and Western defenses.

Integral to this process were two further developments: the emergence of an effective strikeforce—the Strategic Air Command—to give credibility to a US defense posture reliant upon nuclear weapons; and the development of effective collaboration with US allies, chiefly the British. Given the vital nature of British bases, close Anglo-American ties at both the operational and policy levels were crucial. With the impetus of the Korean War, it became all the more urgent. But while US and British interests apparently converged, underlying stresses and strains always threatened to sour the relationship. Like the United States, the European allies eventually found the burdens of a conventional military buildup more than they could reasonably bear. But the British became the first to develop a rationale—one that anticipated the American "new look" associated with the Eisenhower years—for the utilization of nuclear weapons to compensate.

THE EMERGENCE OF SAC

Of the Korean War's various legacies, none had more far-reaching consequences than the rapid expansion of SAC. On the eve of the war, SAC was a force of 71,000 personnel, 19 bomber wings (some without planes), and about 900 aircraft, of which fewer than a third (264) were equipped for atomic bombing. By 1953, SAC's personnel had more than doubled in size, while at the same time its operational capabilities had increased to over 1,600 aircraft (nearly all atomic-capable) organized into 39 wings and 23 separate squadrons.[1] As the 1950s progressed, SAC would grow even larger, becoming in the words of one historian "an air force within the Air Force."[2] Although the results might well have been the same even without the war's stimulus, the Korean struggle and its spin-off effects clearly assured SAC a special niche atop the military hierarchy. There it would stay for the next several decades.

From late 1948 to 1957, Lt. Gen. (later General) Curtis E. LeMay was the driving force behind SAC's early development. What LeMay found when he took command of SAC was an ill-equipped, ill-trained, and ill-organized operation, barely able to pose a credible threat to any would-be aggressor. Built around the 509th Composite Bombardment Group (the only one then in the Air Force flying SILVERPLATE B-29s capable of air-atomic warfare), SAC was a rather motley collection of personnel and equipment with dubious capabilities. Apart from the 509th, the remaining SAC units flew conventionally configured B-29s of World War II–vintage or a somewhat improved version of the same plane (designated the B-50) that became operational in the summer of 1948. The B-29 had a combat radius of less than 2,000, the most advanced B-50 a radius only slightly greater. Neither had sufficient range to attack intercontinental targets. And since SAC had access at this time to few suitable overseas bases, its ability to respond in a serious emergency would have been sorely lacking. Later, in 1948, as a means of extending its reach, SAC began to organize its first squadrons of tanker aircraft (modified B-29s, designated KB-29Ms) for inflight refueling. Around the same time, SAC also took delivery of its first operational B-36s, allegedly with a range of 8,000 miles. But because of the plane's numerous and well publicized defects, its reliability and effectiveness were open to question. "As a deterrent to aggression in its early years," concluded one senior Air Force officer, "SAC was far more symbol than reality."[3]

LeMay's advent in 1948, which coincided with a budgetary policy that placed enhanced stress on strategic bombing, was the turning point in SAC's fortunes. An architect of the air campaigns against Germany and Japan in

World War II, LeMay regarded strategic bombardment as the most potent weapon in the American arsenal. SAC, he believed, would be the force most likely to restrain Russia's aggressive behavior. "SAC," he argued, "is what they are afraid of." Emphasizing his command's nuclear capabilities, LeMay wanted to be able "to deliver a decisive atomic attack in the minimum possible time interval." In practical terms, this meant developing the capacity to deliver 80 percent of the US nuclear arsenal on the Soviet Union in one concerted blow. The entire campaign, he estimated, should last not more than thirty days.[4]

As David Alan Rosenberg has pointed out, LeMay was not a sophisticated strategist. His philosophy of warfare derived from practical considerations rather than from elaborate conceptual models or insights garnered from reading Clausewitz or other military thinkers.[5] The first of his concerns, as during World War II, was to minimize losses to his aircraft and crews and to maximize the impact of the offensive on the enemy, if necessary by striking first. "Any responsible Air Force officer will not advocate a preventive war," he told an interviewer in 1950, shortly after Gen. Orvil Anderson had been relieved for voicing such thoughts, "but you do have to risk it and be ready to fight."[6] Accordingly, in preparing for whatever contingency might arise, LeMay gave priority to improving combat proficiency through rigorous training that stressed realistic flying missions. But despite being a demanding taskmaster, LeMay also paid close attention to the welfare of his men—their housing, food, working conditions, and especially their morale—in the belief that if SAC could satisfy personal needs, airmen would perform better and be more likely to re-enlist.[7]

Not surprisingly, LeMay assembled a like-minded staff ardently devoted to strategic bombing. As long as he commanded SAC, LeMay insisted that it be in the hands of what he termed the "right people," usually meaning friends and colleagues from World War II, including Thomas S. Power, LeMay's subordinate in the Pacific and deputy and successor as commanding general of SAC. Others who figured prominently in SAC's buildup were Walter "Cam" Sweeney, Emmett "Rosie" O'Donnell, Francis "Grizzy" Griswold, J. B. Montgomery, and Clarence "Bill" Irvine, LeMay's maintenance expert during the war and the man upon whom he relied initially as commander of the 509th to guarantee SAC an effective nuclear capability. As LeMay recalled, "I started gathering the old boys in, fast as I could."[8] The result was a group of senior officers who not only knew one another well and worked comfortably together, but who also brought a similar mindset to almost any problem they encountered.

LeMay and his command faced formidable challenges. Funding restrictions and chronic equipment shortages, especially in aircraft engines and spare parts, often kept planes and crews from meeting their training schedules. "As you well know," LeMay complained to his superiors in 1950, "for the past two years we have been operating, materiel-wise, on a hand-to-mouth basis to keep the Strategic Air Command going at only a peace-time rate." Though the increased budgets of the Korean buildup helped to alleviate these problems, the demands on limited contractor production capacity meant that SAC could not always count on getting what it needed on time. So great, in fact, did the shortage of B-50 engines become in the fall of 1950 that LeMay estimated that SAC might be grounded by the end of the year.[9]

The lack of reliable intelligence on Soviet targets further complicated the task of SAC planners. Existing maps in the late 1940s and early 1950s were generally old and untrustworthy, some dating from as far back as czarist days, owing to the absence (until the appearance of the U-2 spy plane in 1956) of direct overhead reconnaissance. Often the only available information on possible targets came from Russian emigrés, returning German POWs, or captured German World War II records, including photographs so outdated as to make synthetic radar target predictions exceedingly difficult.[10] As a result, Air Force planners, in line with accepted targeting doctrine, initially concentrated targeting on some 70 urban-industrial targets—in part because they were thought to be crucial to the Soviet warmaking economy, but also because they were the most readily identifiable to find and hit.[11] Similar targeting procedures, using conventional munitions, had been employed with devastating effect in World War II, both by RAF Bomber Command in the area-bombing of Germany and toward the end of the war by the US Twentieth Air Force in the fire-raids against Japan. With the increasing availability of nuclear weapons, the results were expected to be greatly magnified, leading some Air Force targeting specialists to speculate that atomic air power could someday have the capacity to "kill a nation."[12]

Despite its handicaps and limitations, the Air Force's strategic bombing capability was the envy of the other military services, especially the Navy. Under the assignment of service functions worked out by Forrestal and the Joint Chiefs at the 1948 Key West and Newport conferences, the Navy acquired access to nuclear weapons and a share in the strategic bombing mission with the Air Force. But with interservice rivalry then at a fever pitch, the Air Force and the Navy found it exceedingly difficult to work out the details of their collaboration. Moreover, because of budget cutbacks the following year, the development of naval capabilities for strategic bombing was further retarded. Not until the fall of 1949 did the Navy take delivery of the first AJ-1 Savage, the first carrier-based plane specifically designed for nuclear operations. Meanwhile, as a stop-gap measure until the AJ-1 proved out, the Navy initiated nuclear training operations in the spring of 1950 with converted P2V-3C Neptune patrol planes, most of which were based aboard carriers operating in the Mediterranean. But with a range of only 600 miles, these planes posed a threat only to Soviet submarine pens and other coastal installations; anything deeper inland was SAC's responsibility.[13] Thus, even though the Navy's capacity for nuclear missions was growing, it was still no match for what SAC had to offer.

THE CONTROVERSY OVER TARGETING DOCTRINE

With a near-monopoly on the nuclear mission, SAC was also able to dominate the targeting process, responsibility for which fell under the Air Intelligence Production Division (AIPD) of the Air Force. While the Army and the Navy had representatives on the AIPD, their input, compared with that of the Air Force, was negligible. Final review and approval of AIPD-produced target lists rested with the Joint Chiefs, but rarely did the Chiefs make significant changes. As a result, Air Force target priorities, concentrating on counter-economy bombing practices developed by the Army Air Forces in World War II—with only token concessions to the other services' interests—predominated. As approved by the JCS in December 1949, the air war against the Soviet Union would involve the delivery of 292 atomic bombs (more than were actually then in the stockpile) and 17,610 tons of conventional bombs against a variety of industrial targets, including petroleum refineries, electric power plants, aircraft, automotive, and submarine factories, transportation, and synthetic ammonia plants.[14]

Nonetheless, the December 1949 targeting decision did not end inter-service problems. Rather, targeting increasingly became a source of tension among the services, each of which had its own idea of what strategic bombing of the Soviet Union should accomplish. The Army, with growing responsibilities for the ground defense of Western Europe, wanted more emphasis on retardation bombing to impede advancing Soviet ground forces in the event of war. As a first step, Army Chief of Staff Gen. J. Lawton Collins lobbied his colleagues on the JCS to include in the 1949 targeting guidance a requirement for retardation bombing to become part of US strategy. By contrast, the Air Force and, to a lesser extent, the Navy thought that strategic bombardment should be directed against the Soviet homeland. But while acceding to the Army's position, the Air Force neatly side-stepped any real responsibility for retardation bombing by insisting that its attacks on Soviet industry and transportation would eventually slow, if not stop, the Soviet advance into Western Europe. Hence, even though US war plans at this time incorporated provision for retardation bombing, there were no specific requirements for holding assets in reserve for this purpose.[15]

In the final analysis, it was SAC's opposition to retardation bombing that ruled Air Force thinking on the subject. Though he sometimes paid it lip service, LeMay never believed that retardation bombing was an essential or intended part of SAC's mission. He believed it necessary, instead, "to realize that SAC is not designed for close or general support of ground forces—that it is designed to deliver an atomic offensive against the heart of an enemy wherever that may happen to be and whenever the situation demands."[16] Elaborating, he argued that too close a distinction between retardation targets and strategic targets would result in "a division of forces" that would end up benefiting no one but the Soviets. "I would point out," he added, "that the targets of both categories . . . are strategic in the classical sense of the word."[17]

LeMay also opposed retardation bombing because it would establish claims on his planes and crews at a time when he believed SAC had to begin planning for a wholly different—and more demanding—future mission. Looking ahead, he alerted his superiors as early as May 1950 that SAC's future targeting priorities would be radically different by mid-1954, the so-called "year of maximum danger" cited in NSC 68 as the date by which the Soviets were expected to have enough nuclear weapons and long-range planes to threaten serious damage to the United States. When that became the case, LeMay argued, the first US attack in mid-1954 should be against Soviet long-range air, with the bombing of economic centers coming thereafter.[18] Here, in embryonic form, were the priorities that would give rise, as the 1950s progressed, to the Air Force doctrine of counterforce and the idea of dealing a decisive strike against the enemy's most threatening opposing forces.

The Joint Chiefs, endeavoring to reconcile continuing differences among themselves over targeting objectives, reached a similar conclusion concerning the allocation of assets for strategic bombing. In August 1950 they established three priority tasks. First came the "blunting," or elimination, of the Soviet Union's air-atomic capabilities; second, retardation bombing of advancing Soviet ground forces; and third, the destruction of key war-supporting facilities in the Soviet urban-industrial complex, with a concentration on liquid fuel, electric power, and atomic energy plants. Subsequently, the JCS gave each of these targeting categories a codename: BRAVO (for blunting), ROMEO (for retardation), and DELTA (for disruption-destruction of industry).[19]

To implement the Joint Chiefs' targeting scheme, SAC planners estimated that they would have to be able to mobilize at least 150 medium bombardment wings or their equivalent within days of the outbreak of war.[20] Because budgetary constraints meant that such a goal could never be met, even with the substantial increases occasioned by Korea, LeMay concluded that a bombardment campaign of sustained operations such as those in Word War II was not practical or feasible. Likewise, for strategic purposes, he discounted the use of conventional munitions and began to focus more closely on the execution of "a large atomic attack" that would inflict devastating blows against the Soviet Union before the Soviets could respond in kind. "All of our efforts," he reported in January 1951, "are being aimed toward this end."[21]

As it happened, SAC's burden of responsibility proved somewhat less than its planners had anticipated. In fact, none of the targets on the first AIPD list prepared in accordance with the Joint Chiefs' August 1950 guidelines fell into either the BRAVO or ROMEO categories.[22] All the same, LeMay objected to this targeting guidance on the grounds that it would require SAC to search out and destroy too many individual targets, thus increasing the risk to his planes and their crews and dissipating the overall effect of the bombing. By early 1951, despite alleged equipment shortages, SAC could deploy and launch an attack utilizing approximately 135 atomic bombs within six days. Just over half this number could be delivered in the first three days of the assault. If prior warning were available, allowing SAC to preposition its forces at forward bases, LeMay estimated that he could launch all 135 bombs within three days. Subsequent attacks would be progressively reduced, depending on the results of bomb damage assessments and new target information. But he worried that under the Joint Chiefs' directive, SAC's assets would be spread too thin to achieve the desired effect of crippling the Soviet Union's warmaking capacity. Any additional missions, he argued, were utterly out of the question. "Intelligence on which to base counter-weapons and retardation attacks," he insisted, "is still practically non-existent."[23]

LeMay agreed with priority on petroleum and atomic weapons, but he saw problems with trying to identify and destroy individual electric power plants. To make the most use of its resources, LeMay argued, SAC should be allowed to concentrate its assault on industrial areas where bombing would yield "bonus" damage to civilian urban centers.[24] After reviewing the matter in early 1951, the USAF Air Staff concurred on the need for a new targeting study—one more in line with LeMay's views, namely that (1) in the DELTA category, urban-industrial complexes rather than specific industries, should be the focus of attack; and

(2) in dealing with BRAVO and ROMEO targets, SAC should have latitude to decide when and where to bomb.[25] Eventually, in July 1951, the Joint Chiefs agreed.[26] From this point on, SAC's control of the targeting process became firmer than ever, a distinct advantage for the Air Force but a source of continuing interservice friction.

PROJECT VISTA

Having failed to lay claim to some of SAC's assets for retardation bombing, the Army turned increasingly, as the 1950s progressed, to developing nuclear fire support of its own. The Army achieved this by exploiting recent breakthroughs in smaller atomic warheads suitable for short-range rockets, missiles, and artillery with battlefield applications. But even though a variety of such weapons had been on the AEC's drawing boards for years, not all Army planners concurred that they would have a viable application. Atomic weapons, some thought, no matter what their designation, were simply too potent and risky for battlefield use. But with the demands of the Korean War and re-armament growing, this line of thinking was beginning to change, as the Army sought to come to terms with the problems of defending Europe and, like the Navy, to establish a claim to the nuclear mission.

As part of this process, the secretaries of the Army, Navy, and Air Force early in 1951 commissioned the California Institute of Technology to study the tactical potential of atomic weapons in defending Europe. Known as Project "Vista," the study gathered together a scientific and technical staff of 113 members, including atomic scientist J. Robert Oppenheimer, and others who had worked with one another in World War II on the Manhattan Project. The thrust of the resulting report, completed in February 1952, was that "the successful defense of Western Europe may hinge mainly on the extent to which the United States and Allied tactical [nuclear] air power is effectively employed." Accordingly, the report urged the building of a NATO tactical nuclear air force of some 10,000 planes to counter Soviet air operations and to provide support for NATO ground forces; and the stock-piling of more tactical-sized nuclear weapons, a proposal especially favored by Oppenheimer, who hoped it would reduce and possibly reverse what he saw as an ominously growing reliance on strategic nuclear forces.[27]

These recommendations promised to solve a host of problems. With budgetary cutbacks ever more likely, reliance on tactical nuclear weapons seemed a fairly easy and economical way to augment firepower for the European land battle, while permitting force reductions. By the spring of

1952, NATO's arsenal of tactical nuclear weapons was on its way to becoming reality. The first installment of delivery vehicles, all deployed to bases in Britain, consisted of one wing of U.S. F-84 fighter-bombers and another wing of B-45 light bombers, all modified to carry relatively small, low-yield atomic bombs.[28]

These developments came about despite objections raised by powerful elements within the Air Force, SAC especially. Because fissionable material was still relatively scarce, LeMay and Secretary of the Air Force Thomas K. Finletter worried that an arsenal of tactical-sized bombs on the scale the Vista study envisioned would interfere with the production of weapons for strategic purposes and thereby jeopardize SAC's effectiveness. As an alternative approach to the problem, LeMay proposed closer coordination between SAC and NATO. In October 1951 he set up a command post called SAC Zebra, stationed in Europe. The functions of this element were to control SAC forces operating in the NATO theater and to coordinate any atomic missions flown in support of allied forces. However, under the ground rules, as many as four commanders, representing not only SAC but also the various command elements in NATO Europe and the Mediterranean, could schedule attacks against the same target. This seemed to auger a great number of duplicating attacks in the event of war. But in view of SAC's pre-eminent interests and position, LeMay assumed that, in the selection of targets and the allocation of assets, SAC would have the dominant and final voice, giving it control of not only the strategic mission but of tactical operations as well. In any case, the acquisition by NATO of a tactical nuclear capability did not, as it turned out, materially impede SAC's capabilities. Indeed, in some respects it promised to enhance them. Nor did it lessen reliance on strategic forces, as Oppenheimer and others who worked on the Vista study hoped would happen.[29]

BRITAIN, BASES, AND BOMBERS

A key factor in SAC's growing confidence was the increasing availability by the early 1950s of overseas bases. Though SAC had not yet attained the intercontinental reach so desired by LeMay and others, progress in that direction was steady. In-flight refueling techniques, carefully planned and flown routes, and the availability of forward staging bases in Britain, the Azores, North America, and elsewhere around the Eurasian land mass, gave SAC planners growing confidence their bombers could strike at any portion of the Russian target complex.[30]

Of all the bases available to SAC, those in the United Kingdom were paramount. Not only were they a principal launch point for attacks on the Soviet Union, they were also the main recycling centers under US war plans for planes and crews returning from missions that originated outside Britain.[31] The presence of SAC bombers in England, as we have already seen, dated from the early days of acute tension surrounding the 1948 Berlin crisis when, as an emergency precaution, the British government had agreed to host two groups of American B-29s. What began as a temporary arrangement, organized as a standard 30-day rotation of planes and crews, soon became permanent, and led the following year (1949) to the routine deployment of nuclear-capable B-29s and B-50s. By 1950, SAC had access to three bases in East Anglia—at Mildenhall, Sculthorpe, and Lakenheath—and wanted access to four more in Oxfordshire.[32] Under the resulting protocol known as the Ambassador's Agreement, signed in April 1950, both countries agreed to share the cost of refurbishing these bases, though the main burden of maintenance expenses (as well a substantial capital outlay on the extension of runways) fell on the British.[33]

London's willingness to undertake these obligations reflected in turn both its heightened concern about the Soviet threat, made all the more evident and urgent by the Soviet atomic test of August 1949, and British defense planners' considerable confidence in the deterrent value of nuclear weapons. For the latter reason, and to shore up Britain's faltering international prestige, the Attlee Government in 1947 had decided to develop an independent nuclear deterrent, a laborious and time-consuming project that was not expected to bear fruit for some years. Subsequently, the RAF initiated design studies of aircraft capable of air-atomic missions. But because of the Ten Year Rule of 1947, mandating cutbacks in military spending, the RAF could not expect to have an advanced jet bomber delivery capability before the mid-1950s.[34]

Britain had no choice, then, but to rely for some time on whatever protection the American nuclear arsenal offered. Indeed, as British Defence Minister Emanuel Shinwell told the cabinet a month before the signing of the Ambassador's Agreement, it was "desirable to persuade the Americans to keep their air forces in the United Kingdom." While Shinwell was committed to obtaining the best deal possible, he also felt that in "the last resort . . . it would be right to make some concessions."[35] Some Britons feared that the presence of American bases would increase chances of the United Kingdom becoming a primary target of a Soviet nuclear attack. However, British defense planners downplayed the immediate danger. They doubted that Moscow's stockpile of atomic bombs (estimated by British intelligence at around ten at the beginning of 1950 and likely to reach no more than 30 by the end of the year) constituted a serious threat. Nor did they believe that the Soviets would risk initiating a war with nuclear weapons, given the American preponderance for retaliation.[36] Not until 1956, at the earliest, did British intelligence foresee any risk of the American advantage being challenged.[37] The British military thus tended to place perhaps even more faith in the atomic arsenal than did their American allies. The overall result, as Margaret Gowing has observed, was to generate "a feeling that atomic weapons were a manifestation of the scientific and technological superiority on which Britain's strength, so deficient if measured in sheer numbers of men, must depend."[38]

At the working level, the Ambassador's Agreement signaled the beginning of the restoration of Anglo-American military ties, which had gone slack since World War II. After years of uneasy relations brought on by misunderstandings over the McMahon Act, the protracted negotiations leading to the 1948 atomic energy *modus vivendi,* espionage revelations, and other impediments, efforts were underway by the spring of 1950 in Washington and London alike to lay aside past differences in favor of strengthening military collaboration. The North Atlantic Treaty, which clearly committed the United States to an active defense role in Europe, had of course formally buttressed the informal Anglo-American alliance. But there were other considerations as well. For the United States, Britain remained the indispensable partner, the essential link in a growing chain of bases that made the American nuclear threat credible. And for Britain, despite the risks involved, the presence of American bombers and bases acted as a powerful deterrent, doing the work that British forces would be incapable of doing until they too acquired a nuclear capability. As a 1950 Foreign Office paper summed up the situation: "We must face the fact that this island is strategically well placed as an advanced air base and we must accept that role."[39]

In Britain, as in the United States, the outbreak of the Korean War in the summer of 1950 touched off a major re-armament effort that quickly exposed major deficiencies. Most glaring, perhaps, was the deplorable condition of the RAF's Bomber Command, which by late 1949 had been reduced to about 160 obsolescent aircraft with neither the range nor the speed to penetrate deep within the Soviet Union.[40] Pending development of a new generation of jet bombers, all of which were still in the design stage, the RAF announced in January 1950 that it had obtained 70 B-29s "on loan" from the United States as part of the US military assistance program for NATO. Unfortunately, none of these planes—designated in Britain as "Washingtons"— could carry atomic bombs; and due to a shortage of spare parts, which hampered training, Bomber Command was never fully able to evaluate their efficiency or effectiveness.[41]

All the same, except for scattered calls from Conservatives in Parliament, Bomber Command found no groundswell of support to restore it to its former strength and glory. By and large, the British experience with strategic bombing in World War II had been an unsatisfactory one. Many Britons felt that what Bomber Command had done, concentrating on "city-busting," had been immoral, counterproductive, and an open invitation for the German *Luftwaffe* to respond in kind. Though they had been exceptionally devastating, such tactics had produced mixed results in terms of deciding the course of the war. Whatever their contribution, the costs to Bomber Command's crews and equipment had been exceedingly heavy.[42] As a result, during the Korean re-armament effort the British Labour government continued to shun Bomber Command. Instead, it preferred to strengthen conventional forces (as favored by the United States for all the NATO allies) and to improve air defenses for the protection of American bomber bases. The latter became its main contribution to the strategic effort. As a cost-saving measure, but indicative at the same time of the low priority it attached to reviving a strategic air component, the government also downgraded the nuclear program, canceled its contract to produce an interim jet-powered replacement for the Washingtons, and put production of the RAF's other new bombers on a par with fighter-interceptors and air-defense guided missiles. But despite this heavy emphasis on conventional capabilities, senior British defense officials never saw conventional forces as a substitute for the deterrent or war-fighting value of American nuclear weapons.[43]

Britain's commitment to a policy of re-arming, not least of all because it accorded with US preferences and interests stressing NSC 68-focused goals of a conventional buildup, earned high praise in Washington and no doubt helped ease the way for even closer Anglo-American collaboration at the strategic level. Following the Truman-Attlee meeting in December 1950, Field Marshal Sir William Slim, Chief of the Imperial General Staff, reported to his colleagues on the Chiefs of Staff Committee that the chairman of the American joint chiefs, Gen. Omar Bradley, "had agreed that planning for the strategic use of the atom bomb in Europe should be carried out jointly between our two countries."[44] Shortly thereafter, contacts intensified appreciably, beginning with "full and complete" briefings for the British Joint Staff Mission in Washington on the situation in Korea. Early the next month, Sir John Slessor, chief of the air staff, came to Washington for the first of what became a regular series of formal exchanges on the situation in the Far East and US strategic air plans. As a reciprocal gesture, Bradley visited the

United Kingdom in May 1951 and gave Slessor a "general indication" of US strategic target systems and the nature of the Soviet and Eastern Bloc installations slated for attack. But he stopped short of revealing either the number of bombs or the number of targets involved.[45]

Having come this far, however, the Americans found themselves under increasing pressure from the British to reveal more and more details. The British were especially anxious to know how and when nuclear weapons might be used, an issue that had bothered Whitehall earlier in connection with reports of the possible US use of atomic weapons in Korea. As Slessor saw it, Britain's lack of full information on US strategic plans—plans that would invariably place Britain in jeopardy—was "quite intolerable."[46] But from the American perspective, the British were making a great deal over nothing. As far as Bradley was concerned, he "had always assumed that we [the United States] could not operate out of British air bases unless the UK were in the war with us since otherwise we would be operating from neutral territory."[47]

In the spring of 1951, as a means of prodding the Americans to reveal more, the British Chiefs of Staff informally passed along to the US State Department a confidential, 22-page paper drafted mainly by Slessor. The paper set forth the Britons' tentative conclusions regarding the possible forms of communist aggression that might necessitate recourse to nuclear weapons.[48] Though not totally successful in eliciting a full disclosure of US plans, the British maneuver did produce a significant clarification of American policy. This took the form of a US paper, similar to that of the British, prepared by representatives of the State Department in collaboration with the Joint Strategic Survey Committee, the senior advisory body to the JCS. The US paper provided hypothetical examples of types of communist aggression that could well provoke a nuclear response. A Soviet attack on Finland or Afghanistan, for example, was unlikely to elicit a US military reaction of any kind; but a Soviet invasion of West Germany would in all probability be strenuously resisted. "In any event," the US report concluded, "the United States must be prepared to use atomic weapons if and when necessary from any and all bases which may be available."[49]

Though never officially adopted in the NSC or endorsed by President Truman as a statement of US policy, this paper became the framework for further Anglo-American discussions. As the talks progressed, Secretary of State Acheson and the Joint Chiefs became somewhat irritated over repeated British requests for information on US war plans. They considered the requests an unwarranted intrusion into American policy and planning. But they also realized that British cooperation, including wartime access to bases in the United Kingdom, remained fundamental for the effective performance of US strategic forces. As Acheson aptly summed up the situation: "We can't successfully take the position that they must give us a blank check. They feel that if a strike takes off from their territory there will be one coming back the other way."[50]

These considerations led to a further series of discussions between senior US and British officials and defense planners in Washington in the early fall of 1951. While less conclusive than the British preferred, these talks did produce an American acknowledgement that the use of British bases affected British sovereignty, and that it was therefore natural that the United States should seek British acquiescence before waging war from the bases. Yet, despite mention of a possible public statement to this effect, nothing materialized at this time. Nor would Washington entertain the idea of a formal commitment which might inhibit its sovereign right to make war should the need arise.[51]

All in all, little was resolved by the 1951 conversations, except to assuage British worries. On this point, obviously, the talks were a qualified success. Even though Whitehall continued to prod and probe, the United States considered the issue closed and was not inclined to offer further concessions or clarifications if it could avoid doing so. Nor, for that matter, did it appear likely that the British government would seek to evict their American visitors. Interdependence on both sides had progressed too far for that, and with international tensions subsiding toward the end of 1951, the concerns that had animated the British in the first place seemed less urgent. Collaboration would continue, but with the clear understanding in both capitals that should an emergency arise, consultations in some form would follow.

THE TWILIGHT OF CONVENTIONAL DETERRENCE

Even while efforts were going forward to guarantee the United States access to bases and facilities for waging nuclear war, American policy aimed at dissuading the NATO allies, including Britain, from becoming too dependent on the US atomic arsenal for their security. As recommended in NSC 68, the United States sought to encourage the European members of NATO to accept the necessity of a conventional buildup that would produce a counterweight to Soviet forces, building what Dean Acheson liked to refer to as "situations of strength." The United States endeavored to set an example—not only by upgrading its own conventional capabilities and by deploying four additional combat divisions to West Germany; but by increasing its military assistance to NATO as a means of subsidizing the heavy burden of re-armament. Except for the British, for whom the United States was willing to make exceptions, as evidenced by providing the B-29s in 1950, American policy discouraged the Europeans from branching out into strategic bombardment; here, an American monopoly was supposed to prevail. Through military aid and other inducements, Washington hoped to persuade its allies to develop and maintain complementary capabilities—tactical air support, air defense, coastal defense, and the "hard core" of NATO's ground forces.[52]

The high point of this policy was the Lisbon meeting of the North Atlantic Council, NATO's senior decision-making organ, in February 1952. In addition to refining plans for West German re-armament through a European Defense Community, the Lisbon meeting endorsed new force-level goals for NATO. The interim aim was a buildup, by the end of 1952, from NATO's current strength of 34 divisions to a total of 51, and a corresponding increase in aircraft from 2,900 to just over 4,000. By the end of 1954 the schedule called for NATO to have an effective force of 89 divisions supported by 9,965 tactical aircraft.[53] Acheson, who had long campaigned for NATO to take these steps, hailed the Lisbon conference as a triumph. But his elation, as he later recalled, was short-lived.[54]

Other than Acheson, in fact, few involved in the Lisbon decision seriously believed that such goals, desirable as they might be, could ever be attained. Well before the conference, W. Averell Harriman, director of the US Mutual Security Program, had warned that the "target for 1954 is unattainable," largely owing to weaknesses in the European allies' economies, but also because of "physical limitations of production of certain types of equipment in the United States."[55] Being more blunt about the Lisbon force goals, one member of the British delegation subsequently described them as "manifestly impossible."[56] Not only was the United States itself in the process of rethinking its re-armament policy, but also there was scant enthusiasm among the Europeans for saddling their economies with heavily increased defense expenditures, beyond those already undertaken at considerable cost in response to Korea. Even with American assistance to defray some of the expense, the Europeans faced daunting costs. The spirit of alliance unity apparently dictated that no one at the time should raise these issues. As a result, the Lisbon goals would remain NATO's benchmark for years to come, but they would never be achieved. In short, the Lisbon formula was a charade, the beginning of the end to NATO's Korean War-inspired re-armament and the eclipse of any hopes of reviving conventional deterrence.[57]

Other strategic solutions quickly presented themselves. One, growing out of the Project Vista findings, placed greater reliance on newly emerging tactical nuclear weapons such as the US Army was studying as an alternative to bombing support from SAC. During preparation of the US FY 1953 military budget, Secretary of Defense Lovett appointed a special interservice panel to report on the strategic impact and practicality of tactical nuclear weapons, a none-too-subtle hint that the services—the Army especially—should pay more attention to these weapons in formulating future budget requests. The panel found that prototype weapons were already available in limited numbers and that more sophisticated production models, suitable for various forms of delivery, would appear within the next several years, helping to reduce the need for large conventional forces.[58]

The first effort to integrate tactical nuclear weapons into battlefield strategy was, however, a miserable disappointment. Known as the Ridgway Plan, it was the product of a series of studies done at NATO headquarters in Europe over the course of 1952 and 1953. Instead of going down, conventional force requirements substantially went up because of planning assumptions that drew on previously accepted conventional troop formations and force concentrations. As one participant in the exercise recalled, the entire plan had an air of unreality about it:

> Every time a nuclear weapon was fired at them, a whole unit or airbase was wiped out, and therefore entire army units and airwings would have to be brought in as replacements. Obviously this plan did not solve the European security problem, and as such it never really saw the light of day.[59]

A more practical and readily available solution—one that for the moment also avoided a choice between conventional forces or tactical nuclear weapons—was that endorsed by the British in the summer of 1952. The previous autumn, British voters had turned out Attlee's Labour government and had brought back the Conservatives, led by the venerable Winston Churchill. Among Churchill's foremost concerns were Britain's diminished stature in world affairs and her chronic financial problems. The latter he and the new chancellor of the exchequer, R. A. Butler, attributed in substantial part to Labour's preoccupation with spending on conventional forces.[60] As a first step toward repairing this situation, Churchill decided to cut defense spending and to let the Americans know that, insofar as Britain's contribution was involved, NATO's re-armament measures would have to follow a new course. "We have to tell them," he noted shortly after resuming the premiership, "that if the rearmament is not spread out over a longer time the nations of Western Europe will be rushing to bankruptcy and starvation."[61]

Churchill's decision stemmed in part from his conviction that a direct East-West confrontation had grown less likely, thereby making possible a reduction in conventional arms. Although Churchill did not rule out the possibility of general war, he calculated that the circumstances in which one might occur were progressively fewer and fewer. According to a conversation recorded by his private secretary, John Colville:

> The Prime Minister said that he did not believe total war was likely. If it came, it would be on one of two accounts. Either the Americans, unable or unwilling any longer to pay for the maintenance of Europe, would say to the Russians you must by certain dates withdraw from certain points and meet us on certain requirements: otherwise we shall attack you. Or, the Russians, realising that safety did not come from being strong, but only from being the strongest, might for carefully calculated and not for emotional reasons, decide that they must attack before it was too late. If they did so their first target would be the British Isles, which is the aircraft carrier. It was for that reason that Mr Churchill was anxious to convert this country from its present status of a rabbit into that of a hedgehog.[62]

In January 1952, Churchill came to Washington with, among other things, hopes of resuming the dialogue, broken off since the previous September, on "strategic air plans and the use of the atomic weapon."[63] Churchill had often stressed the strategic importance of nuclear weapons, calling them on one occasion "the only lever" the West had for assuring peace and security vis-à-vis the Soviet Union.[64] While in Washington, Churchill received "a highly privileged briefing at the Pentagon," said to include as much information on US war plans as Acheson knew. More importantly, he also received assurances from Truman that it had always been the President's "personal feeling that allies should be consulted" before any decision to use nuclear weapons.[65] Reaffirming their eagerness to cooperate, Truman and Churchill acknowledged in a communiqué that there was now an "understanding" that the use of British bases by the United States "in an emergency would be a matter for joint decision."[66] The first formal announcement of its kind, the statement stopped short of specifying how or when consultations would take place, an obvious disappointment to the British, but reassuring nonetheless that the Americans recognized their obligation.

Churchill returned to Britain and set in motion a defense review supervised by his military assistant, Sir Ian Jacob. The other principal participants were Slessor, Slim, and Sir Rhoderick Robert McGrigor, the First Sea Lord. So as not to be unduly influenced by aides and staff, they concluded their deliberations in extreme privacy, at Greenwich. The outcome of the conference was a new strategic concepts paper, "Defence Policy and Global

Strategy," a paper that was comparable in effect to NSC 68 and the precursor in many respects to the American "new look" of the following year.[67]

The drafting of the global strategy paper brought to the surface many of the same interservice tensions and worries that had plagued the British chiefs' American counterparts for years. Prone from the outset to protect their services' roles and importance (not to mention their budget shares), the army and navy chiefs were not inclined to accept any radical alterations in strategy or policy. But with budget cutbacks looming and the prime minister's preferences evident, the outcome became almost a foregone conclusion. According to Slessor:

> Slim, McGrigor and I were not in full agreement in the Spring of 1952; but we shut ourselves up and left the day-to-day work to our Vice-Chiefs until we *were* able to agree and submit to the Cabinet a comprehensive recommendation on British Global Strategy, of a kind which I think should precede every White Paper.[68]

The principal thesis of the global strategy paper centered on the premise that nuclear weapons had revolutionized warfare. Given this dramatic change, Britain had to seize the opportunity to reconfigure its defense posture accordingly. This conclusion reinforced the British chiefs' already well established faith in the value of nuclear weapons as a deterrent. Now it was combined with their increasing certainty, as tensions generated by Korea lessened, that war with the Soviet Union might not necessarily be imminent. Indeed, the chiefs thought that cold war tensions between East and West might last indefinitely. They therefore concluded that the most effective and affordable defense posture for Britain to achieve and maintain for any length of time was one relying in the first instance on the retaliatory threat of long-range air power and atomic weapons.[69] Instead of the more than 300,000 soldiers that Britain would be required to maintain by 1954 under the Lisbon goals, the chiefs calculated that the British contribution could be reduced to as few as 50,000.[70] But it was not for fiscal reasons alone that the British chiefs embraced the proposed change in strategy. "The main reason why we should concentrate on the new strategy," Slessor explained,

> is that it is the one which holds out the best chance of preventing war. . . . Even if these 96 [sic] divisions and thousands of aircraft could be trained and equipped which we don't think they could, they certainly could not be maintained without continuing American aid on a vast scale. We cannot possibly hope to compete on level terms with Russia and China on the basis of manpower. We can, however, hope not only to defeat them in war but prevent them going to war by

maintaining and increasing our superiority in the strategic field. . . . We shall not do that if we expend our resources in a 1955 version of the 1914 war.[71]

In truth, Britain remained far from being able to implement a strategy of nuclear deterrence. Although the first test of a British nuclear device was scheduled for October 1952, it would still be another year before the RAF began to receive deliverable weapons. Nor was the first effective penetrating bomber expected to become operational before 1955. In reality, then, the British chiefs expected the United States to shoulder the major share of responsibility until Britain's own deterrent stood ready. Even once it was in place, no one expected that Britain's nuclear striking power would come close to matching that of either the United States or the Soviet Union. Within British planning circles, 1,000 atomic bombs were judged sufficient to knock the Soviet Union out of a war, though if only 600 found their aim points, they might do the job just as well. Of the latter number, the British expected the United States to be able to deliver two-thirds on target, leaving the United Kingdom to make up the rest.[72] Whether 200 bombs—the projected delivery capacity of Britain's nuclear stockpile—would make a significant difference either in deterring the Soviets or in deciding the outcome of a war remained open to question. To this extent, then, the global strategy paper contained a degree of wishful thinking, but it was wishful thinking of the sort that was aimed not only at policymakers in London but at those in Washington as well.

In July 1952, Slessor visited Washington and gave a round of briefings on the global strategy paper. He soon discovered that, with the exception of senior US Air Force officers, who greeted the paper most warmly, American defense planners were exceedingly skeptical of the proposed strategy.[73] Many thought that the British were trying to renege on earlier promises, and that they placed excessive trust in the efficacy of nuclear retaliation. "I believe," remarked General Bradley during one of the briefings, ". . . it would be a terrific blow against the Soviets, but we are not all convinced that it would be decisive."[74] Within a year, American attitudes, along with American policy, would change. But for the time being, with the Truman administration still in office, the immediate inclination (except for the Air Force, of course) was to spurn the British proposals, not least because they rubbed against lingering American prejudices, from Truman on down, against reliance on nuclear weapons.

Nevertheless, American strategists could ill afford to ignore the British strategy paper. Apart from the challenge it represented to the Lisbon force-goals agreement, the paper raised the more fundamental issue of trying to restore some semblance of a conventional balance in the face of increasingly effective—possibly even decisive—strategic nuclear capabilities. As Slessor described it to his British colleagues, Washington simply could not continue "superimposing the new atomic strategy on the old conventional strategy."[75] At some point, one or the other was bound to give way, and in the British view it was destined to be the latter. The Americans, who were better acquainted with the complexities and limitations of nuclear weapons, were not nearly so confident. Nor were they sure how the British strategy could be applied in situations other than the defense of Western Europe. But with the American commitment to a nuclear-oriented defense posture well established and continuing to grow, such concerns would over time become less urgent. If massive retaliation was not yet the official American policy, it was nonetheless the looming reality.

THE H-BOMB AND BEYOND

During its last months in office, the Truman administration continued to pursue an ambivalent policy toward nuclear weapons. As much as he disliked the bomb, Truman knew that without it the United States would be spending more on defense and perhaps be receiving less in return. Nuclear weapons had become not only a means to an end, they had become in a very real sense an end in themselves, the ultimate expression of American military prowess and the foremost area in which the United States enjoyed marked superiority over the Soviet Union. Kennan's arguments to the contrary notwithstanding, the United States had reached the point where pursuing a viable strategy of containment, especially from a military standpoint, depended directly on nuclear power. Though there were those who worried that nuclear weapons would become a wasting asset, losing their military and political significance as the Soviets acquired more atomic weapons of their own, that time seemed distant and therefore was not a matter for serious concern. And with the conventional buildup giving all appearances of having run its course, leveling off well below most expectations, nuclear weapons became the logical way to make up expected weaknesses and shortcomings in the defense posture. Dependence on the atomic arsenal was, of course, by no means total and irreversible, but with each passing day that prospect became more real.

Thus while Truman may have privately winced at what his seven years in the Oval Office had produced, he could not turn back the clock. Nor did he appear interested in trying to do so anyway. Decisions having been made, he resolved to see them through to their logical conclusion. One such instance occurred on November 1, 1952, with the world's first thermonuclear test. Despite an 11th-hour appeal from a group of State Department consultants on disarmament, headed by J. Robert Oppenheimer, to forego the test, Truman elected to proceed. All the same, he hoped that the detonation could be delayed until after the presidential election. When the delay proved impossible for weather and logistical reasons, he settled for a two-week official news blackout on the story.[76] An awesome demonstration yielding over ten megatons of destructive power, the explosion, held in the Pacific, evaporated the entire atoll on which the test device was housed. Afterward, Robert LeBaron, chairman of the Military Liaison Committee, dryly remarked that the magnitude of the explosion raised "many questions of national policy."[77]

Yet despite the proven feasibility of an H-bomb, the Truman administration had no immediate plans to seize upon this opportunity to create an arsenal of thermonuclear weapons. Indeed, the device tested in the Pacific was scarcely more than a laboratory model. Weighing some 60 tons, it was wholly unsuitable for air delivery and thus of dubious military value at the moment. Months before the experiment took place, though, Senator Brien McMahon, chairman of the Joint Committee on Atomic Energy, had urged Truman to waste no time setting production dates and requirements for H-bombs. Looking ahead, McMahon speculated that the H-bomb should be "our primary nuclear weapon" and the A-bomb "a secondary or special-purpose weapon."[78] Yet, instead of acting on McMahon's suggestion to pursue production, Truman referred it for further study to the NSC where the proposal languished—still unresolved by the time the President left office in January 1953. Of his senior advisors, only Secretary of Defense Robert Lovett clearly favored the stockpiling of thermonuclear weapons. The others either took no position on the matter, apparently preferring to leave it up to the next administration to decide, or, like the Joint Chiefs, chose to withhold judgment pending further research and development on a usable weaponized version.[79] In any case, according to unofficial sources, the stockpiling of deliverable H-bombs did not begin until 1954-1955.[80]

In fact, even without a stockpile of H-bombs, the Korean War buildup had already yielded significant improvements in America's defense posture by the time Truman left office. Not only was the strategic nuclear deterrent stronger and more effective than ever, but also major strides had been made in developing more potent conventional capabilities, as Acheson and the authors of NSC 68 had hoped. In addition to the increased size and readiness of ground and naval forces, tactical air power had expanded as well, making for a more balanced US defense establishment. And with American foreign military assistance on the rise, Western capabilities in general looked decidedly better than at any time since World War II.

Even so, questions remained as to whether much had changed in the overall strategic balance. Only in the nuclear field did the United States enjoy a potentially decisive advantage. It remained to be seen whether this advantage could be translated into more effective solutions to East-West problems short of all-out war. As he stepped down from the presidency, Truman passed along to his successor an NSC staff study (NSC 141), known as the "legacy paper," that attempted to address these questions. But its findings displayed a noticeable lack of optimism. With respect to perhaps the administration's major accomplishment—demonstrating the feasibility of an H-bomb—the paper doubted that the United States had accomplished a great deal other than to buy a little time. "If the U.S.," it argued,

> but not the U.S.S.R., should develop a thermonuclear capability during the period 1954-55, it appears that the free world would possess for the duration of this monopoly an enhanced deterrent to general war. Whether this margin of superiority would permit us, through the adoption of bolder initiatives, favorably to resolve a number of outstanding issues in the cold war is, however, problematical."[81]

In the event, America's monopoly on the H-bomb was even shorter-lived than its monopoly on the A-bomb. In August 1953, the Soviet Union detonated a device that the AEC acknowledged to be of thermonuclear design. It now seems clear, however, that with a yield of around 300 kilotons (compared with the ten megatons of the first American thermonuclear test), the Soviet experiment was not a true thermonuclear or fusion explosion, but more probably a "boosted" fission bomb, using tritium and other elements to enhance its yield. All the same, the test marked a substantial increase in the power of the Soviet nuclear arsenal and allowed the Soviets to acquire deliverable fusion-type weapons about the same time as the United States.[82]

For some, the Soviet Union's acquisition of a thermonuclear capability merely confirmed that nuclear weapons were indeed a wasting asset. But to the incoming Eisenhower administration, it was further evidence of an escalating East-West competition in nuclear arms which the West could not afford to lose. With the increases in production capacity initiated during the Truman years, Eisenhower capitalized on America's strength in nuclear weapons and turned it into the centerpiece of his foreign and defense policies. To be sure, Eisenhower's foremost reason for stressing nuclear weapons remained their relatively low cost to procure and maintain compared with conventional forces. As early as 1952, the explosive effect of one ton of TNT costing $1,700 could be obtained from fissionable material costing as little as $23.[83] According to a popular saying of the 1950s, nuclear weapons gave "more bang for the buck." But there was another reason for Eisenhower's policy: the inability of the United States and its allies, as amply demonstrated during the Truman years, to find a mutually acceptable and equally effective conventional alternative to reliance on nuclear weapons. Learning from this experience, Eisenhower made no attempt whatsoever to try again where Truman had failed. Looking back, Paul Nitze concluded that what the Truman administration had tried to do during the Korean War buildup—i.e., strengthen the West's conventional components—amounted simply to "too little too late."[84]

The changes Eisenhower contemplated and proceeded to implement were made all the easier by a marked shift in the public's outlook on nuclear weapons. In contrast to the dire predictions that followed the news of Hiroshima and Nagasaki, informed opinion by the early 1950s generally accepted reliance on nuclear weapons—to one degree or another—as an accomplished, unavoidable fact, the way of the future. And among a certain group of intellectuals and scientists, tactical nuclear weapons in particular were seen as offering the key to Western security. Writing to his friend and fellow scientist J. Robert Oppenheimer in February 1952, James B. Conant, president of Harvard University and a recent participant in Project Vista, insisted that "at some time not too distant the defense of Europe on the ground becomes a much more feasible undertaking for the NATO powers because of tactical air support with atomic weapons." Such a system of defense, Conant argued, would inherently favor the West because "the advantage of the use of tactical weapons would be a) on the side of those who were holding the line against an offensive, and b) for those who had first started manufacturing atomic weapons, as presumably their stockpile would for some time be greater than that of an enemy."[85]

As Conant's observations suggest, nuclear weapons—or at least certain kinds of nuclear weapons—were gaining respectability. Having worked on the Manhattan Project in World War II, Conant was, of course, somewhat biased in favor of nuclear energy to begin with. He wanted to demonstrate that it had a variety of uses. But at the same time, like many other scientists who had been part of the wartime effort, he had experienced second thoughts about his actions and was especially concerned by recent developments like the advent of the H-bomb and the rise of SAC. Tactical nuclear weapons, on the other hand, offered an alternative that Conant, Oppenheimer, and like-minded others found appealing. Such weapons could not only help to compensate for conventional deficiencies, but, more importantly, they might even lessen or preclude the need for large strategic forces and lower the threshold of violence.

From Truman's standpoint, however, the problem was never quite so easy. Faced with an array of competing demands and interests—the budget, domestic needs, congressional preferences, interservice rivalries, the ever-present dangers of the cold war—he was often forced to make compromises that went against his better judgment. Even so, he never rued a decision. "It has been [one] crisis after another since I've been here," he observed toward the end of his presidency, "and we've met them and are still going strong."[86] What he left as his most important legacy was not only the strategic strikeforce and nuclear arsenal that would make the massive retaliation policy of the 1950s more than mere rhetoric. He also left a new way of thinking about national security, a mindset that for the first time in American history accorded primacy to maintaining a large and ready defense establishment. The burden, it turned out, would be felt for generations to come.

NOTES

1. Hopkins and Goldberg, *Development of SAC,* 16, 37; D. Condit, *Test of War,* 463.
2. John T. Greenwood, "The Emergence of the Postwar Strategic Air Force, 1945-1953," in Alfred F. Hurley and Robert C. Ehrhart (eds.), *Air Power and Warfare* (Washington, D.C.: Office of Air Force History, 1979), 236.
3. Lt. Gen. Walter E. Todd, "Evolution of Aerospace Power," *Air University Quarterly Review* 12 (Winter-Spring 1960-61): 11. On the development and capabilities of SAC aircraft, see Knaack, *Post-World War II Bombers;* and Lloyd S. Jones, *U.S. Bombers, 1920-1980s* (Fallbrook, Calif.: Aero Publishers, 3rd ed., 1980).
4. Quotations from an interview of Gen. LeMay by Mr. McNeil, Scripps-Howard Papers, Oct. 20, 1950, LeMay Papers, box 103, Diary No. 2 folder, L.C. For SAC's bombing strategy, see ltr, Col. E. Vandevanter, Plans Div., D/Plans HQ SAC, to Col. G.W. Martin, Exec., Office SecAF, May 15, 1950, with Presentation to SecAF and Charts, RG 340 (Office of the Secretary of the Air Force), Num.-Subj. file 50, box 3, NARA; and Rosenberg, "Origins of Overkill," 19.
5. Rosenberg, "Toward Armageddon," 162.
6. McNeil interview with LeMay, Oct. 20, 1950, LeMay Papers, box 103, Diary no. 2 folder, L.C.
7. Borowski, *Hollow Threat,* 163-164, 173-178.
8. Gen. Curtis E. LeMay, with McKinlay Kantor, *Mission with LeMay: My Story* (Garden City, N.Y.: Doubleday, 1965), 431.
9. Ltr, LeMay to Vandenberg, Sep. 21, 1950, Vandenberg Papers, box 44, Command Letters (1) folder, L.C. Also see the entry for Sept. 20, 1950, Commanding General's Diary, LeMay Papers, box 103, Diary No. 2 folder, L.C.

10. Rosenberg, "Origins of Overkill," 15; ltr, Lt. Gen. Curtis LeMay, CG SAC, to Gen. Nathan Twining, Vice CoS, sub: Reec and Intelligence Capabilities, Apr. 26, 1951, Twining Papers, box 54, Reading File May 1951, L.C.; William S. Borgiasz, "Struggle for Predominance: Evolution and Consolidation of Nuclear Forces in the Strategic Air Command, 1945-1955 (Ph.D. diss., American University, 1991), 197-219.

11. K. Condit, *JCS and National Policy, 1947-49*, 285-293. For a contemporary analysis of targeting policy, see Col. John H. de Russy, "Selecting Target Systems and Targets," *Air University Quarterly Review* 1 (Spring 1947): 69-78.

12. Futrell, *Ideas, Concepts, Doctrine, 1907-1960*, 237.

13. Rosenberg, "Toward Armageddon," 173; Paul Bracken, *The Command and Control of Nuclear Forces* (New Haven, Conn.: Yale University Press, 1983), 79.

14. Poole, *JCS and National Policy, 1950-52*, 164.

15. K. Condit, *JCS and National Policy, 1947-49*, 297-300.

16. Ltr, LeMay to Vandenberg, Jan. 26, 1951, Vandenberg Papers, box 45, Command—Strategic (5) folder, L.C.

17. Ltr, LeMay to Maj. Gen. Thomas D. White, 7 May 1951, LeMay Papers, box B-197, folder B-10934, L.C.

18. Memo, Finletter to Vandenberg, May 12, 1950, [sub: LeMay's Views on SAC's Mission], Vandenberg Papers, box 84, Selected Memos folder, L.C.

19. JCS 2056/7, Aug. 12, 1950, and decision on Aug. 15, 1950, RG 218, CCS 373.11 (12-14-48), sec. 2; Rosenberg, "Toward Armageddon," 156.

20. Entry, Jan. 16, 1951, LeMay Diary, LeMay Papers, box 103, Diary No. 3 folder, L.C.; memo, LeMay to Vandenberg, Jan. 20, 1951, sub: Force Requirements of the Strategic Offensive, LeMay Papers, box B-197, B-9328 folder, L.C. Exactly how many planes this would involve LeMay did not specify.

21. Memo, LeMay to Vandenberg, Jan. 20, 1951, sub: SAC Capabilities, LeMay Papers, box B-197, B-9327 folder, L.C.

22. Rosenberg, "Toward Armageddon," 163.

23. Ltr, LeMay to Vandenberg, Jan. 15, 1951, LeMay Papers, box B-197, B-9226 folder, L.C.

24. LeMay Diary, Jan. 23, 1951, LeMay Papers, box 103, Diary no. 3 folder, L.C.

25. Mins., 3rd Mtg USAF Target Panel, Jan. 23, 1951, LeMay Papers, box 197, folder B-10174; ltr, LeMay to Gen. E. Moore, Assist. for Production, Directorate of Intelligence, Hq USAF, Mar. 3, 1951, sub: Target Panel Study, LeMay Papers, box B-197, folder B-10018; and ltr, Moore to LeMay, Mar. 8, 1951, same subj., LeMay Papers, box B-197, folder B-10174, L.C. Also see Rosenberg, "Toward Armageddon," 163-165.

26. Poole, *JCS and National Policy, 1950-52*, 166.

27. David C. Elliot, "Project Vista and Nuclear Weapons in Europe," *International Security* 11 (Summer 1986): 163-183; Matthew Anthony Evangelista, "Technological Innovation and the Arms Race: A Comparative Study of Soviet and American Decisions on Tactical Nuclear Weapons" (Ph.D. diss., Cornell University, 1986), 259-283, 296.

28. Futrell, *Ideas, Concepts, Doctrine, 1907-1960*, 328-330; and May, "American Commitment to Germany," 455-456.

29. Futrell, *Ideas, Concepts, Doctrine, 1907-1960*, 434; Walton S. Moody, "Building a Strategic Air Force, 1945-1953," (MS) ch.9.

30. See "Report on Strategic Air Command Capabilities to Initiate and Sustain Combat Operations," Mar. 20, 1951, LeMay Papers, box B-197, B-10647 folder, L.C.

31. Poole, *JCS and National Policy, 1950-52*, 169-170.

32. Duke, *US Defence Bases in the United Kingdom*, 47-56.

33. FO 371/112055, Ltr, Pierson Dixon, F.O., to Sec., Chiefs of Staff Committee, Nov. 30, 1950, PRO.

34. Andrew Brookes, *V-Force: The History of Britain's Airborne Deterrent* (London: Jane's, 1982), 21.

35. Quoted in Duke, *US Defence Bases in the United Kingdom*, 56.

36. Wheeler, "British Nuclear Weapons and Anglo-American Relations, 1945-54," 73.

37. See DEFE 4/16, for example J.P.(48)70 (Final), Report by the Joint Planning Staff, CoS Committee, sub: World Strategic Review, Sep. 11, 1948, enclosure to C.O.S. (48) 128th Mtg Chiefs of Staff Committee, Sep. 14, 1948, P.R.O.

38. Gowing, *Independence and Deterrence*, I, 184.

39. Memo by Minister of State to Defence Committee, Jan. 4, 1950, sub: U.S. airforce groups in U.K., quoted in Wheeler, "British Nuclear Weapons and Anglo-American Relations, 1945-54," 72.

40. "Manpower Requirements of the R.A.F. During 1949," n.d., annex III to P.P.O. (P. 48), Rpt to the Chiefs of Staff Committee by the Principal Personnel Officer's Committee, Sep. 28, 1948, sub: Manpower Requirements of the Armed Forces During 1949, DEFE 4/16, P.R.O.

41. Brookes, *V-Force*, 32-33; DEFE 7/669, P.D.P.(53)3, Note by the Air Ministry, Feb. 7, 1953, sub: Progress Report for 1952, P.R.O.

42. Much of the criticism fell personally on the architect of the bombing campaign, Air Marshal Sir Arthur Harris. See Dudley Saward, *Bomber Harris: The Story of Marshal of the Royal Air Force Sir Arthur Harris* (Garden City, N.Y.: Doubleday, 1985).

43. Brookes, *V-Force*, 33-34; Clark and Wheeler, *British Origins of Nuclear Strategy, 1945-1955*, 143-144.

44. Quoted from Mins, Chiefs of Staff Comte. Mtg., Dec. 14, 1950, *Documents on British Policy Overseas*, series II, vol. IV, *Korea, June 1950-April 1951*, 255n.

45. Acheson to Bevin, Jan. 26, 1951, *FRUS 1951*, I, 807-808; Nitze memcon, June 12, 1951, *ibid.*, 842.

46. Quoted in Gowing, *Independence and Deterrence*, I, 315.

47. Jessup memcon, Jan. 15, 1951, *FRUS 1951*, I, 806.

48. *Ibid.*, 826n.

49. Paper Prepared by the Joint Strategic Survey Committee and Representatives of the State Dept., Aug. 3, 1951, sub: U.S. Position on Considerations Under

Which the United States Will Accept War and on Atomic Warfare, *ibid.,* 866-874.

50. Ferguson memcon between Acheson and JCS, Aug. 6, 1951, sub: Discussions with the British regarding the use of atomic weapons, *ibid.,* 875-880.
51. Gowing, *Independence and Deterrence,* I, 317-318; *FRUS 1951,* I, 880-894.
52. Rearden, *Formative Years,* 482. The best account of U.S. military assistance is Lawrence S. Kaplan, *A Community of Interests* (Washington, D.C.: Historical Office, Office of the Secretary of Defense, 1980). Also see James A. Huston, *Outposts and Allies: U.S. Army Logistics in the Cold War, 1945-1953* (London: Associated University Presses, 1988); and Chester A. Pach, Jr., *Arming the Free World: The Origins of the United States Military Assistance Program, 1945-1950* (Chapel Hill: University of North Carolina Press, 1991).
53. "Summary of Temporary Council Committee Report," Feb. 6, 1952, *FRUS, 1952-54,* V, 204; D. Condit, *Test of War,* 376-377.
54. Acheson, *Present at the Creation,* 625.
55. Ltr, Harriman to Eisenhower, Nov. 17, 1951, Harriman Papers, box 278, SHAPE-SACEUR folder, L.C.
56. Evelyn Shuckburgh, *Descent to Suez: Diaries, 1951-56* (New York: W.W. Norton, 1986), 35.
57. May, "American Commitment to Germany," 448-450. Also see Lawrence S. Kaplan, *The United States and NATO: The Formative Years* (Lexington: University Press of Kentucky, 1984), 145-175.
58. D. Condit, *Test of War,* 268.
59. Robert C. Richardson III, "NATO Nuclear Strategy: A Look Back," *Strategic Review* 9 (Spring 1981): 38.
60. Clark and Wheeler, *British Origins of Nuclear Strategy, 1945-53,* 156.
61. Quoted in diary entry, Jan. 4, 1952, Lord Moran, *Churchill Taken from the Diaries of Lord Moran: The Struggle for Survival, 1940-1965* (Boston: Houghton, Mifflin, 1966), 376.
62. John Colville, *The Fringes of Power: 10 Downing Street Diaries, 1939-1955* (New York: W. W. Norton, 1985), 636.
63. Churchill to Truman, Dec. 23, 1951, *FRUS 1952-1954,* VI, 718.
64. Quoted from a 1950 speech in Martin Gilbert, *Winston S. Churchill,* vol. VIII, *"Never Despair," 1945-1965* (London: Heinemann, 1988), 575.
65. Mins., Second Formal Mtg of Truman and Churchill, Jan. 7, 1952, *FRUS 1952-54,* VI, 763.
66. Communiqué Issued by Truman and Churchill, Jan. 9, 1952, *ibid.,* 837.
67. Charles J. V. Murphy, "A New Strategy for NATO," *Fortune* (Jan. 1953): 80-83; Andrew J. Pierre, *Nuclear Politics: The British Experience with an Independent Strategy Force, 1939-1970* (London: Oxford University Press, 1972), 86-87.
68. Quoted in Clark and Wheeler, *British Origins of Nuclear Strategy, 1945-1955,* 161. Emphasis in original.

69. Cable, Twining to Norstad, July 31, 1952, sub: JCS Mtg with Slessor, RG 341, DCS/Ops, Dir. of Plans, OPD, 323.361, sec. 6 Annex (16 Aug 50), NARA. Also see Pierre, *Nuclear Politics,* 87-89.

70. R. N. Rosecrance, *Defense of the Realm: British Strategy in the Nuclear Epoch* (New York: Columbia University Press, 1968), 162-163.

71. CoS Comte Mtg, July 5, 1952, quoted in Wheeler, "British Nuclear Weapons and Anglo-American Relations, 1945-54," 76.

72. Brookes, *V-Force,* 21.

73. See Air Staff Study on "Defence Policy and Global Strategy," July 24, 1952, Tab 7 to Memo, Maj. Gen. Herbert B. Thatcher to Gen. Nathan Twining, July 28, 1952, sub: Rpt of UK Chiefs of Staff on UK Defense Policy and Global Strategy, RG 341, DCS, Ops, Dir. of Plans, OPD 323.361, sec. 6, Annex (16 Aug 50).

74. Poole, *JCS and National Policy, 1950-52,* 309.

75. Quoted in Clark and Wheeler, *British Origins of Nuclear Strategy, 1945-1955,* 164.

76. For an interesting analysis of the behind-the-scenes maneuvering over the H-bomb test and the consultants' role, see Barton J. Bernstein, "Crossing the Rubicon: A Missed Opportunity to Stop the H-Bomb?" *International Security* 14 (Fall 1989): 132-160.

77. D. Condit, *Test of War,* 480.

78. Ltr, McMahon to Truman, May 30, 1952, *FRUS 1952-54,* II, 955-957.

79. D. Condit, *Test of War,* 480-481.

80. Cochran, Arkin, and Hoenig, *Nuclear Weapons Databook,* I, 11.

81. NSC 141, "Reexamination of U.S. Programs for National Security," Jan. 19, 1953, p. 73, RG 273, NARA.

82. David Holloway, "Soviet Thermonuclear Development," *International Security* 4 (Winter 1979-80): 192-197.

83. D. Condit, *Test of War,* 472.

84. Ltr, Nitze to Joseph Alsop, July 1, 1954, in Kenneth W. Thompson and Steven L. Rearden (eds.), *Paul H. Nitze on National Security and Arms Control* (Lanham, Md.: University Press of America, 1990), 50.

85. Ltr, Conant to Oppenheimer, Feb. 15, 1952, Oppenheimer Papers, James B. Conant file, box 27, L.C.

86. Ltr, Truman to Ethel Noland, May 11, 1952, in Ferrell (ed.), *Off the Record,* 249.

VIII

Conclusion

When Harry S. Truman left the Oval Office in January 1953, nuclear weapons were America's first line of defense. This dependence on nuclear weapons was not intended and was not a foregone conclusion with the coming of either the cold war or the nuclear age. Rather, it was the logical outcome of Truman's policies and practices since the first nuclear explosion in the summer of 1945.

The bomb's paramount role in American policy emerged hesitantly. As World War II ended many people—including many senior American policymakers and military leaders—expected the bomb, like mustard gas, to be banned or placed under some regimen of international control. The result of this uncertainty was to throw the ultimate fate of nuclear weapons into limbo for at least the next year-and-a-half. As awesome a weapon as the atomic bomb may have been, its availability for military purposes was not assured. The scarcity of fissionable material, the Air Force's stumbling assimilation of the new weapon into its operational plans and doctrine, the extensive secrecy surrounding atomic matters, and interservice feuding also contributed to the virtual absence before 1948 of serious planning for atomic war.

Yet if the bomb's future military role remained unclear in the immediate aftermath of the war, its impact on the world political environment did not. Mere possession of the bomb added immensely to America's already considerable prestige, and paradoxically convinced other countries—Great Britain and the Soviet Union, initially—that they must also become nuclear powers in order to participate in great power politics. In these circumstances, the political significance of nuclear weapons often outweighed whatever military advantages they presumably conferred. This fact became increasingly apparent in the UN debates over international control that took place during 1946. But with the subsequent deterioration in East-West relations after 1947, the prospects for international control steadily dimmed. As the cold war intensified, it virtually assured that nuclear competition would become an integral part of the larger East-West rivalry.

Whether international control would have made a difference remains conjecture. Possibly, as Secretary of War Henry L. Stimson and other proponents of international control believed, agreement would have removed atomic energy from the growing list of divisive issues contributing to East-West tensions. To this extent, international control might have produced a less potentially volatile postwar international order. On the other hand, failure to achieve international control should not be exaggerated. The chances were at best problematic. Simply put, the odds were so strongly against international control that, in retrospect, it seems surprising that the entire enterprise prospered as long as it did. While the United States made the initial proposals, the conditions attached to the Baruch Plan were bound to frustrate, if not infuriate, the Soviets. Not only did American interests come first, but these interests would also remain protected and predominant under the only system of international control that Washington would contemplate.

Nor is it clear that the Soviets really wanted international control. An early accord might have worked to Moscow's advantage initially, especially as it sought to narrow the West's lead in atomic technology. But as part of Stalin's long-range strategy, international control would have been counterproductive, since it would have impeded his goal of acquiring a nuclear capability to offset the West's. Thus, while the United Nations debated the Baruch Plan and other measures, Stalin pressed vigorously to manufacture a bomb of his own. Using espionage and deception to help further their effort, the Soviets sacrificed scarce resources that might otherwise have contributed to swifter recovery from the devastation of World War II. Stalin desperately wanted the bomb and would have paid almost any price to have it.

As the international control debate continued, Washington also began to discover that possessing the bomb did not readily translate into the political leverage that some imagined. Truman may have briefly believed, at the time of the 1945 Potsdam Conference, that the bomb could be applied as a diplomatic lever. But he soon came to regard it more as a hindrance than as a help in working out a satisfactory relationship with the Soviet Union. Secretary of State James Byrnes and others who hoped in 1945 to wring concessions from the Soviets through "atomic diplomacy" were soon woefully disappointed. The Soviets may have feared the bomb. But they disguised their concern and convinced Western policymakers that they would not be easily intimidated.

In the emerging atomic diplomacy, Truman's behavior and attitude were crucial, perhaps decisive. They set not only the tone but substantive content of American nuclear policy. As Colin McInnes points out, the President looked upon the bomb as a terror weapon that would be more effective against civilian than military targets.[1] Having ordered the destruction of Hiroshima and Nagasaki, he was not eager to confront another such decision. Although he assured his advisors at the time of the 1948 Berlin crisis of his willingness to use the bomb, his position remained couched in qualifications. Nor did it receive much clarification from NSC 30, the official statement of policy. Truman consciously distanced himself from nuclear matters, not even allowing atomic energy information (officially known as "Restricted Data") to be stored in White House safes. Indeed, Truman's apprehensions and prudence about the bomb were strikingly evident throughout his presidency, while his fiscal policies increasingly encouraged additional reliance upon an atomic-oriented defense posture.

A major turning point in American policy came in 1948 with the convergence of the Berlin crisis and disputes in Washington over the FY 1950 military budget. Berlin not only seemed to demonstrate the deterrent effect of nuclear weapons; it also gave urgency to preparations for atomic warfare that had previously been desultory. Moreover, the Berlin experience suggested that America's nuclear capability had resolved the crisis by keeping the Soviets from escalating the pressure. It had thus lessened the danger of war. From this it was not hard to conclude that a larger nuclear stockpile would be even more effective, a definite and distinct asset in any possible future confrontation. Furthermore, with the breakthroughs achieved by the SANDSTONE tests, that larger nuclear arsenal now became possible. Curiously, though, few Americans before the H-bomb debate in late 1949 gave serious thought to the Soviets' ability to duplicate these feats, or to what might happen if they did. Initially, the prospect of a nuclear stalemate—though not unimaginable—appeared too distant for most policymakers, including Truman, to contemplate or fear.

The budget process also helped solidify America's nuclear dependence. As much as Truman said he disliked relying on nuclear weapons, he disliked deficits and taxes even more. His conservative fiscal and budgetary policies left little leeway in choosing weapons and strategy. The steady deterioration of Soviet-American relations finally convinced Truman by 1948 that bold economic and political initiatives, such as the Greek-Turkish aid program and the Marshall Plan, would not restore an international order favorable to the United States. But these same conditions did not persuade him that a surge in defense spending, as urged by Forrestal and the Joint Chiefs, was the right answer. Had nuclear weapons never been invented the choices would, of course, have been quite different. But with Truman determined to hold down the defense budget, a nuclear-oriented defense policy and primary reliance on the Air Force's strategic bombing capability appeared an acceptable and less expensive alternative.

Ironically, Truman's professed preference for a conventional option helped to obscure the impact that White House-mandated budget limitations were actually having on the development of the U.S. force posture. The Chief Executive's fiscal prudence progressively narrowed his range of choices. Thus his fiscal orthodoxy effectively forged a military strategy that rested on the most readily available and relatively cheapest source of military might—the nuclear stockpile. Not everyone agreed that this was a satisfactory course of action. The Bureau of the Budget, straining to stay within the President's spending guidelines, still raised objections, as did the Navy, which bitterly resented and continually challenged the Air Force's monopoly of the nuclear mission. Yet the atomic option increasingly seemed the most viable solution to America's defense needs, not least because it had the strong support of an economy-minded, pro-airpower Congress.

Personalities also influenced these decisions. Truman respected Forrestal but never developed the close working relationship with him that he had first with Marshall and later with Acheson. Truman and Forrestal differed repeatedly, over service unification, over procedural questions such as the role and importance of the National Security Council, and over policy matters. In 1948, when Truman refused to give the military custody of atomic weapons, his growing skepticism of Forrestal's advice reinforced his preference for civilian control. In the ensuing battle over the FY 1950 defense budget, Forrestal clearly lacked the President's confidence. To be sure, had someone else been secretary of defense, the budget results would in all likelihood have been essentially the same, given Truman's priorities and mindset at the time. Yet a different defense secretary—one Truman fully trusted—might still have prevailed in securing budgetary concessions which, to some degree, would have contributed to a more balanced force posture.

As it happened, though, the FY 1950 defense budget considerably boosted reliance on strategic air power and nuclear weapons. As 1949 progressed, the trend-lines became ever clearer. Not only was the Air Force the ascendent service, but also it had a monopoly on the key element in a defense policy that now accorded primacy to technology in assuring American security. With the decision to develop the H-bomb, the commitment to a nuclear-dependent defense posture became even stronger. If the description "massive retaliation" was not yet appropriate, the trend was certain and reliance on nuclear weapons unmistakable.

Efforts to reverse this pattern were, by and large, unsuccessful, mainly because no one ever seriously pursued them. Despite NSC 68 and the massive Korean War buildup, the change in priorities was always more apparent than real. Larger conventional forces did not really alter the situation. The longer the buildup lasted, the more anxious Truman became that it would do irreparable harm to the economy, discredit his other policies, and plunge the nation into fiscal chaos. Though he now accepted the need for a stepped-up level of military spending, his inclination during the crucial first year-and-a-half of the buildup was to curb growth in conventional capabilities whenever possible in favor of relying on air-atomic power. Atomic forces were, to be sure, less expensive to maintain over the long term, but they also represented the most potent element in the American arsenal. Moreover, Truman approved increases in production facilities for atomic weapons not just once, but three times, thereby assuring that future administrations need not be troubled by the lack of bombs and warheads. As a result, the Korean re-armament effort simply confirmed and accelerated the policy and strategy that had been evolving since 1948.

This course of events carried with it disturbing implications which officials in Washington were either reluctant to accept or prone to overlook. The British were more realistic. Occupying the front line of a possible East-West atomic conflict, London wanted clearer assurances as to how, where, and when nuclear weapons would be used, assurances that the United States would not—indeed, could not—provide. The British also took the lead in suggesting a strategy whereby nuclear weapons might substitute for other forces, in effect anticipating the "new look" of the Eisenhower administration. This maturity of strategic thinking had yet to arrive in Washington, and when it did, in the summer of 1952, the initial reaction (except, of course, among Air Force leaders) was one of consternation and skepticism. To American policymakers during the Truman years, nuclear weapons may not have been the solution per se to security needs, but they provided a convenient means to avoid tough decisions and painful choices.

The early evolution of American nuclear weapons policy invites several further observations. First, the action-reaction model so often used by historians and political scientists to study cold war US-Soviet relations, particularly in the area of strategic arms competition, must be reconsidered. Although certain aspects of the atomic problem—the H-bomb decision, for example—may fit such an interpretation, the overall picture is far more complex. Well before the Soviet achievement of an atomic capability in

1949, the United States had already opted for reliance on an atomic strategy. Had the Soviet explosion never occurred, US defense policy would probably not have changed. In fact, even the H-bomb was a more than likely possibility at some future point. The real significance of the Soviet atomic achievement was to compress time and thus speed up American decisions.

Second, as atomic weapons became more plentiful, they tended to lose their "special" status for senior policymakers. What made reliance on the nuclear strategy such an appealing prospect was not only its apparent deterrent effect on Soviet ambitions but also its practical utility. Out of the give-and-take of the budget process, especially, came the operating assumption that nuclear weapons, though clearly more powerful, were essentially no different from other weapons. Although there were notable dissents from this view, in particular from the Navy, the proffered alternative (i.e., a strengthening of conventional capabilities) remained inherently unacceptable because of the additional expense it would entail. At a time when holding down costs took priority, the appeal of an effective and economical nuclear-oriented defense posture became irresistible. Moreover, it would continue to be so for years to come, until the 1960s when the soaring cost of delivery vehicles made it less attractive.

Related to this is a third observation: that technological innovations such as atomic weapons can obscure but not resolve the gaps in an ambivalent strategic policy. In fact, the defense policy that emerged during Truman's presidency recognized no distinct difference between conventional and nuclear war, even though the administration's behavior after the Baruch Plan suggested otherwise. Then came the Korean War and the return to ambiguity. Korea did, of course, compel a clarification to some extent, resulting in a de facto action policy that all but ruled out the use of atomic weapons in limited engagements. For anything less than an all-out conflict, the deterrent effect of the atomic stockpile was virtually negated. Ironically, this refinement of policy occurred at roughly the same time that the first generation of "tactical" nuclear weapons went into production. As a practical matter, however, tactical atomic weapons were obsolete before they appeared. Clearly, under the rules of engagement laid down by Korea, they were unsuitable for the very same purposes for which they had been conceived and developed.

Finally, there is the lesson of how leaders adopt policies they actually seek to avoid. It may well be, as Arthur M. Schlesinger, Jr., has argued, that the United States by Truman's day was entering the era of the "imperial presidency."[2] But a more apt and accurate characterization in the area of defense and nuclear policy would seem to be the "bureaucratic presidency." As eager as Truman may have been to avoid reliance on nuclear weapons, he never really had that option. Rather, it rested with aides and subordinates who, in evaluating what they could do with available resources, made the choices for him. For Truman, the ultimate irony was that he wound up embracing an atomic strategy he never sought and certainly never wanted. Four decades later, despite the dramatic changes in the international arena that the end of the cold war has brought, his successors are still struggling to reverse the effects of his unintended policy choices.

NOTES

1. Colin McInnes, "Nuclear Strategy," in Colin McInnes and G. D. Sheffield (eds.), *Warfare in the Twentieth Century: Theory and Practice* (London: Unwin Hyman, 1988), 146.
2. See Arthur M. Schlesinger, Jr., *The Imperial Presidency* (Boston: Houghton Mifflin, 1973).

NOTE ON SOURCES AND SELECT BIBLIOGRAPHY

PRIMARY SOURCES: MANUSCRIPT COLLECTIONS

This book is the outgrowth of an earlier support study that the authors prepared in 1975 for the US Department of Defense in connection with a larger, more comprehensive survey of US-Soviet strategic arms competition since World War II. At that time many of the primary sources, including government records pertaining to atomic energy, strategic planning, and high-level decision-making, were still closed to all but official researchers. Since then, ongoing declassification efforts have made most of these records publicly available. For an overview of the documentary record and its accessibility, see Robert A. Wampler, *Nuclear Weapons and the Atlantic Alliance: A Guide to U.S. Sources* (College Park, Maryland: Center for International Security Studies at Maryland and the Nuclear History Program, 1989).

The most important records for our purposes were those in the custody of the National Archives and Records Administration, Washington, D.C. Our starting point was Record Group (RG) 330, Records of the Office of the Secretary of Defense, which yielded significant documentation on the policy aspects of nuclear energy. For strategic planning, RG 218, Records of the Joint Chiefs of Staff, and RG 341, Records of the Headquarters, United States Air Force, were indispensable. On a selected basis, we also consulted RG 340, Records of the Office of the Secretary of the Air Force; RG 59, Records of the Department of State, concerning policy development; and RG 51, Records of the Bureau of the Budget, for fiscal and budgetary matters. RG 273, Records of the National Security Council, was useful in supplementing materials in the presidential libraries.

Another important Washington repository was the Manuscript Division of the Library of Congress, which houses the papers of most of the postwar Air Force chiefs of staff, including Generals Carl A. Spaatz, Hoyt S. Vandenberg, Nathan Twining, and Curtis E. LeMay. Included in LeMay's papers is his diary, which provides a running commentary on SAC's Korean

War buildup, the targeting controversy, and other pertinent Air Force matters. Also at the Library of Congress are the diary of Fleet Admiral William D. Leahy; the W. Averell Harriman papers, a large but disappointing collection of miscellaneous documents, heavily censored, on postwar policy; the papers of Secretary of War Robert P. Patterson; the papers of legislative clerk Byron S. Miller, which provided interesting congressional background on passage of the 1946 Atomic Energy Act; the papers of Vannevar Bush, science advisor to President Roosevelt; and the papers of atomic scientist J. Robert Oppenheimer.

Outside Washington, the most useful sources were the pre-presidential papers of Dwight D. Eisenhower at the Eisenhower Library in Abilene, Kansas; the unpublished diary of Secretary of Defense James Forrestal at Princeton, New Jersey; the papers and diary of Secretary of War Henry L. Stimson at the Yale University Library in New Haven, Connecticut (also available on microfilm through the Library of Congress); and the various collections of presidential papers at the Harry S. Truman Library in Independence, Missouri. The Truman papers are arranged in three basic parts: an Official File (OF), generally containing unclassified materials; a Confidential File (CF) for more sensitive records; and the President's Secretary's File (PSF), subdivided into collections on the National Security Council, the intelligence community, and other security agencies. Other collections of personal papers at the Truman Library that proved helpful were those of Secretary of State Dean Acheson; Donald F. Carpenter, first civilian chairman of Military Liaison Committee; White House counsel Clark M. Clifford; George Elsey, who served as Clifford's deputy; White House aide Eben A. Ayers; Under Secretary of the Navy Dan A. Kimball; and budget director Frederick J. Lawton. The University of Virginia in Charlottesville is custodian of Louis Johnson's papers, which unfortunately have been extensively purged and contain little on his tenure as secretary of defense.

Our research at archives outside the United States centered on the British Public Records Office at Kew, near London. While our effort was by no means exhaustive, it did turn up some very useful material that helped to flesh out the story on Anglo-American collaboration. The most important documentation was in the run of minutes and memoranda of the Chiefs of Staff Committee (DEFE 4 and 5), the Air Ministry and Bomber Command (AIR 8), and scattered documents from the Foreign Office on American base rights (FO 371). For a full account of the PRO's holdings and potential for further research, see Ian Clark and Philip Sabin, *Sources for the Study of British Nuclear History* (College Park, Maryland: Center for International Security Studies at Maryland and the Nuclear History Program, 1989).

PUBLISHED DOCUMENTS

Cole, Alice C, et al., eds. *The Department of Defense: Documents on Establishment and Organization, 1944-1978.* Washington, D.C.: Historical Office, Office of the Secretary of Defense, 1978.

Etzold, Thomas H., and John Lewis Gaddis, eds. *Containment: Documents on American Policy and Strategy.* New York: Columbia University Press, 1978.

Gallup, George. *The Gallup Poll.* 3 vols. New York: 1972.

Loewenheim, Harold D., and Manfred Jonas, eds. *Roosevelt and Churchill: Their Secret Wartime Correspondence.* New York: Saturday Review Press, 1975.

Public Papers of the Presidents of the United States: Harry S. Truman, 1945-1953. 8 vols. Washington, D.C.: G.P.O., 1961-1966.

Smyth, Henry D. *Atomic Energy for Military Purposes: The Official Report on the Development of the Atomic Bomb Under the Auspices of the United States Government, 1940-1945.* Princeton, N.J.: Princeton University Press, 1946.

Thompson, Kenneth W., and Steven L. Rearden, eds. *Paul H. Nitze on National Security and Arms Control.* Lanham, Md: University Press of America, 1990.

U.S. Bureau of the Census. *Historical Statistics of the United States: Colonial Times to 1957.* Washington, D.C.: G.P.O., 1960.

U.S. Department of State. *Foreign Relations of the United States, 1945-1954* (annual volumes). Washington, D.C.: G.P.O., 1967-1985.

U.S. President's Air Policy Commission. *Survival in the Air Age.* Washington, D.C.: The Commission, Jan. 1, 1948.

U.S. Strategic Bombing Survey. *Summary Report (Pacific War)*. Washington, D.C.: G.P.O., 1946.

Wolf, Richard I., ed. *The United States Air Force: Basic Documents on Roles and Missions*. Washington, D.C.: Office of Air Force History, 1987.

Yasamee, H.J., and K.A. Hamilton. *Documents on British Policy Overseas, series II*, vol. IV, *Korea, June 1950-April 1951*. London: HMSO, 1991.

MEMOIRS, AUTOBIOGRAPHIES, DIARIES

Acheson, Dean. *Present at the Creation: My Years in the State Department*. New York: W.W. Norton, 1969.

Anders, Roger M., ed. *Forging the Atomic Shield: Excerpts from the Office Diary of Gordon E. Dean*. Chapel Hill and London: University of North Carolina Press, 1987.

Baruch, Bernard. *The Public Years*. New York: Holt, Rinehart and Winston, 1960.

Blum, John Morton, ed. *The Price of Vision: The Diary of Henry A. Wallace, 1942-1946*. Boston: Houghton, Mifflin, 1973.

Bohlen, Charles E. *Witness to History, 1929-1969*. New York: W. W. Norton, 1973.

Byrnes, James F. *Speaking Frankly*. New York: Harper and Brothers, 1947.

Churchill, Winston S. *The Hinge of Fate,* vol. 4 of *The Second World War*. Boston: Houghton, Mifflin, 1950.

Clifford, Clark, with Richard Holbrooke. *Counsel to the President: A Memoir*. New York: Random House, 1991.

Colville, John R. *The Fringes of Power: 10 Downing Street Diaries, 1939-1955*. New York: W. W. Norton, 1985.

Ferrell, Robert H., ed. *Dear Bess: The Letters from Harry to Bess Truman, 1910-1959*. New York: W. W. Norton, 1983.

Ferrell, Robert H., ed. *The Eisenhower Diaries*. New York: W.W. Norton, 1981.

Ferrell, Robert H., ed. *Off the Record: The Private Papers of Harry S. Truman.* New York: Harper and Row, 1980.

Ferrell, Robert H., ed. *Truman in the White House: The Diary of Eban A. Ayers.* Columbia: University of Missouri Press, 1991.

Groves, Leslie R. *Now It Can Be Told: The Story of the Manhattan Project.* New York: Harper and Brothers, 1962.

Kennan, George F. *Memoirs, 1925-1950.* Boston: Little, Brown, 1967.

Krock, Arthur. *Memoirs: Sixty Years on the Firing Line.* New York: Funk and Wagnalls, 1968.

Lilienthal, David. *The Journals of David Lilienthal,* vol. II, *The Atomic Energy Years, 1945-1950.* New York: Harper and Row, 1964.

Lord Moran. *Churchill Taken from the Diaries of Lord Moran: The Struggle for Survival, 1940-1965.* Boston: Houghton, Mifflin, 1966.

Millis, Walter, ed., with E. S. Duffield. *The Forrestal Diaries.* New York: Viking Press, 1951.

McLellan, David S., and David C. Acheson, eds. *Among Friends: Personal Letters of Dean Acheson.* New York: Dodd, Mead, 1980.

Nichols, K.D. *The Road to Trinity.* New York: William Morrow, 1987.

Nitze, Paul H., with Ann M. Smith and Steven L. Rearden. *From Hiroshima to Glasnost: At the Center of Decision—A Memoir.* New York: Grove Weidenfeld, 1989.

Rotblat, Joseph. "Leaving the Bomb Project." *Bulletin of the Atomic Scientists* 41 (August 1985): 16-19.

Rusk, Dean, with Richard Rusk. *As I Saw It.* New York: W.W. Norton 1990.

Shuckburgh, Evelyn. *Descent to Suez: Diaries, 1951-56.* New York: W. W. Norton, 1987.

Stimson, Henry L. "The Decision to Use the Atomic Bomb." Reprinted in Robert A. Divine, ed. *Causes and Consequences of World War II.* Chicago: Quadrangle Books, 1969.

Stimson, Henry L., and McGeorge Bundy. *On Active Service in Peace and War.* New York: Harper and Brothers, 1947.

Szilard, Leo. "Reminiscences." *Perspectives in American History* II (1968): 94-151.

Truman, Harry S. *Memoirs,* vol. I, *Year of Decisions.* Garden City, New York: Doubleday, 1955.

Truman, Harry S. *Memoirs,* vol. II, *Years of Trial and Hope.* Garden City, New York: Doubleday, 1956.

Truman, Harry S. *Mr. Citizen.* New York: Bernard Geis Associates, 1960.

Truman, Margaret. *Harry S. Truman.* New York: Morrow, 1973.

Vandenberg, Arthur H., Jr., with Joe Alex Morris, eds. *The Private Papers of Senator Vandenberg.* Boston: Houghton, Mifflin, 1952.

Weisskopf, Victor F. "Looking Back on Los Alamos." *Bulletin of the Atomic Scientists* 41 (August 1985): 20-22.

SECONDARY WORKS: BOOKS

Alperovitz, Gar. *Atomic Diplomacy: Hiroshima and Potsdam.* New York: Random House, 1965; rev. ed. 1985.

Anders, Roger M. *Institutional Origins of the Department of Energy: The Office of Military Application.* Washington, D.C.: U.S. Dept. of Energy, 1980.

Ball, Desmond, and Jeffrey Richelson, eds. *Strategic Nuclear Targeting.* Ithaca and London: Cornell University Press, 1986.

Baxter, James Phinney, 3rd. *Scientists Against Time.* Cambridge, Mass.: M.I.T. Press, 1952; reprint of the 1946 original.

Blum, John Morton. *V Was For Victory: Politics and American Culture During World War II.* New York: Harcourt Brace Jovanovich, 1976.

Borklund, Carl W. *Men of the Pentagon: From Forrestal to McNamara.* New York: Frederick A. Praeger, 1966.

Bracken, Paul. *The Command and Control of Nuclear Forces.* New Haven: Yale University Press, 1983.

Brodie, Bernard, ed. *The Absolute Weapon: Atomic Power and World Order.* New York: Harcourt, Brace, and World, 1946.

Bundy, McGeorge. *Danger and Survival: Choices About the Bomb in the First Fifty Years.* New York: Random House, 1988.

Burns, James MacGregor. *Roosevelt: The Soldier of Freedom, 1940-1945.* New York: Harcourt Brace Jovanovich, 1970.

Callahan, David. *Dangerous Capabilities: Paul Nitze and the Cold War.* New York: Harper Collins, 1990.

Caraley, Demetrios. *The Politics of Military Unification.* New York: Columbia University Press, 1966.

Clark, Ian, and Nicholas J. Wheeler. *The British Origins of Nuclear Strategy, 1945-1955.* Oxford: Clarendon Press, 1989.

Cochran, Thomas B., William M. Arkin, and Milton M. Hoenig. *Nuclear Weapons Databook,* vol. I, *U.S. Nuclear Forces and Capabilities.* Cambridge, Mass.: Ballinger, 1984.

Condit, Doris M. *History of the Office of the Secretary of Defense: The Test of War, 1950-1953.* Washington, D.C.: Historical Office, Office of the Secretary of Defense, 1988.

Condit, Kenneth W. *History of the Joint Chiefs of Staff: The Joint Chiefs of Staff and National Policy,* vol. II, *1947-1949.* Washington, D.C.: Historical Division, Joint Secretariat, Joint Chiefs of Staff, 1976.

Craven, Wesley Frank, and James Lea Cate. *The Army Air Forces in World War II,* vol. V, *The Pacific: Matterhorn to Nagasaki, June 1944 to August 1945.* Washington, D.C.: Office of Air Force History, 1983 (new imprint).

Darling, Arthur B. *The Central Intelligence Agency: An Instrument of Government, to 1950.* 2 vols. Washington, D.C.: Historical Staff, Central Intelligence Agency, 1953, released 1989.

Davis, Vincent. *Postwar Defense Policy and the U.S. Navy, 1943-1946.* Chapel Hill: University of North Carolina Press, 1966.

Donovan, John C. *The Cold Warriors: A Policy-Making Elite.* Lexington, Mass.: D.C. Heath, 1974.

Donovan, Robert J. *Conflict and Crisis: The Presidency of Harry S. Truman, 1945-1948.* New York: W. W. Norton, 1977.

Donovan, Robert J. *Tumultuous Years: The Presidency of Harry S. Truman, 1949-1953.* New York: W. W. Norton, 1982.

Drea, Edward J. *MacArthur's ULTRA: Codebreaking and the War Against Japan, 1942-1945*. Lawrence, Kan.: University Press of Kansas, 1992.

Duke, Simon. *US Defence Bases in the United Kingdom: A Matter for Joint Decision?* New York: St. Martin's Press, 1987.

Feis, Herbert. *From Trust to Terror: The Onset of the Cold War, 1945-1950*. New York: W.W. Norton, 1970.

Ferrell, Robert H. *George C. Marshall*. Vol. XV in Robert H. Ferrell and Samuel Flagg Bemis, eds. *The American Secretaries of State and Their Diplomacy*. New York: Cooper Square, 1966.

Freedman, Lawrence. *The Evolution of Nuclear Strategy*. New York: St. Martin's Press, 1981; rev. ed. 1989.

Freedman, Lawrence. *U.S. Intelligence and the Soviet Strategic Threat*. 2d. ed. Princeton, New Jersey: Princeton University Press, 1986.

Fursdon, Edward. *The European Defence Community: A History*. New York: St. Martin's Press, 1979.

Futrell, Robert Frank. *Ideas, Concepts, Doctrine: Basic Thinking in the United States Air Force, 1907-1984*. Rev. ed. 2 vols. Maxwell Air Force Base, Alabama: Air University Press, 1989.

Gaddis, John Lewis. *The Long Peace: Inquiries into the History of the Cold War*. New York: Oxford University Press, 1987.

Gaddis, John Lewis. *Strategies of Containment: A Critical Appraisal of Postwar American National Security Policy*. New York: Oxford University Press, 1982.

Gaddis, John Lewis. *The United States and the Origins of the Cold War, 1941-1947*. New York: Columbia University Press, 1972.

Gardner, Lloyd C. *Architects of Illusion: Men and Ideas in American Foreign Policy, 1941-1949*. Chicago: Quadrangle Books, 1970.

George, Alexander L., and Richard Smoke. *Deterrence in American Foreign Policy: Theory and Practice*. New York: Columbia University Press, 1974.

Gilbert, Martin. *Winston S. Churchill*, vol. VIII, *"Never Despair," 1945-1965*. London: Heineman, 1988.

Gilbert, Martin. *Winston S. Churchill,* vol. VII, *Road to Victory, 1941-1945.* Boston: Houghton, Mifflin, 1986.

Goudsmit, Samuel. *Alsos.* New York: Henry Schuman, 1947.

Gowing, Margaret. *Independence and Deterrence: Britain and Atomic Energy, 1945-1952,* vol. I, *Policy Making.* New York: St. Martin's Press, 1974.

Hamby, Alonzo L. *Beyond the New Deal: Harry S. Truman and American Liberalism.* New York: Columbia University Press, 1973.

Hammond, Paul Y. *Organizing for Defense: The American Military Establishment in the Twentieth Century.* Princeton: Princeton University Press, 1961.

Haynes, Richard F. *The Awesome Power: Harry S. Truman as Commander in Chief.* Baton Rouge: Louisiana State University Press, 1973.

Heller, Francis H., ed. *The Truman White House.* Lawrence: Regents Press of Kansas, 1980.

Herken, Gregg. *The Winning Weapon: The Atomic Bomb in the Cold War, 1945-1950.* New York: Knopf, 1980.

Hewlett, Richard G., and Oscar E. Anderson. *A History of the United States Atomic Energy Commission,* vol. I, *The New World, 1939-1946.* Washington, D.C.: U.S. Atomic Energy Commission, 1972.

Hewlett, Richard G., and Francis Duncan. *A History of the United States Atomic Energy Commission,* vol. II, *Atomic Shield, 1947-1952.* Washington, D.C.: U.S. Atomic Energy Commission, 1972.

Hinsley, F. H., et al. *British Intelligence in the Second World War: Its Influence on Strategy and Operations.* 3 vols. London: HMSO, 1981-1988.

Holloway, David. *The Soviet Union and the Arms Race.* New Haven and London: Yale University Press, 1983.

Hoopes, Townsend, and Douglas Brinkley. *Driven Patriot: The Life and Times of James Forrestal.* New York: Knopf, 1992.

Hopkins, J. C., and Sheldon A. Goldberg. *The Development of Strategic Air Command, 1946-1986.* Offutt Air Force Base: Office of the Historian, Headquarters Strategic Air Command, 1986.

Huntington, Samuel P. *The Common Defense: Strategic Programs in National Politics*. New York: Columbia University Press, 1961.

Huston, James A. *Outposts and Allies: U.S. Army Logistics in the Cold War, 1945-1953*. London and Toronto: Associated University Presses, 1988.

Isaacson, Walter, and Evan Thomas. *The Wise Men: Six Friends and the World They Made*. New York: Simon and Schuster, 1986.

Jervis, Robert. *The Illogic of American Nuclear Strategy*. Ithaca, N.Y.: Cornell University Press, 1984.

Jervis, Robert. *The Meaning of the Nuclear Revolution: Statecraft and the Prospect of Armageddon*. Ithaca, N.Y.: Cornell University Press, 1989.

Jones, Joseph Marion. *The Fifteen Weeks (February 21-June 5, 1947)*. New York: Viking, 1955.

Jones, Vincent. *Manhattan: The Army and the Atomic Bomb*. Washington, D.C.: Center of Military History, 1985.

Jungk, Robert. *Brighter Than a Thousand Suns*. New York: Harcourt, Brace, 1958.

Kaplan, Lawrence S. *A Community of Interests: NATO and the Military Assistance Program, 1948-1951*. Washington, D.C.: Historical Office, Office of the Secretary of Defense, 1980.

Kaplan, Lawrence S. *NATO and the United States: The Enduring Alliance*. Boston: Twayne Publishers, 1988.

Kaplan, Lawrence S. *The United States and NATO: The Formative Years*. Lexington: University Press of Kentucky, 1984.

Kepley, David R. *The Collapse of the Middle Way: Senate Republicans and the Bipartisan Foreign Policy, 1948-1952*. New York: Greenwood Press, 1988.

Kinnard, Douglas. *The Secretary of Defense*. Lexington, Ky.: University Press of Kentucky, 1980.

Knaack, Marcelle Size. *Encyclopedia of U.S. Air Force Aircraft and Missile Systems*, vol. II, *Post-World War II Bombers, 1945-1973*. Washington, D.C.: Office of Air Force History, 1988.

Larson, Deborah Welch. *Origins of Containment: A Psychological Explanation*. Princeton, N.J.: Princeton University Press, 1985.

Leffler, Melvyn P. *A Preponderance of Power: National Security, the Truman Administration, and the Cold War*. Stanford, Calif.: Stanford University Press, 1992.

Lieberman, Joseph I. *The Scorpion and the Tarantula: The Struggle to Control Atomic Weapons, 1945-1949*. Boston: Houghton Mifflin, 1970.

MacIsaac, David. *Strategic Bombing in World War Two: The Story of the United States Strategic Bombing Survey*. New York: Garland Publishing, 1976.

McCullough, David. *Truman*. New York: Simon and Schuster, 1992.

May, Ernest R. *"Lessons" of the Past: The Use and Misuse of History in American Foreign Policy*. New York: Oxford University Press, 1973.

Mayers, David A. *George Kennan and the Dilemmas of U.S. Foreign Policy*. New York and London: Oxford University Press, 1988.

Messer, Robert L. *The End of an Alliance: James F. Byrnes, Roosevelt, Truman, and the Origins of the Cold War*. Chapel Hill: University of North Carolina Press, 1982.

Milward, Alan S. *The Reconstruction of Western Europe, 1945-1951*. Berkeley: University of California Press, 1984.

Moss, Norman. *Klaus Fuchs: The Man Who Stole the Atom Bomb*. New York: St. Martin's Press, 1987.

Mueller, John. *Retreat from Doomsday: The Obsolescence of Major War*. New York: Basic Books, 1989.

Neufeld, Jacob. *The Development of Ballistic Missiles in the United States Air Force, 1945-1960*. Washington, D.C.: Office of Air Force History, 1990.

Pach, Chester J., Jr. *Arming the Free World: The Origins of the United States Military Assistance Program, 1945-1950*. Chapel Hill: University of North Carolina Press, 1991.

Pash, Boris T. *The Alsos Mission*. New York: Award House, 1969.

Paterson, Thomas G. *Meeting the Communist Threat: Truman to Reagan*. New York: Oxford University Press, 1988.

Patterson, James T. *Mr. Republican: A Biography of Robert A. Taft.* Boston: Houghton, Mifflin, 1972.

Pierre, Andrew J. *Nuclear Politics: The British Experience with an Independent Strategic Force, 1939-1970.* London: Oxford University Press, 1972.

Pogue, Forrest C. *George C. Marshall: Statesman, 1945-1959.* New York: Viking Press, 1987.

Poole, Walter S. *The History of the Joint Chiefs of Staff: The Joint Chiefs of Staff and National Policy,* vol. IV, *1950-1952.* Washington, D.C.: Historical Division, Joint Secretariat, Joint Chiefs of Staff, 1976.

Powaski, Ronald E. *March to Armageddon: The United States and the Nuclear Arms Race, 1939 to the Present.* New York: Oxford University Press, 1987.

Prados, John. *Keepers of the Keys: A History of the National Security Council from Truman to Bush.* New York: W. Morrow, 1991.

Prados, John. *The Soviet Estimate: U.S. Intelligence Analysis and Russian Military Strength.* New York: Dial Press, 1982.

Rearden, Steven L. *The Evolution of American Strategic Doctrine: Paul H. Nitze and the Soviet Challenge.* Boulder, Colo.: Westview Press and the Johns Hopkins Foreign Policy Institute, 1984.

Rearden, Steven L. *History of the Office of the Secretary of Defense: The Formative Years, 1947-1950.* Washington, D.C.: Historical Office, Office of the Secretary of Defense, 1984.

Rhodes, Richard. *The Making of the Atomic Bomb.* New York: Simon and Schuster, 1986.

Ries, John C. *The Management of Defense.* Baltimore: Johns Hopkins University Press, 1964.

Rosecrance. Richard N. *Defense of the Realm: British Strategy in the Nuclear Epoch.* New York: Columbia University Press, 1968.

Ross, Steven T. *American War Plans, 1945-1950.* New York: Garland, 1988.

Rothwell, Victor. *Britain and the Cold War, 1941-1947.* London: J. Cape, 1982.

Sagan, Scott D. *Moving Targets: Nuclear Strategy and National Security.* Princeton: Princeton University Press, 1989.

Schnabel, James F. *History of the Joint Chiefs of Staff: The Joint Chiefs of Staff and National Policy,* vol. I, *1945-1947.* Wilmington, Del.: Michael Glaser, 1979.

Schnabel, James F. *United States Army in the Korean War: Policy and Direction—The First Year.* Washington, D.C.: Office of the Chief of Military History, 1972.

Sherry, Michael S. *Preparing for the Next War: American Plans for Postwar Defense, 1941-1945.* New Haven: Yale University Press, 1977.

Sherry, Michael S. *The Rise of American Air Power: The Creation of Armaggedon.* New Haven: Yale University Press, 1987.

Sherwin, Martin J. *A World Destroyed: The Atomic Bomb and the Grand Alliance.* New York: Random House, 1975.

Shlaim, Avi. *The United States and the Berlin Blockade, 1948-1949.* Berkeley, Calif.: University of California Press, 1983.

Sigal, Leon V. *Fighting to a Finish: The Politics of War Termination in the United States and Japan, 1945.* Ithaca: Cornell University Press, 1988.

Siracusa, Joseph M. *Rearming for the Cold War.* Los Angeles: Center for the Study of Armament and Disarmament, 1983.

Smith, Perry McCoy. *The Air Force Plans for Peace, 1943-1945.* Baltimore: Johns Hopkins University Press, 1970.

Spanier, John W. *The Truman-MacArthur Controversy and the Korean War.* Cambridge, Mass.: Harvard University Press, 1959.

Thomas, Hugh. *Armed Truce: The Beginnings of the Cold War, 1945-1946.* New York: Atheneum, 1987.

Ulam, Adam B. *The Rivals: America and Russia Since World War II.* New York: Viking Press, 1971.

Williams, Robert Chadwell. *Klaus Fuchs, Atom Spy.* Cambridge, Mass.: Harvard University Press, 1987.

Wolk, Herman S. *Planning and Organizing the Postwar Air Force, 1943-1947.* Washington, D.C.: Office of Air Force History, 1984.

Yergin, Daniel. *Shattered Peace: The Origins of the Cold War and the National Security State.* Boston: Houghton, Mifflin, 1977.

York, Herbert F. *The Advisors: Oppenheimer, Teller, and the Superbomb.* San Francisco: W.H. Freeman and Co., 1976.

SECONDARY WORKS: ARTICLES

Alperovitz, Gar. "More on Atomic Diplomacy." *Bulletin of the Atomic Scientists* 41 (December 1985): 35-39.

Berger, Henry W. "Bipartisanship, Senator Taft, and the Truman Administration." *Political Science Quarterly* 90 (Summer 1975): 221-237.

Bernstein, Barton J. "Crossing the Rubicon: A Missed Opportunity to Stop the H-Bomb?" *International Security* 14 (Fall 1989): 132-160.

Bernstein, Barton J. "Eclipsed by Hiroshima and Nagasaki: Early Thinking About Tactical Nuclear Weapons." *International Security* 15 (Spring 1991): 149-173.

Bernstein, Barton J. "Roosevelt, Truman, and the Atomic Bomb, 1941-1945: A Reinterpretation." *Political Science Quarterly* 90 (Spring 1975).

Buhite, Russell D., and William Christopher Hamel. "War for Peace: The Question of an American Preventive War against the Soviet Union, 1945-1955." *Diplomatic History* 14 (Summer 1990): 367-384.

Combs, Jerald A. "The Compromise That Never Was: George Kennan, Paul Nitze, and the Issue of Conventional Deterrence in Europe, 1949-1952. *Diplomatic History* 15 (Summer 1991): 361-386.

DeConde, Alexander. "George Catlett Marshall." In Norman A. Graebner, ed. *An Uncertain Tradition: American Secretaries of State in the Twentieth Century.* New York: McGraw-Hill, 1961.

Dingman, Roger. "Atomic Diplomacy During the Korean War." *International Security* 13 (Winter 1988/89): 50-91.

Dockrill, M. L. "The Foreign Office, Anglo-American relations and the Korean War, June 1950-June 1951." *International Affairs* (London) 62 (Summer 1986).

Elliot, David C. "Project Vista and Nuclear Weapons in Europe." *International Security* 11 (Summer 1986): 163-183.

Erskine, Hazel Gaudet. "The Polls: Atomic Weapons and Nuclear Energy." *Public Opinion Quarterly* 27 (Summer 1963): 155-190.

Foot, Rosemary J. "Nuclear Coercion and the Ending of the Korean Conflict." *International Security* 13 (Winter 1988/89): 92-112.

Hammond, Paul Y. "NSC-68: Prologue to Rearmament," in Warner R. Schilling, Paul Y. Hammond, and Glenn H. Snyder. *Strategy, Politics, and Defense Budgets*. New York: Columbia University Press, 1962.

Holloway, David. "Soviet Thermonuclear Development." *International Security* 4 (Winter 1979-80): 192-197.

Kennan, George F. "The Sources of Soviet Conduct." *Foreign Affairs* 25 (July 1947): 566-582.

Kuehl, Daniel T. "Refighting the Last War: Electronic Warfare and U.S. Air Force B-29 Operations in the Korean War, 1950-53." *Journal of Military History* 56 (January 1992): 87-111.

Maier, Charles S. "Revisionism and the Interpretations of Cold War Origins," *Perspectives in American History* IV (1970): 311-347.

May, Ernest R. "The American Commitment to Germany, 1949-1955." *Diplomatic History* 13 (Fall 1989): 431-460.

May, Ernest R. "The Cold War." In Joseph S. Nye, Jr., ed. *The Making of America's Soviet Policy*. New Haven: Yale University Press, 1984.

Messer, Robert L. "New Evidence on Truman's Decision." *Bulletin of the Atomic Scientists* 41 (August 1985): 50-56.

Miscamble, Wilson D. "George F. Kennan, the Policy Planning Staff and the Origins of the Marshall Plan." *Mid-America* 62 (April-July 1980): 75-89.

Morton, Louis. "The Decision to Use the Atomic Bomb." In Kent Roberts Greenfield, ed. *Command Decisions*. Washington, D.C.: Center of Military History, 1984.

Murphy, Charles J. V. "A New Strategy for NATO." *Fortune* (January 1953): 80f.

Nelson, Anna Kasten. "President Truman and the Evolution of the National Security Council." *Journal of American History* 72 (September 1985): 360-378.

Nitze, Paul H. "The Development of NSC 68." *International Security* 4 (Spring 1980): 170-176.

Nitze, Paul H. "Military Power: A Strategic View." *The Fletcher Forum* 5 (Winter 1981).

Nitze, Paul H. "The Relationship of Strategic and Theater Nuclear Forces." *International Security* 2 (Fall 1977): 122-132.

Norris, Robert S., Thomas B. Cochran, and William M. Arkin. "History of the Nuclear Stockpile." *Bulletin of the Atomic Scientists* 41 (August 1985): 106-109.

Poole, Walter S. "From Conciliation to Containment: The Joint Chiefs of Staff and the Coming of the Cold War." *Military Affairs* 42 (1978): 12-16.

Postbrief, Sam. "Departure from Incrementalism." *Naval War College Review* 33 (March-April 1980): 34-57.

Rearden, Steven L. "Congress and National Defense, 1945-1950." In Richard H. Kohn, ed. *The United States Military under the Constitution of the United States*. New York: New York University Press, 1991.

Richardson, Robert C., III. "NATO Nuclear Strategy: A Look Back." *Strategic Review* 9 (Spring 1981): 35-43.

Rosenberg, David Alan. "American Atomic Strategy and the Hydrogen Bomb Decision." *Journal of American History* 66 (June 1979): 62-87.

Rosenberg, David Alan. "The Origins of Overkill: Nuclear Weapons and American Strategy, 1945-1960." *International Security* 7 (Spring 1983): 3-71.

Rosenberg, David Alan. "U.S. Nuclear Stockpile, 1945 to 1950." *Bulletin of the Atomic Scientists* 38 (May 1982): 25-30.

Sander, Alfred D. "Truman and the National Security Council, 1945-1947." *Journal of American History* 59 (September 1972): 369-388.

Schlesinger, Arthur, Jr. "Origins of the Cold War." *Foreign Affairs* 46 (October 1967): 22-52.

Shlaim, Avi. "Britain, the Berlin Blockade and the Cold War." *International Affairs* (London) 60 (Winter 1983/4): 1-14.

Trachtenberg, Marc. "A 'Wasting Asset': American Strategy and the Shifting Nuclear Balance." *International Security* 13 (Winter 1988/89): 5-49.

Walker, J. Samuel. "The Decision to Use the Bomb: A Historiographical Update." *Diplomatic History* 14 (Winter 1990): 97-114.

Wells, Samuel F., Jr. "The Origins of Massive Retaliation." In Robert H. Connery and Demetrios Caraley, eds. *National Security and Nuclear Strategy*. New York: Academy of Political Science, 1983.

Wells, Samuel F., Jr. "Sounding the Tocsin: NSC 68 and the Soviet Threat." *International Security* 4 (Fall 1979): 116-158.

Werrell, Kenneth P. "The Strategic Bombing of Germany in World War II: Costs and Accomplishments." *Journal of American History* 73 (Dec. 1986): 702-713.

Wheeler, N.J. "British Nuclear Weapons and Anglo-American Relations, 1945-54." *International Affairs* (London) 62 (Winter 1985/86): 71-86.

UNPUBLISHED AND OTHER WORKS

Borgiasz, William Stephen. "Struggle for Predominance: Evolution and Consolidation of Nuclear Forces in the Strategic Air Command, 1945-1955." Ph.D. diss., American University, 1991.

Cornell, Cecilia Stiles. "James V. Forrestal and American National Security Policy, 1940-1949." Ph.D. diss., Vanderbilt University, 1987.

Evangelista, Matthew Anthony. "Technological Innovation and the Arms Race: A Comparative Study of Soviet and American Decisions on Tactical Nuclear Weapons." Ph.D. diss., Cornell University, 1986.

Legere, Lawrence, Jr. "Unification of the Armed Forces." Ph.D. thesis, Harvard University, 1950.

Little, R. D. *The History of Air Force Participation in the Atomic Energy Program, 1943-1953,* vol. II, *Foundations of an Atomic Air Force and Operation Sandstone, 1946-1948.* Bound MS (Sanitized), USAF Historical Division, n.d., available through the Office of Air Force History, Bolling Air Force Base, Washington, D.C.

Mahoney, Leo J. "A History of the War Department Scientific Intelligence Mission (Alsos), 1943-1945." Ph.D. diss., Kent State University, 1981.

Meigs, Montgomery Cunningham. "Managing Uncertainty: Vannevar Bush, James B. Conant and the Development of the Atomic Bomb, 1940-1945." Ph.D. diss., University of Wisconsin, 1982.

Moody, Walton S. "Building a Strategic Air Force, 1945-1953." MS, Office of Air Force History, 1989.

O'Brien. L. D. "National Security and the New Warfare: Defense Policy, War Planning, and Nuclear Weapons, 1945-50." Ph.D. diss., The Ohio State University, 1981

Rosenberg, David Alan. "Toward Armageddon: The Foundations of United States Nuclear Strategy." Ph.D. diss., University of Chicago, 1981.

INDEX